How to Protect Your Children from Child Abuse: A Parent's Guide

Boy Scouts of America

Introduction

Our children are often faced with choices that affect their development and safety. As parents, we can do our best to provide education and guidance to prepare our children to make the best decisions. One way we do this is to talk with our children. Some subjects are easy to discuss with our children—sports, their grades in school, their friends, and many other features of our daily lives. Other things are more difficult for us to discuss, including child abuse—especially child sexual abuse.

Although discussing child abuse with your children may be difficult for you, it is very important. Perhaps the most important step parents can take to protect their children from abuse is to have open communication in the home. Research has shown that children whose parents talk to them about preventing abuse are more effective at fending off assaults. Your role is very important.

More than three million reports of child abuse are received each year, including half a million reports of *child sexual abuse.* As a major youth-serving organization, the Boy Scouts of America has a unique opportunity to help protect the youth of our nation. This booklet is designed to give you essential information that should help you teach your children how to protect themselves.

If your son is a new Boy Scout, this might be the first time that you have seen this *Parent's Guide.* If you have other sons in Scouting, or if your son has advanced in Boy Scouting, we hope that you are familiar with this guide and have discussed its contents with your children. In either case, we encourage you to make this information part of a continuing family effort that reinforces the concepts included in this guidebook.

We do not expect that your son will become a victim of child abuse. It is extremely important, however, that if he is ever confronted with an abusive situation, he will know that there are adults in his life who will listen and respond in a supportive manner. The purpose of this booklet is to help you and your son establish, or reinforce, open communication on this sensitive topic.

Section I.
Information for Parents

Using This Booklet

This booklet is divided into two sections. The first section is for your information. It contains information about child abuse and provides some tips to help parents talk with their Boy Scout–age sons about child abuse. The second section is for you to share with your son. Some of the activities listed in the second section are requirements your son needs your help to complete before he can join his Boy Scout troop.

> *Youth Protection Troop Joining Requirement:* For your son to join a Boy Scout troop, he must complete the exercises included in Section II of this pamphlet.

It is important that you read the entire booklet before you and your son do any of the exercises together. You might be tempted to hand this booklet to your son and tell him to read it. We urge you to resist this temptation. Your son needs to know that he can openly discuss difficult topics with you.

Child Abuse:
Basic Information for Parents

An abused or neglected child is a child who is harmed, or threatened with physical or mental harm, by the acts or lack of action of a person responsible for the child's care. There are several forms of abuse: physical abuse, emotional abuse, and sexual abuse. Child neglect is a form of abuse that occurs when a person responsible for the care of a child is able, but fails, to provide necessary food, clothing, shelter, or care. Each state has its own definitions and laws concerning child abuse and child neglect.

Child abuse and neglect are serious problems for our society. The number of cases reported has increased each

3

year since 1976, when statistics were first kept. Brief discussions of each form of abuse are presented below.

Neglect

A child is neglected if the persons this child depends on do not provide food, clothing, shelter, medical care, education, and supervision. When these basic needs are *deliberately withheld,* not because the parents or caregivers are poor, it is considered neglect. Often parents or caregivers of neglected children are so overwhelmed by their own needs that they cannot recognize the needs of their children.

Physical Abuse

Physical abuse is the deliberate injury of a child by a person responsible for the child's care. Physical abuse often stems from unreasonable punishment, or by punishment that is too harsh for the child. Sometimes it is the result of a caregiver's reaction to stress. Drinking and drug abuse by caretakers have become more common contributing factors in physical abuse cases.

Physical abuse injuries can include bruises, broken bones, burns, and abrasions. Children experience minor injuries as a normal part of childhood, usually in predictable places such as the shins, knees, and elbows. When the injuries are in soft-tissue areas on the abdomen or back, or don't seem to be typical childhood injuries, physical abuse becomes a possibility.

Physical abuse happens to children of all age groups; however, youth ages 12 to 17 have the highest rate of injury from physical abuse. This is possibly due to increasing conflict between parents and children as children become more independent.

Emotional Abuse

Emotional abuse is harder to recognize, but is just as harmful to the child as other forms of abuse. Emotional abuse damages the child's self-esteem and, in extreme cases, can lead to developmental problems and speech disorders. A child suffers from emotional abuse when constantly ridiculed, rejected, blamed, or compared unfavorably with brothers or sisters or other children.

Expecting too much from the child in academics, athletics, or other areas is a common cause of emotional abuse by parents or other adults. When a child can't meet these expectations, the child feels that he or she is never quite good enough.

Sexual Abuse

When an adult or an older child uses his or her authority over a child to involve the child in sexual activity, it is sexual abuse, and that person is a child molester. The molester might use tricks, bribes, threats, or force to persuade the child to join in sexual activity. Sexual abuse includes any activity performed for the sexual satisfaction of the molester, including acts ranging from exposing his or her sex organs (exhibitionism), observing another's sex organs or sexual activity (voyeurism), to fondling and rape.

Here are a few facts you should know about child sexual abuse:

- Child sexual abuse occurs to as many as 25 percent of girls and 14 percent of boys before they reach 18 years of age.

- Boys and girls could be sexually abused at any age; however, most sexual abuse occurs between the ages of 7 and 13.

- Children are most likely to be molested by someone they know and trust.

- Eighty to 90 percent of sexually abused boys are molested by acquaintances who are nonfamily members.

- Females perform 20 percent of the sexual abuse of boys under age 14 (prepubescents).

- Few sexually abused children tell anyone that they have been abused. Children are usually told to keep the abuse secret. This could involve threats, bribes, or physical force.

- Children might feel responsible for the abuse and fear an angry reaction from their parents.

5

Preteen and teenage boys are especially at risk for sexual abuse. The physical and hormonal changes caused by puberty, and their natural curiosity about their new emotions and feelings, make these youth likely targets for child molesters. The normal desire of boys this age to show their independence from their parents' control adds to the risk. This combination might keep boys this age from asking their parents for help when faced with sexual abuse.

Sexual Molestation by Peers

Approximately one-third of sexual molestation occurs at the hands of other children. If your child tells you about club initiations in which sexual activity is included, or if your child tells you about inappropriate or tricked, pressured, or forced sexual activity by other children, this is a form of sexual abuse and you need to take steps to stop the activity. This kind of sexual misconduct is serious and should not be ignored.

Children who molest other children need professional help. They are much more likely to respond to treatment when young than are adults who were molesters as children and received no treatment, and continue to molest children as adults.

Parents and other adults who work with children need to distinguish between sexual behavior that is a normal part of growing up, and sexual behavior that is abusive. If you find your child has engaged in sexual behavior that might not be abusive, but which bothers you, use the opportunity to discuss the behavior and help your child understand *why* it bothers you.

Signs of Sexual Abuse

The best sign that a child has been sexually abused is his statement that he was. Children often do not report their abuse, so parents should be alert for other signs. These are some signs to watch for:

- *Hints, indirect messages*—Refusing to go to a friend's or relative's home for no apparent reason; for example, "I just don't like him anymore."

- *Seductive or provocative behavior*—Acting out adult sexual behavior or using sexual language a child his age is unlikely to know.

- *Physical symptoms*—Irritation of genital or anal areas.

The following are common signs that children are upset. If present for more than a few days, these signs could indicate that something is wrong and your child needs help and parental support. They might also be signs that your child is being sexually abused:

- *Self-destructive behavior*—Using alcohol or drugs, deliberately harming himself, running away, attempting suicide, or sexual recklessness or promiscuity.

- *Unhappiness*—Undue anxiety and crying, sleep disturbances, or loss of appetite.

- *Regression*—Behaving like a younger child, thumb sucking, or bed-wetting.

- *Difficulty at school*—Sudden drop in grades, behavioral problems, or truancy.

Preventing Child Abuse

Except for sexual abuse of boys, the great majority of child abuse occurs within families. Prevention efforts for emotional and physical abuse as well as neglect generally focus on helping abusers, often the parents, change their behavior.

Some physical and emotional abuses are reactions by parents to the stresses in their lives. By learning to recognize these stresses, and then taking a time-out when the pressures mount, we can avoid abusing those we love. The next page lists some alternatives to physical and emotional abuse for overstressed parents. These suggestions come from the National Committee to Prevent Child Abuse.

In addition to the alternatives on the next page, parents and other child caregivers may want to think about the following questions* suggested by Douglas Besharov, the first director of the U.S. National Center on Child Abuse and Neglect, regarding the methods of discipline they use.

- Is the purpose of the punishment to educate the child or to vent the parent's anger?

- Is the child capable of understanding the relationship between his behavior and the punishment?

- Is the punishment appropriate and within the bounds of acceptable discipline?

- Is a less severe, but equally effective, punishment available?

- Is the punishment degrading, brutal, or extended beyond the limits of what the child can handle?

- If physical force is used, is it done carefully to avoid injury?

These questions help to define the boundaries between acceptable discipline and child abuse. Other causes of child abuse inside the family might be much more complex and require professional help to resolve.

*Adapted from Douglas J. Besharov. *Recognizing Child Abuse: A Guide for the Concerned*. New York: Free Press, 1990.

8

Alternatives to Child Abuse

The next time everyday pressures build up to the point where you feel like lashing out—**Stop!** Try any of these simple alternatives. You'll feel better . . . and so will your child:

- Take a deep breath. And another. Then remember you are the adult.

- Close your eyes and imagine you're hearing what your child is about to hear.

- Press your lips together and count to ten; or, better yet, to twenty.

- Put your child in a time-out chair. (Remember this rule: One time-out minute for each year of age.)

- Put yourself in a time-out chair. Think about why you are angry: Is it your child, or is your child simply a convenient target for your anger?

- Phone a friend.

- If someone can watch the children, go outside and take a walk.

- Splash cold water on your face.

- Hug a pillow.

- Turn on some music. Maybe even sing along.

- Pick up a pencil and write down as many *helpful* words as you can think of. Save the list.

Few parents mean to abuse their children. When parents take time out to get control of themselves before they grab hold of their children, everybody wins.

Talking with Your Child About Sexual Abuse

Some parents would almost rather have a tooth pulled than talk with their children about sexual abuse. This reluctance seems to increase with the age of the child. To help you in this regard, the information in Section II focuses on sexual abuse prevention.

The following information should help you and your child talk about sexual abuse prevention:

- *If you feel uncomfortable discussing sexual abuse with your child, let him know.* When you feel uncomfortable discussing sexual abuse with your children and try to hide your uneasiness, your children might misinterpret the anxiety and be less likely to approach you when they need help. You can use a simple statement like, "I wish we did not have to talk about this. I am uncomfortable because I don't like to think that this could happen to you. I want you to know that it's important and you can come to me whenever you have a question or if anybody ever tries to hurt you."

- *Children at this age are developing an awareness of their own sexuality and need parental help to sort out what is and is not exploitive.* Children at this age need specific permission to ask questions about relationships and feelings. Nonspecific "good touch, bad touch" warnings are insufficient, since most of the touching they experience might be "confusing touch." Adolescents also need parental help to set boundaries for their relationships with others—an awareness of when they are being controlling or abusive.

- *Many children at this age feel it is more important to be "cool" than it is to ask questions or seek parental assistance.* Your son might resist discussing the material in this booklet with you. He might be giggly, unfocused, or restless. He might tell you that he already knows about sexual abuse. That's all right. The point of discussing sexual abuse with him is to let him know that if and when he has questions or problems he can't handle by himself, you will help him. If he tells you he already knows about sexual abuse, you can ask him to tell you what he knows.

Today's teenagers and preteens receive a lot of misinformation about sexuality, relationships, and sexual abuse. Their role models are likely to be rock stars and other media personalities. As influential as these are, surveys of young people indicate that parents continue to be a strong influence in their lives.

When a Child Tells You About Abuse

If your child becomes a victim of abuse, your first reaction can be very important in helping him through the ordeal. The following guidelines may help you:

- **Don't** panic or overreact to the information your child tells you.

- **Don't** criticize your child or tell your child he misunderstood what happened.

- **Do** respect your child's privacy and take your child to a place where the two of you can talk without interruptions or distractions.

- **Do** reassure your child that he is not to blame for what happened. Tell him that you appreciate being told about the incident and will help to make sure that it won't happen again.

- **Do** encourage your child to tell the proper authorities what happened, but try to avoid repeated interviews that can be stressful to the child.

- **Do** consult your family doctor or other child abuse authority about the need for medical care or counseling for your child.

You should show real concern, but NOT alarm or anger, when questioning your child about possible sexual abuse.

Finally, if your child has been sexually abused, do not blame yourself or your child. People who victimize children are not easy to identify. They come from all walks of life and all socioeconomic levels. Often they have a position of status—they go to church, hold regular jobs, and are active in the community. Child molesters are sometimes very skilled at controlling children, often by giving excessive attention, gifts, and money.

Child molesters use their skills on parents and other adults, disguising their abusive behavior behind friendship and care for the child.

Resources

BSA Youth Protection Materials

A Time to Tell is a videotape produced by the BSA to educate boys 11 to 14 years of age about sexual abuse. This video introduces the "three Rs" of Youth Protection. Boy Scout troops are encouraged to view the video once each year. It is available from your BSA local council. A meeting guide supporting its use can be found in the *Scoutmaster Handbook* (beginning with the 1995 edition).

For Scouting's leaders and parents, the BSA has a videotaped training program, *Youth Protection Guidelines: Training for Volunteer Leaders and Parents.* This also is available from your BSA local council, and regular training sessions are scheduled in most districts. It addresses many questions that Scout volunteers and parents ask regarding child sexual abuse.

In addition to these videotaped materials, the BSA sometimes provides Youth Protection information to its members and families through *Boys' Life* and *Scouting* magazines.

Other Sources of Child Abuse Prevention Information

National Center for Child Abuse and Neglect
U.S. Department of Health and Human Services
P.O. Box 1182
Washington, DC 20013
800-394-3366

National Committee to Prevent Child Abuse
332 South Michigan Avenue, Suite 1600
Chicago, IL 60604-4537
312-663-3520

National Center for Missing and Exploited Children
2101 Wilson Boulevard, Suite 550
Arlington, VA 22201
800-843-5678

Section II.
Information for Youth

(Youth Protection Troop Joining Requirements)

The *Child's Bill of Rights* outlines some specific strategies your child can use to protect himself. You should discuss these and the "three Rs" of Youth Protection with your child before completing the Youth Protection joining requirements. These could provide the information that your son needs to help him respond to the situations in the exercises.

Child's Bill of Rights

When feeling threatened, you have the right to

- Trust your instincts or feelings.

- Expect privacy.

- Say no to unwanted touching or affection.

- Say no to an adult's inappropriate demands and requests.

- Withhold information that could jeopardize your safety.

- Refuse gifts.

- Be rude or unhelpful if the situation warrants.

- Run, scream, and make a scene.

- Physically fight off unwanted advances.

- Ask for help.

It's important to remember that these are protective actions that will give your son the power to protect himself.

The Boy Scouts of America bases the Youth Protection strategies it teaches its members on the "three Rs" of Youth Protection.

"Three Rs" of Youth Protection

- **Recognize** that anyone could be a child molester and be aware of situations that could lead to abuse.

- **Resist** advances made by child molesters to avoid being abused.

- **Report** any molestation or attempted molestation to parents or other trusted adults.

The "three Rs" of Youth Protection provide a useful tool for parents when they talk with their 11- to 14-year-old children about sexual abuse. Children of this age are less apt than younger children to respond to a list of child safety rules. They need to develop the problem-solving skills necessary to evaluate situations and come up with their own responses. Parents need to help their children develop these skills.

You can help your children develop their personal safety skills. Read the following material with your son. Use the "three Rs" of Youth Protection and the *Child's Bill of Rights* as references.

Personal Protection Rules for Computer On-line Services

When you're on-line, you are in a public place, among thousands of people who are on-line at the same time. Be safe by following these personal protection rules and you will have fun:

- Keep on-line conversations with strangers to public places, not in e-mail.

- Do not give anyone on-line your real last name, phone numbers at home or school, your parents' workplaces, or the name or location of your school or home address unless you have your parent's permission first. Never give your password to anyone but a parent or other adult in your family.

- If someone shows you e-mail with sayings that make you feel uncomfortable, trust your instincts. You are probably right to be wary. Do not respond. Tell a parent what happened.

- If somebody tells you to keep what's going on between the two of you secret, tell a parent.

- Be careful whom you talk to. Anyone who starts talking about subjects that make you feel uncomfortable is probably an adult posing as a kid.

- Pay attention if someone tells you things that don't fit together. One time an on-line friend will say he or she is 12, and another time will say he or she is 14. That is a warning that this person is lying and may be an adult posing as a kid.

- Unless you talk to a parent about it first, never talk to anybody by phone if you know that person only on-line. If someone asks you to call—even if it's collect or a toll-free, 800 number—that's a warning. That person can get your phone number this way, either from a phone bill or from caller ID.

- Never agree to meet someone you have met only on-line any place off-line, in the real world.

- Watch out if someone on-line starts talking about *hacking,* or breaking onto other people's or companies' computer systems; *phreaking* (the "ph" sounds like an "f"), the illegal use of long-distance services or cellular phones; or *viruses,* on-line programs that destroy or damage data when other people download these onto their computers.

- Promise your parent or an adult family member and yourself that you will honor any rules about how much time you are allowed to spend on-line and what you do and where you go while you are on-line.

1. Child Abuse and Being a Good Scout

When a boy joins the Scouting program, he assumes a duty to be faithful to the rules of Scouting as represented in the Scout Oath, Scout Law, Scout motto, and Scout slogan.

The rules of Scouting don't require a Scout to put himself in possibly dangerous situations—quite the contrary, we want Scouts to "be prepared" and to "do their best" to avoid these situations.

We hope that you will discuss these rules with your Scout and be sure that he understands that he should not risk his safety to follow the rules of Scouting.

The Scout Oath includes the phrase "To help other people at all times." The Scout Law says that "A Scout is helpful," and the Scout slogan is "Do a Good Turn Daily." There are many people who need help, and a Boy Scout should be willing to lend a hand when needed.

Sometimes people who really do not need help will ask for it in order to create an opportunity for abuse. Boy Scouts should be very familiar with the rules of safety so that they can recognize situations to be wary of. For example:

- It is one thing to stand on the sidewalk away from a car to give directions, and something else to get in the car with someone to show them the way. A Scout should never get into a car without his parent's permission.

- It may be okay for a Scout to help carry groceries to a person's house, but he should never enter the house unless he has permission from his parents.

The Scout Law also states that a Scout is obedient—but a Scout does not have to obey an adult when that person tells him to do something that the Scout feels is wrong or that makes the Scout feel uncomfortable. In these situations, the Scout should talk with his parent about his concerns.

2. Practicing the "Three Rs" of Youth Protection

The following stories will help your son understand how to use the "three Rs" of Youth Protection. These situations might be more detailed than you feel comfortable with; however, if children are going to learn about sexual abuse, they must be able to identify and discuss specific acts.

Jeff's Story

I am a 12-year-old boy in the sixth grade at my middle school. Every afternoon after school, I go to a recreation center until my mom gets home from work. One of the guys who works at the center has been spending a lot of time with me lately. He's really nice, and he told me that he would teach me how to wrestle. He said that wrestling would be a good sport for me because it has different weight classes and I'm so small I would be wrestling other kids my own size. I've got to admit that I like to wrestle. But there's something bothering me. This guy who's teaching me to wrestle wants me to come to the center on Sunday when no one else is there. He said that we would have the place to ourselves, and he could really teach me a lot. I'd like to, but I've been noticing that when he's teaching me, he holds me down and sometimes grabs me between the legs. He makes like it's a real funny joke, but I'm not so sure that I like it.

- **What is risky about this situation?**

  —History of unwanted touching of private parts.

  —Touching will probably become more serious if allowed to continue.

  —Individual coaching on Sunday would put Jeff alone at the center with a possible molester.

18

- **How would you resist?**

  —Tell the person to stop grabbing you and do not wrestle with him any longer.

  —Make sure that you are not alone with him, and if he grabs you yell "Stop that!" loud enough so that everyone will hear.

- **How would you report this situation?**

  —Tell the individual's supervisor and ask that someone else help you with wrestling.

  —Ask your parents to file a report with the police. What he is doing is abuse and it is illegal.

Mario's Story

I am a 13-year-old boy with a problem—my 17-year-old uncle, Roy. Roy stays with me when my parents go out of town. The last time, he started to act really strange. He wouldn't let me out of his sight. Even when I took a shower, he insisted that I keep the bathroom door open. When I turned around, Roy was taking a picture of me in the shower. He told me there wasn't any film in the camera and that it was a joke. I don't think it was funny, though. On the last night he was there, he told me to come into his bedroom and watch TV with him—only it wasn't TV, it was sex stuff. He told me not to tell anyone because if I did he would be in trouble *and so would I.*

- **Does the fact that Roy is a member of Mario's family and only 17 years old mean that he could not be a possible child molester?**

  —Remember that a child molester could be anyone. Most are family members or someone else the child knows.

  —Many child molesters begin molesting others when they are teenagers.

- **Does the fact that Roy has not touched Mario mean that sexual abuse did not happen?**

  —Roy violated Mario's privacy by taking a picture that Mario did not want taken—this is one form of abuse.

—Showing Mario pornographic videos is a form of sexual abuse and is usually a forerunner of sexual contact.

- **Should Mario get into trouble if he tells on Roy?**

   —Mario should not be blamed. He did nothing wrong.

   —Anytime that sexual abuse occurs, the abuser is the one who is responsible.

Steven's Story

My name is Steven. I go to junior high school and make pretty good grades, so I'm not stupid. But the other day something happened that made me feel really dumb. A group of guys decided that they wanted to start a secret club. Only a few kids would be able to join their club. It was a fun thing, and the only way that you could join was to be asked by one of the members of the club. Well, one of my friends belonged and asked me to join. I was really flattered, and I really wanted to join. He told me that the club was meeting in one of the storage buildings on campus and that we could get high and have some fun—then he grabbed my crotch and laughed.

- **What do you suppose Steven's friend meant when he said, "We could get high and have some fun," and then grabbed Steven's crotch?**

   —Secret clubs are often used by child molesters to gain access to unsuspecting boys.

   —Using drugs and alcohol to lower resistance to sexual abuse also is quite common.

- **Suppose that Steven went to the club meeting and ended up being sexually molested by one of the other guys there. How do you think he would feel?**

   —A lot of boys feel very embarrassed when they realize that they have been fooled. Often they are afraid that others will think that they are homosexual if they have been sexually abused by another guy.

   —Embarrassment might cause Steven and other boys in his situation to not report their abuse.

Family Meeting
(Not Part of Joining Requirement)

A child must feel comfortable telling his parent about any sensitive problems or experiences in which someone approached him in an improper manner, or in a way that made him feel uncomfortable. Studies have shown that more than half of all child abuse incidents are never reported because the victims are too afraid or too confused to report their experiences.

Your children need to be able to talk freely about their likes and dislikes, their friends, and their true feelings. You can create open communication through family meetings where safety issues can be talked about by the entire family. The Youth Protection materials could be discussed in a family meeting.

No. 46-015

1998 Printing

BOY SCOUT HANDBOOK

ELEVENTH EDITION

BOY SCOUTS OF AMERICA

Dedicated to the American Scoutmaster
who makes Scouting possible

In appreciation

This handbook, the official BSA manual, is based
on the experience of the Boy Scouts of America
in the United States since its founding in 1910,
and is administered under the leadership of

Edward E. Whitacre Jr., *President*

Jere B. Ratcliffe, *Chief Scout Executive*

Copyright © 1998
Boy Scouts of America
Irving, Texas
Printed in U.S.A.   750M1298
No. 33105

Eleventh Edition • First Printing
Total copies of eleventh edition—750,000
Total printing since 1910—36,760,000

Library of Congress Cataloging-in-Publication Data

Boy Scouts of America.
        Boy Scout handbook.   11th ed.
        p.   cm.
    Includes index.
    ISBN 0-8395-3105-2
    1. Boy Scouts of America—Handbooks, manuals, etc. 2. Boy
Scouts—United States—Handbooks, manuals, etc. I. Title.
HS3313.B69   1998
369.43—ddc21

98-40936
CIP

FROM THE CHIEF SCOUT EXECUTIVE . . .

Fellow Scouts:

The *Boy Scout Handbook* you are holding is the road map to your Scouting adventure. It will show you how to be an expert in camping, hiking, and other activities in the great outdoors— all while having a great deal of fun with your friends.

Your handbook will also give you step-by-step information on how to advance to the rank of Eagle Scout. It will show you how to help make your neighborhood, community, and nation better places in which to live and how to become the best person you can be.

This *Boy Scout Handbook* is designed to go wherever you go. Don't leave it at home. Take it with you and refer to it often. It will get tattered and torn, but it will remain a wonderful tool to help you get the most from the magic of Scouting.

As you explore this handbook you will feel a sense of pride in your journey along the Scouting trail.

Good luck and good Scouting!

Jere B. Ratcliffe
Chief Scout Executive
Boy Scouts of America

CONTENTS

SCOUTING

THE ULTIMATE ADVENTURE

THE ADVENTURE BEGINS

TRAILHEAD

1

Millions of boys have been Scouts. They joined because they liked what the Boy Scouts of America had to offer. Now, Scouting welcomes you.

WELCOME TO THE BOY SCOUTS OF AMERICA

SCOUTING promises you the great outdoors. As a Scout, you can learn how to camp and hike without leaving a trace and how to take care of the land. You'll study wildlife up close and learn about nature all around you. There are plenty of skills for you to master, and you can teach others what you have learned. Everyone helping everyone else—that's part of Scouting, too.

SCOUTING promises you friendship. Members of the troop you join might be boys you already know, and you will meet many other Scouts along the way. Some could become lifelong friends.

SCOUTING promises you opportunities to work toward the Eagle Scout rank. You will set positive goals for yourself and then follow clear routes to achieve them.

SCOUTING promises you tools to help you make the most of your family, your community, and your nation. The good deeds you perform every day will improve the lives of those around you. You will be prepared to help others in time of need.

SCOUTING promises you experiences and duties that will help you mature into a strong, wise adult. The Scout Oath and the Scout Law can guide you while you are a Scout and throughout your life.

Adventure, learning, challenge, responsibility—the promise of Scouting is all this and more. Are you ready for the adventure to begin? Then turn the page and let's get started.

THE ADVENTURE OF SCOUTING

"Every boy delights in the adventure of a hike into the woods. He loves to explore caves, to climb hills, to wander through and spy out unknown territory."

Handbook for Scoutmasters, 2nd edition, 1920

COMPASS

Adventures are a big part of Scouting, and one of the best adventures is going camping. Let a First Class Scout tell you about his latest trip:

"I've been a Scout for almost a year, and I've been on plenty of hikes and campouts. We went on a weekend canoe trip, too. It was awesome.

"At our last patrol meeting we decided to go camping at a lake near our city. We made a list of the gear and food we would need and figured out how to reach the lake.

"Saturday we laced up our boots, swung our packs onto our shoulders, and hiked into the woods. I used a map and compass to lead the way. The trail was steep at first, but we kept a steady pace and put some miles behind us. We spotted a beaver dam in the stream below the lake, and during a rest break we watched a couple of hawks circling high above the trees.

"When we reached our campsite we pitched our tents, hauled water, and lit our camp stoves. We made stew for supper with our patrol's own secret recipe, then baked biscuits that we ate hot out of the pan with butter and jam. You can't believe how great everything tasted!

"Some of us went fishing, and at one point I thought I'd caught a whopper. When I reeled it in, though, it was pretty small so I let it go. My friends and I laughed about it, but next time I really am going to hook a big one.

"After dark we sat by the lake telling stories. The weather was kind of cold, so when I finally crawled into my sleeping bag I pulled on a warm hat and some wool socks.

"Early the next morning I looked out of the tent and saw a deer by the lake. My buddy and I went down there, being real quiet and hiding behind trees and bushes. We got close enough to see the deer's breath in the cold air, and we watched it eating grass. Its ears were twitching around and it must have heard us, because all of a sudden it ran away.

"We ate a big breakfast, then packed up and headed for home. The tents are stored again at our Scoutmaster's house, but they won't be there long. We're already planning our next adventure, and I can hardly wait!"

HOW TO BECOME A BOY SCOUT

✓ **Here's all you need to do to become a Boy Scout:**

MEET AGE REQUIREMENTS.
Be a boy who has completed the fifth grade or is 11 years old, or has earned the Arrow of Light Award but is under 18 years old.

COMPLETE A BOY SCOUT APPLICATION AND HEALTH HISTORY SIGNED BY YOUR PARENT OR GUARDIAN.

FIND A SCOUT TROOP NEAR YOUR HOME.

REPEAT THE PLEDGE OF ALLEGIANCE.

DEMONSTRATE THE SCOUT SIGN, SALUTE, AND HANDSHAKE.

DEMONSTRATE TYING THE SQUARE KNOT
(a joining knot).

UNDERSTAND AND AGREE TO LIVE BY THE SCOUT OATH OR PROMISE, LAW, MOTTO, AND SLOGAN, AND THE OUTDOOR CODE.

DESCRIBE THE SCOUT BADGE.

COMPLETE THE PAMPHLET EXERCISES.
With your parent or guardian, complete the exercises in the pamphlet *How to Protect Your Children from Child Abuse: A Parent's Guide.*

PARTICIPATE IN A SCOUTMASTER CONFERENCE.
Turn in your Boy Scout application and health history form signed by your parent or guardian, then participate in a Scoutmaster conference.

When you have done these things, the Scoutmaster will give you a certificate of membership, and you can proudly wear the badge and uniform that show you are a member of the Boy Scouts of America.

A graduating Webelos Scout who has earned the Arrow of Light Award has completed most of the Boy Scout joining requirements. With the approval of his Scoutmaster, he will receive the Boy Scout badge upon joining the troop.

FIND A SCOUT TROOP NEAR YOUR HOME

If you don't know of a troop in your area, look for the Boy Scouts of America in your telephone directory, or contact the national office at the following address and telephone number:

Boy Scout Division
Boy Scouts of America
1325 West Walnut Hill Lane
P.O. Box 152079
Irving, TX 75015-2079
972-580-2000

You can also use the Internet to find your Boy Scouts of America (BSA) local council. The web page of the BSA national office follows:

http://www.bsa.scouting.org

If you live in a remote area where there is no troop, you can still take part in the Scouting program by becoming a Lone Scout. For more information on the Lone Scout program, contact the national office at the address listed above.

REPEAT THE PLEDGE OF ALLEGIANCE

Pledge of Allegiance

I pledge allegiance to the flag of the United States of America and to the republic for which it stands, one nation under God, indivisible, with liberty and justice for all.

The Meaning of the Pledge of Allegiance

When you pledge allegiance to the flag, you promise loyalty and devotion to your nation:

I pledge allegiance . . . You promise to be true

. . . to the flag . . . to the emblem of your country

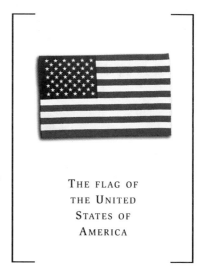

THE FLAG OF
THE UNITED
STATES OF
AMERICA

. . . of the United States of America . . . a nation made up of fifty states and several territories, each with certain rights of its own

. . . and to the republic . . . a country where the people elect representatives from among themselves to make laws for them

. . . for which it stands, . . . the flag represents the United States of America

. . . one nation under God, . . . a country whose people are free to believe in God

. . . indivisible, . . . the nation cannot be split into parts

. . . with liberty and justice . . . with freedom and fairness

. . . for all. . . . for every person in the country—you and every other American.

DEMONSTRATE THE SCOUT SIGN, SALUTE, AND HANDSHAKE

Scout Sign

The Scout sign shows you are a Scout. Give it each time you recite the Scout Oath and Law. When a Scout or Scouter raises the Scout sign, all Scouts should make the sign, too, and come to silent attention.

To give the Scout sign, cover the nail of the little finger of your right hand with your right thumb, then raise your right arm bent in a 90-degree angle, and hold the three middle fingers of your hand upward. Those fingers stand for the three parts of the Scout Oath. Your thumb and little finger touch to represent the bond that unites Scouts throughout the world.

Scout Salute

The Scout salute shows respect. Use it to salute the flag of the United States of America. You may also salute a Scout leader or another Scout.

Give the Scout salute by forming the Scout sign with your right hand and then bringing that hand upward until your forefinger touches the brim of your hat or the arch of your right eyebrow. The palm of your hand should not show.

Scout Handshake

The Scout handshake is made with the hand nearest the heart and is offered as a token of friendship. Extend your left hand to another Scout and firmly grasp his left hand. **The fingers do not interlock.**

SQUARE KNOT

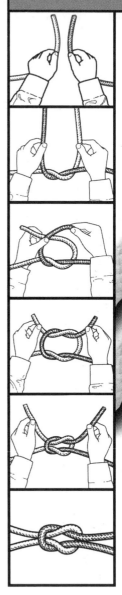

DEMONSTRATE TYING THE SQUARE KNOT

The square knot is also known as a joining knot because it can join together two ropes and because it is the first knot Scouts learn when they join the BSA. It has many uses—from securing bundles, packages, and the sails of ships to tying the ends of bandages.

To tie a square knot, hold one rope end in each hand. Pass the right end over and under the rope in your left hand and pull it snug. Next, pass the rope now in your left hand over and under the one now in your right, and pull it snug. Remember, **right over left, left over right.**

UNDERSTAND AND AGREE TO LIVE BY THE SCOUT OATH OR PROMISE, LAW, MOTTO, AND SLOGAN, AND THE OUTDOOR CODE

Scout Oath or Promise

On my honor I will do my best
To do my duty to God and my country
and to obey the Scout Law;
To help other people at all times;
To keep myself physically strong,
mentally awake, and morally straight.

Scout Law

A Scout is trustworthy, loyal,
helpful, friendly, courteous, kind,
obedient, cheerful, thrifty, brave,
clean, and reverent.

Scout Motto

Be Prepared.

Scout Slogan

Do a Good Turn Daily.

> SCOUT MOTTO
>
> **BE PREPARED.**
>
> SCOUT SLOGAN
>
> **DO A GOOD TURN DAILY.**

(For further explanation of the Scout Oath or Promise, Law, motto, and slogan, see chapter 3, "Tenderfoot Scout," pages 45–55 **T**.)

Outdoor Code

As an American, I will do my best to
Be clean in my outdoor manners,
Be careful with fire,
Be considerate in the outdoors, and
Be conservation-minded.

(For more on the Outdoor Code, see chapter 9, "Camping," page 219 **A**.)

DESCRIBE THE SCOUT BADGE

The badge is shaped like the north point on an old compass. The design resembles an arrowhead or a *trefoil*—a flower with three leaves. It is also known by the French name *fleur-de-lis*, which means lily or iris flower. It is the basic shape of the badges used by Scout organizations in other countries, too.

The **three points** of the trefoil stand for the three parts of the Scout Oath.

The **eagle and shield** stand for freedom and a Scout's readiness to defend that freedom.

There are **two stars** on the badge. They symbolize truth and knowledge.

The **shape** of the Scout badge means that a Scout can point the right way in life as truly as does a compass in the field.

The **scroll** bearing the Scout motto is turned up at the ends as a reminder that a Scout smiles as he does his duty.

The **knot** at the bottom of the scroll represents the Scout slogan, Do a Good Turn Daily.

COMPLETE THE PAMPHLET EXERCISES

With your parent or guardian, complete the exercises in the pamphlet *How to Protect Your Children from Child Abuse: A Parent's Guide.*

The pamphlet found inside the cover of this handbook is part of the BSA's commitment to ensuring the safety of young people wherever they might be. It explains ways that adults can help protect children, and so should be shared by you with your parent or guardian.

PARTICIPATE IN A SCOUTMASTER CONFERENCE

After you finish the joining requirements, your Scoutmaster will want to have a conference with you. He or she will also sit down and talk with you after you finish the requirements for each Scout rank. These Scoutmaster conferences are opportunities for you to review how you are doing and to look ahead with your Scoutmaster toward what happens next in your life as a Scout. You can ask questions, share what you like about being a Scout, and together figure out ways it can be even better.

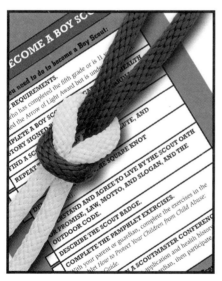

Friendly visits with your troop leader help open the way for your success as a Scout.

SCOUT UNIFORM

"... putting on the uniform does not make a fellow a Scout, but putting on the uniform is a sign to the world that one has taken the Scout obligations and folks expect Scout-like acts from one wearing it."

Handbook for Boys, 3rd edition, 1927

Like the Scout badge, the uniform is an emblem of Scouting. It might be brand-new, or it might be an experienced uniform already worn by another Scout to many meetings and campouts. Old or new, wear your uniform proudly whenever you are taking part in Scout activities. By dressing alike, Scouts show they are equals. Your uniform is also a sign to yourself and to others that you are a person who can be trusted. You can be counted on to lend a hand when help is needed. Dressed as a Scout, you will want to act as a Scout.

The complete official uniform includes the Scout long-sleeved or short-sleeved shirt, Scout pants or shorts, Scout belt and buckle, Scout socks or knee socks. A neckerchief and cap or campaign hat

are optional. Wear full uniform for all cere-
monial and indoor activities, such as troop
meetings, courts of honor, and most other
indoor functions. The uniform should also
be worn during special outdoor occasions,
such as Scout shows, flag ceremonies, and
special times at summer camp.

For outdoor activities, Scouts may wear
troop or camp T-shirts with the Scout pants
or shorts.

How to Wear a Neckerchief

Roll the long edge
of a neckerchief
until it is about six
inches from the tip.
Place the necker-
chief smoothly
around your neck,
either over or
under your collar
depending on the
custom of your
troop. Hold the
neckerchief in
place with a slide.

EAGLE
AWARD

THE RANKS OF SCOUTING

SCOUTING provides many opportunities for you to learn skills and take part in terrific adventures. The Boy Scouts of America will recognize your achievements by awarding badges of rank. The first three are Tenderfoot, Second Class, and First Class. Next come Star and Life. The highest rank is Eagle.

The requirements to earn each rank are more challenging than the one before it. Each prepares you to be a better camper, hiker, Scout, and citizen. When you complete the requirements for a rank, you will find that you can use your new knowledge on patrol and troop outings. You will also have the background you need for achieving even more as you begin the next rank.

Setting out to advance through the ranks of Scouting and become an Eagle Scout is an ambitious goal. Learning all the skills and completing all the requirements will take dedication and hard work. But the journey will be worth it as the ideals and adventures of Scouting become a part of your life.

You may pass any of the requirements for Tenderfoot, Second Class, and First Class at any time. For example, if you fulfill a First Class requirement before you are a Second Class Scout, you may check off the First Class requirement as completed. Though you can advance at your own pace, active Scouts will usually earn First Class within a year of joining a troop.

Earning badges can be very satisfying. However, badges are not the most important part of Scouting. Of greater value is what the badges represent. The skills you master, the wisdom you gain, and the experiences you enjoy are what really count. The merit badge program provides you the opportunity to meet and work with adult leaders in your community. It also introduces you to potential new hobbies and vocations.

EAGLE SCOUT

 LIFE

STAR

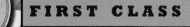

FIRST CLASS

SECOND CLASS

TENDERFOOT

YOUR PATROL AND TROOP

TRAILHEAD

2

Your patrol is a team of good friends working together to make things happen. Several patrols make up a troop, the community of Scouts you can call your own.

YOUR PATROL AND TROOP

YOUR PATROL

Patrols are the building blocks of Scouting. Your patrol is a team of six to eight boys who make things happen. With the help of a *patrol leader*, you plan together, learn together, and all of you pitch in to turn exciting plans into action. Together, members of your patrol can achieve much more than each of you could on your own. You can invite your non-Scout friends to join the troop and become patrol members, too.

Adventures with your patrol will help you develop as a Scout and as a leader.

Patrols are such an important part of Scouting that a part of every troop meeting should be set aside for each patrol to meet by itself. At other times your patrol might get together in the home of one of its members or at a special patrol site.

A patrol is just the right size for outdoor adventures. On camping trips, a few tents will shelter everyone, and a couple of backpacking stoves are enough for cooking hearty meals. Patrol members can learn to roam the backcountry together without leaving any sign that they were ever there.

Because all of you are different, each member of your patrol will have much to share. You can teach each other the skills you know. As friends, you can look out for one another. Friendship, fun, adventure—that's what a Scout patrol is all about.

The New-Scout Patrol

"A good Patrol is a gang of good friends, standing together shoulder to shoulder whatever comes. 'All for One—One for All'—that's the spirit of a Scout Patrol."

Handbook for Patrol Leaders, 1950

The new-Scout patrol is a group of boys who have just become Scouts. They are helped by a *troop guide*—an older, experienced Scout who can show the way. An *assistant Scoutmaster* assigned to the patrol gives it added support.

Members of a new-Scout patrol choose their patrol leader, plan what they want to do, and take part in outings and troop meetings just like any patrol. They can also learn the basic skills they need in order to enjoy hiking, camping, and other Scout adventures. Before long, members of a new-Scout patrol will discover that they are passing many of the requirements for the ranks of Tenderfoot, Second Class, and First Class.

PATROL BADGES

Patrols for Experienced Scouts

Scouts who have entered the seventh grade or who hold the rank of First Class or higher may become members of patrols for experienced Scouts. Older Scouts who have not yet reached First Class may join experienced Scout patrols and then continue their work on the First Class requirements.

Venture Patrols

Many troops have a Venture patrol—a special patrol for older Scouts. Venture patrols plan and take on rugged outdoor adventures and special sports activities. The opportunities within a Venture patrol give older Scouts every reason to stay active in their troop and to use their Scouting knowledge. (For more on Venture patrols, see page 420–21.)

Patrol Activities

Patrols are fueled by real adventures. Some happen indoors, such as planning trips; making camp equipment; and practicing first aid, knots and lashings, and other Scouting skills. But most happen outdoors: Your patrol will go hiking and camping with other patrols in the troop. With the permission of your Scoutmaster and your parent or guardian, your patrol may go on its own to camp, hike, and conduct special projects.

Hikes and campouts give your patrol the opportunity to put its knowledge to good use. Away from home and school, you'll also have time to focus on your friendships with other Scouts and on your enjoyment of the outdoors.

Patrol Name, Flag, and Emblem

Every patrol has a name. Yours might be the Silver Fox Patrol, or you might be called the Hawks, Bears, Sharks, or Coyotes. Some patrols name themselves for trees (Pine Tree Patrol, or the Giant Redwood Patrol) or a person (the Daniel Boone Patrol).

Each patrol has a flag it can carry at troop meetings and on campouts, and an emblem for the members to wear on the right sleeve of their Scout shirts. Some patrols mark their camping gear with their emblem.

Patrol Yell

Every patrol has a yell, too. A patrol that is named for an animal could use the animal's sound—the howl of a wolf, for example, or the hoot of an owl. Patrols not named for animals may also choose an animal's call, or they can decide on some other yell that identifies them.

Give your yell when your patrol wins a contest during a troop meeting or performs well at any other competitive event.

Patrol Leader

Your patrol will elect one of its members to serve as patrol leader. He will be in charge of the patrol at troop meetings and during outdoor adventures, and he represents the patrol on the patrol leaders' council. He suggests Good Turns and service projects, then encourages the patrol to pitch in. When spirits are low, he gets the members going again. Working with the senior patrol leader, he finds ways all patrol members can make progress in Scouting.

A patrol leader will expect everyone in the patrol to help make things happen, and his goal is to bring out the best in his patrol. He might invite a Scout who writes well to keep a journal of patrol meetings. He might ask other Scouts to repair and store camping gear. He might want you to help him come up with menus for a campout, songs and skits for a campfire, or information about conservation projects the patrol can do.

While there is only one patrol leader, every member of a patrol shares the duties of leadership. You could be the one who finds the way on a hike, who is the chief cook in camp, or who teaches other Scouts how to tie a knot. Those experiences let you practice being in charge. Someday you might become a patrol leader, too.

As a member of a patrol, you will discover many ways to be of service to others.

NATIONAL HONOR PATROL AWARD

The National Honor Patrol Award is given to patrols whose members make an extra effort to have the best patrol possible. Your patrol can earn the award by doing the following over a period of three months:

☑

HAVE A PATROL NAME, FLAG, AND YELL.
Put your patrol design on equipment and use your patrol yell. Keep patrol records up to date.

HOLD TWO PATROL MEETINGS EVERY MONTH.

TAKE PART IN AT LEAST ONE HIKE, OUTDOOR ACTIVITY, OR OTHER SCOUTING EVENT.

COMPLETE TWO GOOD TURNS OR SERVICE PROJECTS APPROVED BY THE PATROL LEADERS' COUNCIL.

HELP TWO PATROL MEMBERS ADVANCE ONE RANK.

WEAR THE FULL UNIFORM CORRECTLY
(at least 75 percent of the patrol's membership).

HAVE A REPRESENTATIVE ATTEND AT LEAST THREE PATROL LEADERS' COUNCIL MEETINGS.

HAVE EIGHT MEMBERS IN THE PATROL OR INCREASE PATROL MEMBERSHIP OVER THE PREVIOUS THREE MONTHS.

The National Honor Patrol Award is an embroidered star worn beneath the patrol medallion, and will spotlight a patrol as a high-standard group. Help your patrol become a National Honor Patrol.

LEADER BADGES

YOUR TROOP

No patrol stands alone. Together, all the patrols make up a troop. Scout troops have the size and leadership to take on projects and adventures larger than those that can be done by a single patrol.

Help keep your troop exciting and lively by coming to meetings on time. Join in every activity with cheerful enthusiasm. Set your sights on becoming one of your troop's best all-around Scouts. The more of yourself that you give to Scouting, the more Scouting will give to you.

Patrol Leaders' Council

The activities of your troop are planned by a *patrol leaders' council* (PLC) made up of your patrol leaders, senior patrol leader, Scoutmaster, and other troop leaders. The PLC discusses future meetings and outings for the whole troop. Your patrol leader shares ideas that have come from you and other Scouts in your patrol. The patrol leaders' council considers the suggestions and needs of all the Scouts, then maps out activities for the troop.

Troop Meetings

When you go to a weekly troop meeting, you can expect it to be packed with activities. There often will be games that improve your Scouting know-how. Patrol demonstrations and contests between patrols will help you learn new skills. There will be fun and good fellowship, too, and perhaps songs, games, and ceremonies.

Troop meetings are not always held at the same place. Now and then a troop might meet at a fire station or police headquarters so that you can learn how your town is protected. On a summer evening you might gather at a local pool to pass some of the swimming requirements for a rank or merit badge. Your troop might meet outdoors to practice outdoor skills.

Troop Camping and Hiking

Every good Scout troop has an exciting outdoor program. Throughout the year, your troop will set off on hikes and camping trips. Troop members attend Scout summer camp together. They might also participate in one of the BSA's council or national high-adventure programs or activities. On most troop outings you will travel and camp with your patrol.

Scout Troop Leaders

Senior Patrol Leader

This top boy leader of a troop is elected by all the Scouts. With guidance from the Scoutmaster, he is in charge of troop meetings and the patrol leaders' council, and does all he can to see that the patrols succeed.

Scoutmaster

The adult leader of your troop is dedicated to bringing learning, adventure, and opportunity to you and other Scouts. Your Scoutmaster will be at troop meetings and go on most hikes and camping trips. The senior patrol leader and the troop's patrol leaders look to the Scoutmaster for advice and direction. You will get to know your Scoutmaster as an adult you can trust for support and guidance.

Assistant Scoutmasters

These are individuals at least 18 years of age who assist your Scoutmaster in making sure your troop's program is interesting and effective and that everyone has a worthwhile time.

Junior Assistant Scoutmasters

These are young men ages 16 and 17 who help the troop achieve its goals.

Troop Committee

This group of parents and other adults are responsible for your troop's welfare.

Chartered Organization

This is a church, synagogue, school, service club, or other religious or civic group that has ownership of the troop to help fulfill aims and goals for the development of youth. The chartered organization provides the troop with a meeting place, leaders, and guidance.

YOUR DISTRICT AND COUNCIL

The geographic area in which your troop is located is called a *district*. A district in a large city might include one or more neighborhoods. In rural areas, it could cover several counties.

One or more districts make up a *council*. The council's professional staff and volunteers help all of the troops have successful programs. Local council service centers and Scout shops sell uniforms, books, and other Scouting goods. Many districts and councils hold camporees so that troops can come together to share the spirit of Scouting.

The biggest council activity of the year is summer camp. You and the rest of your troop can spend a week or more learning and using Scout skills. Many camps offer swimming, boating, canoeing, and other water activities. Most also have opportunities for hiking, camp cooking, nature study, and much more.

Mountains, prairies, rivers, seashores— every part of America offers great country for Scout activities.

CLIMBING

T TENDERFOOT
SCOUT

TRAILHEAD

3

TENDERFOOT SCOUT

TENDERFOOT is the first rank you will earn as a Boy Scout. The requirements offer a taste of the great adventures awaiting you in Scouting, and can give you the basic skills you'll need to begin taking part in those adventures. There is a lot of challenge in earning the Tenderfoot badge, and you might soon find yourself doing things you had only dreamed about before.

1. Present yourself to your leader, properly dressed, before going on an overnight camping trip. Show the camping gear you will use. Show the right way to pack and carry it.

2. Spend at least one night on a patrol or troop campout. Sleep in a tent you have helped pitch.

3. On the campout, assist in preparing and cooking one of your patrol's meals. Tell why it is important for each patrol member to share in meal preparation and cleanup, and explain the importance of eating together.

MY FIRST CAMPOUT

Date _____

Where did we go? _____

Who else went along? _____

_____

What did we see? _____

What did we eat? _____

How was the weather? _____

What did I like most about the campout? _____

_____

What did I not like? _____

_____

What will I do differently next time? _____

_____

Your first campout with your patrol or troop is one of the most exciting experiences in Scouting. You might go to a park near your home or to a Scout camp far away. You might be able to look out and see mountains, farm fields, or the skyline of your city. Expect plenty of fun and adventure.

Your Scoutmaster, patrol leader, troop guide, and others will help you get ready for your first campout. (For more information on what to wear for outdoor adventures, turn to chapter 8, "Hiking," beginning on page 197 [image]. For information on choosing, packing, and carrying camping gear; pitching a tent; and preparing for a great adventure, see chapter 9, "Camping," starting on page 217 [image]. Read about meal preparation and cleanup in chapter 10, "Cooking," starting on page 247 [image].)

Whatever happens, your first campout will be special to you. Make a few notes about it on the previous page so that you can always remember when your outdoor adventures as a Boy Scout began.

TENDERFOOT RANK REQUIREMENTS

✓	
	1. Present yourself to your leader, properly dressed, before going on an overnight camping trip. Show the camping gear you will use. Show the right way to pack and carry it.
	2. Spend at least one night on a patrol or troop campout. Sleep in a tent you have helped pitch.
	3. On the campout, assist in preparing and cooking one of your patrol's meals. Tell why it is important for each patrol member to share in meal preparation and cleanup, and explain the importance of eating together.
	4a. Demonstrate how to whip and fuse the ends of a rope.
	4b. Demonstrate that you know how to tie the following knots and tell what their uses are: two half hitches and the taut-line hitch.
	5. Explain the rules of safe hiking, both on the highway and cross-country, during the day and at night. Explain what to do if you are lost.
	6. Demonstrate how to display, raise, lower, and fold the American flag.

TENDERFOOT RANK REQUIREMENTS

7. Repeat from memory and explain in your own words the Scout Oath, Law, motto, and slogan.

8. Know your patrol name, give the patrol yell, and describe your patrol flag.

9. Explain why we use the buddy system in Scouting.

10a. Record your best in the following tests:

Current results	**30 days later**
Push-ups _____	Push-ups _____
Pull-ups _____	Pull-ups _____
Sit-ups _____	Sit-ups _____
Standing long jump (_____ feet _____ inches)	Standing long jump (_____ feet _____ inches)
¼-mile walk/run _____	¼-mile walk/run _____

10b. Show improvement in the activities listed in requirement 10a after practicing for 30 days.

11. Identify local poisonous plants; tell how to treat for exposure to them.

12a. Demonstrate the Heimlich maneuver and tell when it is used.

12b. Show first aid for the following:

- Simple cuts and scratches
- Blisters on the hand and foot
- Minor burns or scalds (first-degree)
- Bites or stings of insects and ticks
- Poisonous snakebite
- Nosebleed
- Frostbite and sunburn

13. Participate in a Scoutmaster conference.

14. Complete your board of review.

NOTE: Alternate requirements for the Tenderfoot rank are available for Scouts with physical or mental disabilities if they meet the criteria listed in the *Boy Scout Requirements* book, No. 33215.

As you complete each requirement, ask your Scoutmaster to initial his or her approval on pages 438–39.

4a. Demonstrate how to whip and fuse the ends of a rope.

Rope is one of mankind's oldest tools. Today it is made by twisting together the stringy fibers of certain plants, or by twisting together or weaving strands of nylon, plastic, or other modern materials.

The ends of a rope sometimes begin coming apart. For a temporary fix, tie a knot in each end or wrap it with duct tape. The permanent way to prevent ropes from unraveling is by whipping or fusing the ends.

Whipping

Cut off any of the rope that has already unraveled. Take a piece of strong string, preferably waxed and at least two feet long, and form a loop in it. Lay the loop near the end of the rope. Tightly wrap, or *whip,* the string around the rope. When the whipping is at least as wide as the rope is thick, slip the end through the loop and pull hard. Trim off the excess string, then whip the rope's other end.

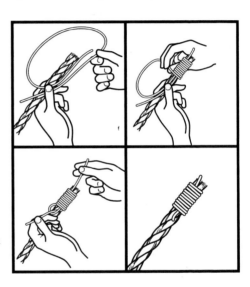

Fusing

Rope and cord made of plastic or nylon will melt when exposed to high heat. Cut away the frayed part of the rope, then, working in a well-ventilated area, hold each end a few inches above a lighted match or candle to melt and fuse the strands together. Melted rope can be hot and sticky—don't touch the end until it has

cooled. Do not try to fuse ropes made of manila, sisal, hemp, cotton, or other natural fibers, because they will burn rather than melt.

"To tie a knot seems to be a simple thing, and yet there are

right ways and wrong ways of doing it, and scouts ought to

know the right way."

—*Baden-Powell,* Scouting for Boys, *1915*

4b. Demonstrate that you know how to tie the following knots and tell what their uses are: two half hitches and the taut-line hitch.

Three tests of a good knot:
1
IT SHOULD BE EASY TO TIE.
2
IT SHOULD STAY TIED.
3
IT SHOULD BE EASY TO UNTIE.

You probably already know how to tie a few knots. At home you tie your shoes, your necktie, and sometimes a package. You will use knots on camping trips to hold gear on your pack, set up tents and dining flies, and keep canoes and boats from drifting away. Knots hold bandages in place. They often play a role during rescues on the water and in the mountains.

After you have learned to tie a knot, practice it often. Carry a piece of cord in your pocket and, several times a day, pull it out and tie the knots you know. When you are able to tie them quickly, even with your eyes closed, you will own those knots and be ready to use them in any situation.

A *hitch* is a knot that ties a rope to something. Friction caused by the wraps of the rope holds the hitch in place.

TWO HALF HITCHES

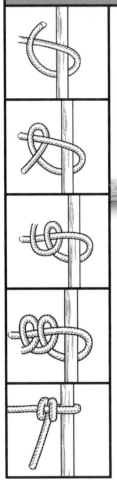

TWO HALF HITCHES

Use two half hitches to tie a rope around a post.

Pass the end of the rope around the post. Bring the end over and under the body of the rope (known as the *standing part)*, then back through the loop thus formed. That makes a *half hitch.* Take the end around the standing part a second time and tie another half hitch. Pull it snug.

TAUT-LINE HITCH

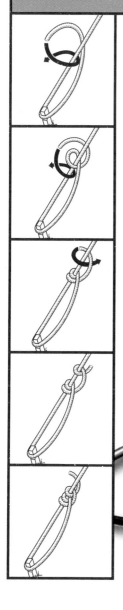

TAUT-LINE HITCH

The taut-line hitch is tied on a line that is tight, or *taut*. Use it to tighten or loosen a tent guyline by pushing the hitch up or down. Here's how: Pass the line around a tent stake. Bring the end under and over the standing part and twice through the loop you have formed. Again bring the rope end under, over, and through a loop, but this time farther up the standing part. Work any slack out of the knot, then slide the hitch to adjust the tension on the line.

5. Explain the rules of safe hiking, both on the highway and cross-country, during the day and at night. Explain what to do if you are lost.

Scout hiking often takes you along trails. Quiet back roads can also be wonderful for walking. When hiking in the city, you can often travel on sidewalks along busy streets. Wherever you go, the most important part of hiking is doing it safely.

When on outings with your patrol or troop, always hike with a buddy. The trip can be more fun, and you will have help if you need it.

HIKING BOOTS

Hiking on Highways and Roads

Anytime you must hike along a highway or road without a sidewalk, stay in single file on the left side, facing the traffic. Light-colored clothing can make it easier for drivers to see you.

If you must hike alongside a road at night, tie strips of white cloth or reflective ribbon around your right arm and leg. Even better are the fluorescent vests often worn by highway workers. Use a flashlight to brighten your way and to alert drivers that you are there.

Never hitchhike. It can be dangerous, it might be illegal, and it spoils the spirit of a hike.

Hiking on Trails and Cross-Country

Following a trail is often the best way to reach the places you want to go. Staying on trails helps you avoid trampling plants or adding to erosion with your footsteps. It is hard to get lost if your feet are on a pathway.

Whether or not your backcountry hikes are on trails or across open ground, watch where you place your feet to avoid slipping or twisting an ankle. Use bridges to cross streams. Wade through water only if there

Backcountry travel often involves problem solving—crossing a stream, finding your way, doing things safely.

is no other way to go, and only if the water is shallow and the current is not too swift. Unfasten the hip belt of your backpack before crossing a stream. If you slip, you'll be able to free yourself from the backpack before it can weigh you down in the water.

Detour around areas that appear to be dangerous, or go back the way you came. **Your safety is always much more important than reaching the destination of a hike.**

(For more about hiking, see chapter 8, "Hiking," beginning on page 197 .)

"Were you ever lost?" someone asked Daniel Boone.

"No," he replied, "but once I was confused for about five

days over where I was."

Staying Found

The best way not to get lost is to know at all times where you are. Before you start out, mark the route of your hike on a map and then study the map to become familiar with the countryside. Find your destination on the map. What landmarks should you be able to see as you are walking?

Pay attention while you are hiking. Notice the direction you are going. Watch for hills, streams, valleys, buildings, and other landscape features. If you have a map and compass, use them to pinpoint your location.

STAY CALM.

THINK.

OBSERVE.

PLAN.

Look back over your shoulder often to see how your route will look on your way back.

What to Do If You Are Lost

One day—even though you know all of the safety rules—you might wander off a trail and not be able to find it again. Or, you might take a wrong turn and not know which way to go. If you think you are lost, stop and follow these *STOP* steps:

STOP

Stay calm.
Think.
Observe.
Plan.

- *Stay calm.* Sit down and have a sip of water and a bite of food. If you are cold, pull on a jacket or sweater. Breathe slowly and steadily.

- *Think.* Try to remember how you got where you are. Get out your map and see what you can learn from the symbols and contour lines.

- *Observe.* Look for your footprints in loose and muddy earth or in the snow. Look around for landmarks that might give clues about your location.

- *Plan.* If you are fairly sure of a route that will take you to a known location, move carefully. If you have a compass, use it to set a bearing in the direction of your destination. In case you need to find your way back, mark your route well with broken branches, piles of stones, or whatever else is handy.

However, if you have no idea where you are or which way to go, **stay put**. People will start looking for you as soon as someone realizes you are missing.

Help searchers find you. The universal distress call is any signal repeated three times. Three shouts, for instance, or three blasts on a whistle. A smoky fire in the daytime and a bright fire at night might also attract attention. For smoke, toss grass or green leaves on the flames. Spread your rain gear and bright-colored equipment in the open to catch the eye of a rescue pilot, or flash a mirror in the direction of aircraft.

Make yourself comfortable. Pitch a tent if you have one, or find shelter against a rock or under a tree. Use what you find in your pack and pockets to stay warm and dry. Hang a T-shirt or some other bright object in a branch above you so that searchers can spot your location even if you are sleeping.

Finally, try not to worry too much. You will survive for several days without water and for several weeks without food. Stay put and stay calm. You will be found.

"The worst thing you can do is to get frightened. The truly dangerous enemy is not the cold or the hunger, so much as the fear. It is fear that robs the wanderer of his judgment and of his limb power. . . . Only keep cool and all will be well."

—*Ernest Thompson Seton, 1912*

6. Demonstrate how to display, raise, lower, and fold the American flag.

The flag of the United States is much more than just red, white, and blue cloth. As the symbol of America, it stands for the past, present,

and future of our country. It represents our people, our land, and our many ways of life.

Respect the flag and the ideals it represents by handling and displaying it correctly.

Flying the Flag

The flag of the United States may be flown every day and, if it is made of weather-resistant material, in any conditions. A flag is usually flown from sunrise to sunset. The flag should be flown on all national and state holidays, and on other days proclaimed by the president.

Show joy and pride in your country by flying the flag at full-staff. Hoist it briskly and lower it slowly.

Fly the flag at half-staff to show sorrow and mourning following a national tragedy, the death of a president or other national or state figure, or to honor those who have sacrificed their lives for their country. Hoist the flag to the top of the pole, hold it for an instant, then lower it to a point half the distance between the top and the bottom of the pole. To take it down, first raise the flag back to the top of the pole, then slowly lower it. On Memorial Day, fly the flag at half-staff until noon, then hoist it to full-staff.

The United States flag should never be flown upside down except as a distress signal to call for help.

Hoisting the Flag

It takes two people to hoist, lower, and fold the flag correctly. For hoisting, one person holds the folded flag and prevents it from touching the ground. The other person attaches the flag to the flag line, or *halyard,* then raises the flag briskly, keeping the line tight. When the flag has left the arms of the first person and is flowing freely, he or she steps back and salutes the flag as the other person ties the halyard to the flagpole.

FOLDED FLAG

Lowering the Flag

One person unfastens the halyard from the pole and slowly lowers the flag while the other salutes. When the flag is within reach, the saluter gathers the flag into his or her arms. The first person removes the flag from the halyard and ties the halyard to the pole.

Folding the Flag

The two people begin by folding the flag in half lengthwise and then again in half lengthwise, keeping the blue field on the outside. Then, while one person holds the flag by the blue field, the other makes a triangular fold in the opposite end and continues folding in triangles until nothing shows but the blue field.

Greeting the Flag

When you are wearing your Scout uniform, with or without a hat, greet the flag with a Scout salute anytime you pass it, it passes you, or you see it being hoisted or lowered. Give the Scout salute when you recite the Pledge of Allegiance, too.

When you are not in uniform, greet the flag by placing your right hand over your heart. If you are wearing a hat, remove it and hold it in your right hand over your heart.

(For more information about flags, see the *Your Flag* book, No. 33188.)

Carrying the Flag

The flag may be carried on a staff in parades, at the beginning and end of a Scout meeting, and during other ceremonies and patriotic events. It is always carried aloft and free, never flat or horizontally.

When the flag is carried by itself, there should be a person serving as an honor guard to its left, or one on each side of it. When carried with other flags, the United States flag should be in front of the others or, if the flags are arranged in a row, the farthest to its own right. The flag of the United States is never dipped in salute to any person or thing.

Displaying the Flag

A few basic rules ensure that the flag will always be displayed in an orderly and respectful manner:

When flags are displayed at different heights, the United States flag flies higher than all the others. It is hoisted first and lowered last.
When flags are displayed at equal heights, the United States flag is either out in front or farthest to its own right.
To display the United States flag flat against a wall, horizontally or vertically, the blue field should be at the top and at the flag's own right (at the observer's left).
In a church, synagogue, temple, or auditorium, the United States flag on a staff may be placed to the clergy's or speaker's right.
When hung over the center of a street, the United States flag should have the blue field to the north in an east-west street and to the east in a north-south street.

International usage forbids the display of the flag of one nation above that of another nation in time of peace. Flags of other nations must be flown from separate flagpoles of equal height, and all flags should be approximately equal in size.

7. Repeat from memory and explain in your own words the Scout Oath, Law, motto, and slogan.

The principles of the Boy Scouts of America are found in the Scout Oath, Scout Law, Scout motto, and Scout slogan. You will be expected to live by these standards while you are a Boy Scout. They will also help guide you throughout all of your life.

The Meaning of the Scout Oath

Before you pledge yourself to any oath or promise, you must know what it means:

Scout Oath

On my honor I will do my best
To do my duty to God and my country
and to obey the Scout Law:
To help other people at all times;
To keep myself physically strong,
mentally awake, and morally straight.

On my honor . . .
By giving your word, you are promising to be guided by the ideals of the Scout Oath.

. . . I will do my best . . .
Try hard to live up to the points of the Scout Oath. Measure your achievements against your own high standards and don't be influenced by peer pressure or what other people do.

. . . To do my duty to God . . .
Your family and religious leaders teach you about God and the ways you can serve. You do your duty to God by following the wisdom of those teachings every day and by respecting and defending the rights of others to practice their own beliefs.

. . . and my country . . .
Help keep the United States a strong and fair nation by learning about our system of government and your responsibilities as a citizen and future voter.

America is made up of countless families and communities. When you work to improve your community and your home, you are serving your country. Natural resources are another important part of America's heritage worthy of your efforts to understand, protect, and use wisely. What you do can make a real difference.

As you study our country's history, you learn about the men and women who made America great. Most of them contributed in quiet, useful ways while others sacrificed their lives. All of them did their part to build the nation we have today.

. . . and to obey the Scout Law; . . .

The twelve points of the Scout Law are guidelines that can lead you toward wise choices. When you obey the Scout Law, other people will respect you for the way you live, and you will respect yourself.

. . . To help other people at all times; . . .

There are many people who need you. Your cheerful smile and helping hand will ease the burden of many who need assistance. By helping out whenever possible, you are doing your part to make this a better world.

. . . To keep myself physically strong . . .

Take care of your body so that it will serve you well for an entire lifetime. That means eating nutritious foods, getting enough sleep, and exercising regularly to build strength and endurance. It also means avoiding harmful drugs, alcohol, tobacco, and anything else that can harm your health.

. . . mentally awake . . .

Develop your mind both in the classroom and outside of school. Be curious about everything around you, and work hard to make the most of your abilities. With an inquiring attitude and the willingness to ask questions, you can learn much about the exciting world around you and your role in it.

. . . and morally straight . . .

To be a person of strong character, your relationships with others should be honest and open. You should respect and defend the rights of all people. Be clean in your speech and actions, and remain faithful in your religious beliefs. The values you practice as a Scout will help you shape a life of virtue and self-reliance.

Scout Spirit

Scout spirit refers to the effort you make to live up to the ideals of Scouting. The Oath, Law, motto, and slogan serve as everyday guidelines for a good life.

Scout Law

A Scout is trustworthy, loyal, helpful, friendly, courteous, kind, obedient, cheerful, thrifty, brave, clean, and reverent.

The Meaning of the Scout Law

The Scout Law is the foundation of Scouting. It is expressed in just twelve simple points, but the standards they set for you are high. Use the Scout Law to guide your actions when you are alone and as a member of your family, community, and nation. The Scout Law will show you how to live as a boy and as a man.

A Scout is **trustworthy.** A Scout tells the truth. He is honest, and he keeps his promises. People can depend on him.

A reputation for being trustworthy is important to you now and in years to come. Trustworthiness will help you make and maintain good friendships. But more than that, your honesty is a sign of your character—the kind of person you are inside. Your parents, teachers, and friends expect you to tell the truth and to keep your promises. They know they can rely upon you to do your best in every situation.

Of course, there will be times when your judgment fails and you make mistakes. Now and then that happens to everyone. Your baseball might smash a window. You might misread your map and come home late from a hike. If you quickly admit what you have done and make good on any damage, others will soon forget the incident. By learning from your errors, you can do better in the future.

You must also have trust in yourself. You know when you have done right and when you have done wrong. Live in such a way that you can respect yourself, and others will respect you, too.

*A Scout is **loyal.*** A Scout is true to his family, friends, Scout leaders, school, and nation.

Loyalty starts at home. You show through your actions that your family can count on you. The success of your Scout troop and patrol also depends upon your loyalty and that of other Scouts as you support your leaders and pitch in to do your share of the work. Your loyalty to the ideals of your school can make the learning experience good for everyone.

Express your loyalty to the United States by respecting the flag and government, and by participating in the democratic process. See where things can be made better and work toward that ideal. Our form of government allows each of us to voice our concerns and act within the system to make changes. Give real meaning to your loyalty by helping improve your community, state, and nation.

*A Scout is **helpful.*** A Scout cares about other people. He willingly volunteers to help others without expecting payment or reward.

You promise in the Scout Oath to help other people at all times. The Scout motto asks you to be prepared. The Scout slogan reminds you to do a Good Turn daily. These three ideals work together: you promise to help, you can help because you have learned how, and you do help because you care about people.

Scouts want the best for everyone, and act to make that happen. While a

1

YOU PROMISE
TO HELP.

2

YOU CAN HELP
BECAUSE YOU HAVE
LEARNED HOW.

3

YOU HELP
BECAUSE YOU
CARE ABOUT
PEOPLE.

Scout might work for pay, he does not expect to receive money for being helpful. A Good Turn that is done in the hope of getting a tip or a favor is not a Good Turn at all.

*A Scout is **friendly.***
A Scout is a friend to all. He is a brother to other Scouts. He offers his friendship to people of all races and nations, and respects them even if their beliefs and customs are different from his own.

Friendship is a mirror. When you have a smile on your face as you greet someone, you will probably receive a smile in return. If you are willing to be a good friend, you will find friendship reflected back to you.

Accept who you are, too, and celebrate the fact that you don't have to be just like everyone else. Real friends will respect the ideas, interests, and talents that make you special.

*A Scout is **courteous.*** A Scout is polite to everyone regardless of age or position. He knows that using good manners makes it easier for people to get along.

"A Scout is courteous" is another way of saying "A Scout is a gentleman." Open a door for someone. Offer your seat on a bus or in a busy waiting room to an elderly person, a pregnant woman, or anyone who needs it more than you. Greet others with a firm handshake. Do your share of family chores in a pleasant way. Say "Please" and "Thank you" or "Pardon me" and "I'm sorry" whenever appropriate.

Being courteous shows that you are aware of the feelings of others. The habits of courtesy that you practice as a Scout will stay with you throughout your life.

*A Scout is **kind**.* A Scout knows there is strength in being gentle. He treats others as he wants to be treated. Without good reason, he does not harm or kill any living thing.

Kindness is a sign of true strength. To be kind you must look beyond yourself and try to understand the needs of others. Take time to listen to people and imagine being in their place.

It should never be difficult to show kindness to those in need and those who cannot defend themselves. What can be harder is being kind to people you don't know or with whom you disagree. We live in a world that has more than its share of anger, fear, and war. Extending kindness to those around you and having compassion for all people is a powerful antidote to the poisons of hatred and violence.

Kindness is not limited to how we feel about people. Be kind to pets and wildlife. Be kind to the earth by protecting natural resources and by using no-trace methods of hiking and camping.

*A Scout is **obedient**.* A Scout follows the rules of his family, school, and troop. He obeys the laws of his community and country. If he thinks these rules and laws are unfair, he tries to have them changed in an orderly manner rather than disobeying them.

Your family cares for you and wants you to be safe. Help them out by following the rules set for you by your parent or guardian.

There are others besides family members to whom you owe obedience. When teachers give you homework, it is usually because the assignments will help you learn. When an employer gives you a task to be done, it is usually for the good of the business. When your Scout leader asks you to do a job, it is because your efforts will help your patrol and troop. Being obedient also means following city, state, and national laws.

Obedience must be guided by good judgment. If someone tells you to cheat, steal, or do something else you know is wrong, you must say no. Trust your own beliefs and obey your conscience when you know you are right.

*A Scout is **cheerful.*** A Scout looks for the bright side of life. He cheerfully does tasks that come his way. He tries to make others happy.

Some people grumble when they are doing homework or losing a game. They might become upset if the weather turns bad on a Scout hike or if the trail is long and dusty. Others are cheerful. They jump at opportunities, and their sense of joy makes everything easier for them and those around them.

You know that you cannot always have your way. Now and then you must do things that you don't like very much. A cheerful attitude can make the time go by more quickly, and can even turn a task you dislike into a lot of fun.

You have the choice of whether or not to enjoy the experiences and challenges of life. You can complain if you want to and be grumpy all the time, but it is easier and much more enjoyable to decide from the start to be cheerful whenever you can. Cheerfulness is infectious—the smile on your face can lift the spirits of those around you.

The Scout Oath and Scout Law are the rules of Scouting and guides for living a good life.

Challenging yourself to overcome your fears is one kind of Scout bravery.

*A Scout is **thrifty.*** A Scout works to pay his way and to help others. He saves for the future. He protects and conserves natural resources. He carefully uses time and property.

On Scout campouts you will learn to live comfortably with little more than the clothes you are wearing and the gear in your pack. Likewise, you can live other parts of your life simply and well, taking care of what you have and being generous to others.

Paying your way with money you have earned gives you independence and pride. When you save your own money to buy a Scout uniform or something else you need, you learn the real value of those items. You will also be sure to take good care of them.

Even if you have only a few dollars, get in the habit every month of saving money in a bank account. Share what you have with others, too, though what you give does not have to be cash. Volunteering your time and talent is just as valuable as donating money.

Another part of thrift is protecting and conserving the earth's natural resources—its soil, water, forests, wilderness areas, and wildlife. Recycle papers, glass, and metal used in your home and community. Do all you can to minimize waste.

A Scout is **brave.** A Scout can face danger although he is afraid. He has the courage to stand for what he thinks is right even if others laugh at him or threaten him.

Since 1910 when Scouting came to America, thousands of Honor Medals have been awarded to Scouts who saved lives at the risk of their own. They proved themselves ready when emergencies arose. They might have been frightened, but each one of them went to the aid of someone in serious trouble.

Saving lives is not the only test of bravery. You are brave every time you do what is right in spite of what others might say. You are brave when you speak the truth and when you admit a mistake and apologize for it. And you show true courage when you defend the rights of others.

A Scout is **clean.** A Scout keeps his body and mind fit. He chooses the company of those who live by high standards. He helps keep his home and community clean.

You can't avoid getting dirty when you work and play hard. But when the game is over or the job is done, that kind of dirt washes off with soap and water.

There's another kind of dirt, though, that can't be scrubbed away. It is the kind that shows up in foul language and harmful thoughts and actions.

Swearwords and dirty stories are often used as weapons to ridicule other people and hurt their feelings. The same is true of racial slurs and jokes that make fun of ethnic groups or people with physical or mental limitations. A Scout knows there is no kindness or honor in such tasteless behavior. He avoids it in his own words and deeds.

*A Scout is **reverent.*** A Scout is reverent toward God. He is faithful in his religious duties. He respects the beliefs of others.

Wonders all around us remind us of our faith in God. We find it in the tiny secrets of creation and in the great mysteries of the universe. It exists in the kindness of people and in the teachings of our families and religious leaders. We show our reverence by living our lives according to the ideals of our beliefs.

Throughout your life you will encounter people expressing their reverence in many different ways. The Constitution of the United States guarantees each of us the freedom to believe and worship as we wish without government interference. It is your duty to respect and defend others' rights to their religious beliefs even when they differ from your own.

> SCOUT
> MOTTO
>
> **BE
> PREPARED.**

Scout Motto

Be Prepared.

The Meaning of the Scout Motto

"Be prepared for what?" someone once asked Baden-Powell, the founder of Scouting.

"Why, for any old thing," he replied.

The training you receive in your troop will help you live up to the Scout motto. When someone has an accident, you are prepared because of your first aid instruction. Because of lifesaving practice, you might be able to save a nonswimmer who has fallen into deep water.

But Baden-Powell wasn't thinking just of being ready for emergencies. His idea was that all Scouts should prepare themselves to become productive citizens and to give happiness to other people. He wanted each Scout to be ready in mind and body for any struggles, and to meet with a strong heart whatever challenges that might lie ahead.

Be Prepared *for life*—to live happily and without regret, knowing that you have done your best. That's what the Scout motto means.

Scout Slogan

Do a Good Turn Daily.

The Meaning of the Scout Slogan

Some Good Turns are big—saving a life, helping out after floods or other disasters, recycling community trash, working with your patrol on conservation projects.

But Good Turns are often small, thoughtful acts—helping a child cross a busy street, going to the store for an elderly neighbor, cutting back brush that is blocking a sign, doing something special for a brother or sister, welcoming a new student to your school.

A Good Turn is more than simple good manners. It is a special act of kindness.

8. Know your patrol name, give the patrol yell, and describe your patrol flag.

By now your patrol should be an important part of your Scout experience. Members of your patrol are your friends at meetings and during adventures. You learn much from them, and they learn from you.

In the spaces below, write information about your patrol:

My Patrol

Patrol name _____

Patrol yell _____

_____

_____

Patrol leader _____

Assistant patrol leader _____

Patrol members _____

_____

_____

Draw your patrol flag:

9. Explain why we use the buddy system in Scouting.

The buddy system is a way for Scouts to look after one another, especially during outdoor adventures. When your troop goes swimming, for example, each Scout will be assigned a buddy. You keep track of what your buddy is up to, and he knows at all times where you are and how you are doing. Now and then a Scout leader might call for a *buddy check*. That means you must immediately hold up the hand of your buddy. If anyone is missing, everyone will know it right away. The buddy system should always be used when a troop or patrol is hiking, camping, and participating in any aquatics activities. It's a way of sharing the good times and preventing the bad.

10a. Record your best in the following tests:

Current results

Push-ups _____

Pull-ups _____

Sit-ups _____

Standing long jump

(_____ feet _____ inches)

¼-mile walk/run _____

30 days later

Push-ups _____

Pull-ups _____

Sit-ups _____

Standing long jump

(_____ feet _____ inches)

¼-mile walk/run _____

10b. Show improvement in the activities listed in requirement 10a after practicing for 30 days.

Hiking, canoeing, bicycling, backpacking—the adventures of Scouting are full of physical activity. To make the most of these and other activities, you'll want to be in shape. Good fitness can also make you more alert, help you fight off illnesses, and increase your enjoyment of life.

Test your current level of fitness by doing as many push-ups, pull-ups, and sit-ups as you can, by seeing what distance you can cover with a standing long jump, and by timing yourself in a ¼-mile walk/run. Practice each of these exercises every day for a month, then test yourself again. You might be surprised how much you have improved, and you will have gotten yourself into the habit of exercising regularly to increase your endurance and strength.

"To carry out all the duties and work of a scout properly a fellow has to be strong, healthy, and active. And he can make himself so if he takes a little care about it."

—*Baden-Powell,* Scouting for Boys, *1915*

11. Identify local poisonous plants; tell how to treat for exposure to them.

Poison ivy, poison oak, and poison sumac are the most common poisonous plants in the United States. Oily sap in their leaves, stems, and roots can irritate your skin and cause it to itch. Your Scout leaders or others who know about plants can show you how to recognize and avoid the poisonous plants in your area.

Here's a little good news. The sap of poison ivy, oak, and sumac must be on your skin for ten to twenty minutes before it binds to the cells and begins causing problems. If you think you have touched a poisonous plant, immediately wash with soap and water. The sap can also stay on clothing, so change clothes and wash the outfit you were wearing. Calamine lotion helps to relieve the itching. Try not to scratch an affected area because that can cause the irritation to spread. (See chapter 11, "First Aid," page 318 ✚.)

POISON IVY

POISON OAK

POISON SUMAC

12a. Demonstrate the Heimlich maneuver and tell when it is used. (See chapter 11, "First Aid," pages 296–97 ✚.)

12b. Show first aid for the following:

Simple cuts and scratches ("First Aid" chapter, page 304 ✚)
Blisters on the hand and foot ("First Aid," page 308 ✚)
Minor burns or scalds (first-degree) ("First Aid," page 306 ✚)
Bites or stings of insects and ticks ("First Aid," page 310 ✚)
Poisonous snakebite ("First Aid," page 313 ✚)
Nosebleed ("First Aid," page 306 ✚)
Frostbite and sunburn ("First Aid," pages 324, 306–7 ✚)

Knowing how to deal with first aid emergencies is an important skill to have around your home, community, and school, and when you and other Scouts are taking part in outdoor activities.

13. Participate in a Scoutmaster conference.

After you finish all the requirements to become a Tenderfoot Scout, you and your Scoutmaster will sit down and talk. You should be gaining confidence in your ability to be a Scout, and Scouting should be fulfilling its promise to you. The Scoutmaster conference is an opportunity to reflect on what you have accomplished so far and to get a bigger picture of how to approach the exciting challenges that lie ahead.

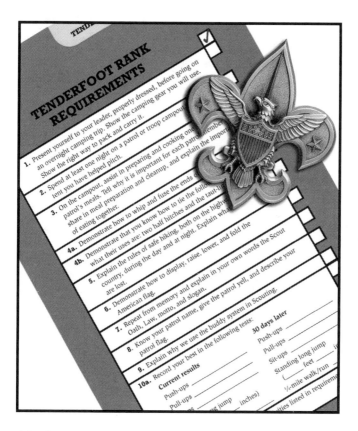

14. Complete your board of review.

Once you have accomplished all the Tenderfoot requirements and have participated in a Scoutmaster conference, your Scoutmaster will arrange a board of review for you. The review board is made up of members of the troop committee. The purpose of the review is to give you the opportunity to talk about how you are getting along in the troop, and to review the Tenderfoot requirements to ensure that they have been met.

2 SECOND CLASS SCOUT

TRAILHEAD

4

Ready for more adventure, learning, and fun?

Then you're ready to move on to becoming a

Second Class Scout.

SECOND CLASS SCOUT

"THE SKILLS I'M LEARNING ARE GREAT!" says a Scout working on his Second Class badge. "I'm going on adventures with my patrol and troop, and I'm having lots of fun."

With the Tenderfoot requirements behind you, you're ready to move ahead toward Second Class. You're about to learn how to use a map and compass. Soon you will know new ways to observe wildlife, and you'll understand when and how to build a campfire.

You'll master the safe use of pocketknives and other woods tools, go on more campouts, take part in troop and patrol activities, and add to your knowledge of first aid. Add swimming and a service project, and you will be well on your way to wearing the Second Class award.

"A trailsman is a fellow who knows how to find his way through the wilds. He hikes through forests, over mountains, across desert lands. His best friends are his compass and his map. They tell him where he is and how to get where he wants to go."

Scout Field Book, 1st edition, 1944

SECOND CLASS
RANK REQUIREMENTS

1a. Demonstrate how a compass works and how to orient a map. Explain what map symbols mean.

1b. Using a compass and a map together, take a 5-mile hike (or 10 miles by bike) approved by your adult leader and your parent or guardian.*

2a. Since joining, have participated in five separate troop/patrol activities (other than troop/patrol meetings), two of which included camping overnight.

2b. On one of these campouts, select your patrol site and sleep in a tent that you pitched.

2c. On one campout, demonstrate proper care, sharpening, and use of the knife, saw, and ax, and describe when they should be used.

2d. Use the tools listed in requirement 2c to prepare tinder, kindling, and fuel for a cooking fire.

2e. Discuss when it is appropriate to use a cooking fire and a light-weight stove. Discuss the safety procedures for using both.

2f. Demonstrate how to light a fire and a lightweight stove.

2g. On one campout, plan and cook over an open fire one hot break-fast or lunch for yourself, selecting foods from the four basic food groups. Explain the importance of good nutrition. Tell how to transport, store, and prepare the foods you selected.

3. Participate in a flag ceremony for your school, religious institution, chartered organization, community, or troop activity.

4. Participate in an approved (minimum of one hour) service project.

5. Identify or show evidence of at least ten kinds of wild animals (birds, mammals, reptiles, fish, mollusks) found in your community.

6a. Show what to do for "hurry" cases of stopped breathing, serious bleeding, and internal poisoning.

*If you use a wheelchair or crutches, or if it is difficult for you to get around, you may substitute "trip" for "hike."

SECOND CLASS
RANK REQUIREMENTS

6b. Prepare a personal first aid kit to take with you on a hike.

6c. Demonstrate first aid for the following:
- Object in the eye
- Bite of a suspected rabid animal
- Puncture wounds from a splinter, nail, and fishhook
- Serious burns (second-degree)
- Heat exhaustion
- Shock
- Heatstroke, dehydration, hypothermia, and hyperventilation

7a. Tell what precautions must be taken for a safe swim.

7b. Demonstrate your ability to jump feetfirst into water over your head in depth, level off and swim 25 feet on the surface, stop, turn sharply, resume swimming, then return to your starting place.†

7c. Demonstrate water rescue methods by reaching with your arm or leg, by reaching with a suitable object, and by throwing lines and objects.† Explain why swimming rescues should not be attempted when a reaching or throwing rescue is possible, and explain why and how a rescue swimmer should avoid contact with the victim.

8. Participate in a school, community, or troop program on the dangers of using drugs, alcohol, and tobacco and other practices that could be harmful to your health. Discuss your participation in the program with your family.

9. Demonstrate Scout spirit by living the Scout Oath (Promise) and Scout Law in your everyday life.

10. Participate in a Scoutmaster conference.

11. Complete your board of review.

†This requirement may be waived by the troop committee for medical or safety reasons.

NOTE: Alternate requirements for the Second Class rank are available for Scouts with physical or mental disabilities if they meet the criteria listed in the *Boy Scout Requirements* book, No. 33215.

As you complete each requirement, ask your Scoutmaster to initial his or her approval on pages 440–41.

1a. Demonstrate how a compass works and how to orient a map. Explain what map symbols mean.

1b. Using a compass and a map together, take a 5-mile hike (or 10 miles by bike) approved by your adult leader and your parent or guardian.

Many Scout hikes will lead to places you know well. You might also want to take off for destinations you've never visited before. Wherever you go, you can find your way with the help of a map and a compass.

WHERE TO GET MAPS

The United States Geological Survey (USGS) makes useful maps for hikers. They are called *topographic* maps—from the Greek *topos,* "place," and *graphein,* "to write." Because they enclose a four-sided area, they are also known as *quadrangle* maps.

Camping and sporting goods stores often sell topographic maps of nearby recreation areas. You can get information about ordering maps by contacting the USGS at the following address, telephone number, or Internet web site:

U.S. Geological Survey
Distribution Branch
Box 25286
Federal Center
Denver, CO 80225

1-800-HELP-MAP

www.usgs.gov

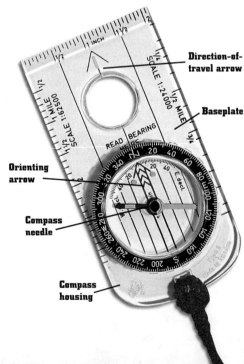

Direction-of-travel arrow

Baseplate

Orienting arrow

Compass needle

Compass housing

WHAT MAP SYMBOLS MEAN

From an airplane you can look down and see roads, rivers, forests, cities, and towns. A map is like a painting of that land. Since mapmakers can't include every detail, they choose information they hope will be valuable to anyone using the map. Some of the most important data are represented by symbols located in a map's margins:

Directions

North is toward the top of most maps. The bottom is *south,* the left side is *west,* and the right side is *east.* A map often will have a *true-north arrow* in its margin.

Distances

Bar scales can be used for measuring feet, meters, and miles on a map.

Scale

The *scale* of a map compares its size to the size of the area it represents. A map scale shown in the margin as 1:24,000 means that one unit of distance on that map (an inch, for example) equals 24,000 like units of distance on the ground (24,000 inches in this example).

Date

A map's *date* tells when it was drawn or last revised. An older map will not show new buildings, roads, trails, or other changes on the land.

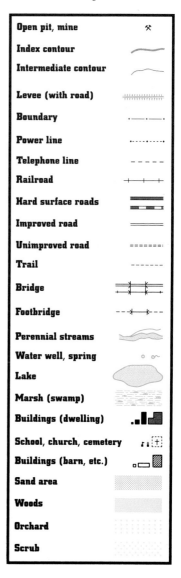

Open pit, mine	
Index contour	
Intermediate contour	
Levee (with road)	
Boundary	
Power line	
Telephone line	
Railroad	
Hard surface roads	
Improved road	
Unimproved road	
Trail	
Bridge	
Footbridge	
Perennial streams	
Water well, spring	
Lake	
Marsh (swamp)	
Buildings (dwelling)	
School, church, cemetery	
Buildings (barn, etc.)	
Sand area	
Woods	
Orchard	
Scrub	

The colors used on a USGS map are also full of meaning:

Green

Green indicates heavy vegetation—areas covered with forests, woodlands, or orchards.

White

White is used for areas that are mostly clear of trees. A white area on a map might be a field, meadow, rocky slope, or other form of open country.

Blue

Blue means water. A large patch of blue is usually a pond or a lake. A blue band is a river, and a blue line is a stream. If the line is broken, the stream it represents doesn't flow all of the time. Marshes and swamps are drawn with broken blue lines and tufts of grass. Names of all water features are given in *italic* type.

Black

Black ink is used on a map to show anything that is the work of humans. Rail lines, bridges, boundaries, and the names of landmarks are printed in black. Roads are shown as parallel black lines—solid for paved and gravel *(improved)* roads, broken for dirt *(unimproved)* roads. A single broken line is a hiking trail.

Black squares and rectangles are buildings. Those that are solid black are inhabited—houses, schools, churches. Those that are just outlined in black are barns, sheds, and other outbuildings.

Brown

Brown is used for *contour lines.* Maps are flat, but the areas they represent might be full of hills, valleys, mountains, and plains. Each contour line represents a specific elevation above sea level; that is, the elevation remains the same at all points along any one contour line. Contour lines allow mapmakers to show the shape of the land.

UNDERSTANDING CONTOUR LINES

Make a fist with one hand. Your fist has length, width, and height—contours just like the land.

Holding your fist steady, draw a level circle around your highest knuckle. (Washable ink will be easy to remove.) Draw another level circle just below that one. Start a third line a little lower. Notice that to keep your line level, your pen might have to encircle another knuckle before the third circle is closed.

Continue to draw level circles, each of them the same distance apart. The lines will wander in and out of the valleys between your fingers, over the broad slope on the back of your hand, and across the steep cliffs above your thumb.

After all the lines are drawn, spread your hand flat. Now, like a map, your hand has only width and length. But by looking at the contour lines you have drawn, you can imagine the shape of your fist. Small circles show the tops of your knuckles. The points at which the lines are close together indicate steep areas; the lines that are farther apart are the more gentle contours of your hand.

The contour lines on a map represent terrain in the same way. Small circles are the tops of hills. Where the lines are close together, a hillside is steep. Where the lines are far apart, the slope of the ground is more gentle.

A note in the map's margin will tell you how far apart the contour lines are spaced. For example, "contour interval 50 feet" means each line is 50 feet higher or lower than its neighboring lines.

INDEX LINES

Every fifth contour line is darker than the other four. Follow one of these *index lines* and you'll find a number—that line's elevation above sea level.

HOW A COMPASS WORKS

The first compasses appeared in China about a thousand years ago and in Europe a few hundred years later. Travelers noticed that a magnetized needle floating on a chip of wood always swung around to point north. Many people believed that the needle moved by magic.

Today we know that Earth itself acts as a huge magnet. One pole of this global magnet is in northern Canada, and one end of every compass needle is drawn toward it. That end is usually painted red or stamped with the letter *N.*

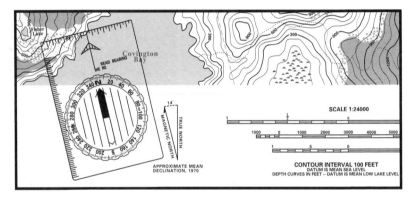

Two Norths

The maps you are most likely to use on Scout hikes are drawn with their tops aimed at *true north.* Extend the boundaries on either side of a map far enough upward and those lines will reach the North Pole. You could say that maps are made to speak the language of true north.

Compass needles, however, do not point to true north. Instead, they are pulled toward *magnetic north,* the area in Canada more than a thousand miles away from the North Pole. Compasses speak magnetic north, a different language from that used by maps.

Arrows drawn in the bottom margin of many maps show the difference. The *true-north arrow* points toward the North Pole. The *magnetic-north arrow* points toward magnetic north. The difference between true north and magnetic north, measured in degrees, is called *declination.*

Drawing magnetic-north lines on a map is one of many ways to deal with declination so that a map and compass can be used together. Depending on the map, methods that involve adding or subtracting the declination from compass bearings can provide more accuracy, though they can also be more difficult to learn.

Another solution is to use a compass that can be adjusted so that its readings are aligned with true north rather than magnetic north. Once the adjustment has been made, the compass uses as its reference any true-north map lines (map borders, lines of longitude, township boundaries, etc.).

(For more on coping with declination, see the *Orienteering* merit badge pamphlet and the BSA's *Fieldbook.*)

Ruling the Map

When you use a map and compass together, declination can cause large errors as you take bearings and try to follow routes. To avoid problems caused by declination, you can change the map so that it and your compass speak the same language.

With a pencil and a long ruler, extend the magnetic-north arrow up to the top of the map. Next, draw other lines a ruler's width apart and parallel to the first line. Use these *magnetic-north lines* to orient the map and find your way.

HOW TO ORIENT A MAP

Hundreds of years ago, European explorers were trying to reach regions of the Far East they called the Orient. Many of their maps had the Orient at the top. Today, most maps are drawn with north at the top, but the act of turning a map to match the landscape is still called *orienting.*

> ### Here are two ways to orient a map:
>
> Look out at the land for features such as buildings, a bridge, and perhaps the top of a hill. On your map, find the symbols for those features. Turn the map until the symbols line up with the landscape features they represent.
>
> If you have a compass, rotate the compass housing until N (360 degrees) touches the *direction-of-travel arrow*. Place the edge of the compass alongside any magnetic-north line on the map or along the magnetic-north arrow in the map's margin. Turn the map and compass as a unit until the compass needle lies directly over the orienting arrow in the compass housing.

USING A COMPASS AND A MAP ON A HIKE OR BIKE TRIP

Orienting a map so that it matches the terrain can give you the guidance you need to walk or pedal over long distances. Stop often to orient the map again and double-check your position.

When traveling in areas that are new to you or when going cross-country, a couple of more advanced map-and-compass skills will show you the way:

Following a Route Drawn on a Map

Step 1. On the map, place the edge of your compass along your planned route. Find the symbols on your map for your current location and for the place you want to reach. Lay your compass on the map with the edge of the *baseplate* touching those two symbols. Be sure the direction-of-travel arrow is pointing in the direction you intend to go. (If the symbols are far apart, connect them with a ruler, pencil a straight line between them, then place the compass edge along that line.)

Step 2. On the compass, set the bearing. Hold the baseplate firmly on the map. Ignore the needle and turn the compass housing until the meridian lines are parallel with any magnetic-north line drawn on your map—probably an extension of the magnetic-north arrow in the margin. The *N* on the compass housing should point toward the top of the map.

Step 3. In the field, follow the compass bearing. Hold your compass in front of you with the direction-of-travel arrow pointing straight ahead. Turn your entire body until the compass needle covers the orienting arrow on the floor of the compass housing (the north end of the needle should be pointing toward north on the housing). The direction-of-travel arrow will point toward your destination.

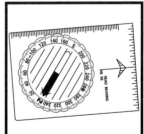

Pick a tree, rock, or something else in line with the direction-of-travel arrow and walk to it. When you reach it, take another compass bearing and head toward another object farther along your route. Repeat, walking from one point to another until you arrive at your destination.

Identifying Landmarks

If you know on the map where you are, you can identify mountains, lakes, buildings, and any other landmarks you can see.

Step 1. Take a bearing on the landmark. Holding the compass in your hand, aim the direction-of-travel arrow at the landmark you want to identify. Turn the compass housing until the needle lines up over the orienting arrow. The north end of the needle should be pointing at *N* on the compass housing.

Step 2. On the map, locate your position. Find the symbol that represents the place where you are standing.

Step 3. Identify the landmark. Place your compass on the map with one edge of the baseplate touching your location. Move the entire compass around until the meridian lines in the housing are parallel with any magnetic-north line drawn on the map. *N* on the compass housing should be pointing toward the top of the map.

Draw a line along the edge of the base-plate starting at your location and going in the direction of travel. Look at the symbols under that line. One of them should represent the landmark you want to identify.

GLOBAL POSITIONING SYSTEMS

A *global positioning system* (GPS) is an electronic receiver that uses the signals of satellites to pinpoint the receiver's location anywhere on Earth. A GPS outfit is especially useful for Scout units involved in search-and-rescue operations, but it's no substitute for learning to use a map and compass.

2a. Since joining, have participated in five separate troop/patrol activities (other than troop/patrol meetings), two of which included camping overnight.

Hikes, bike rides, swimming, service projects, field trips, campouts—patrols and troops take part in all sorts of activities you won't want to miss. For more information on a few of these, see chapter 8, "Hiking," beginning on page 197 , and chapter 9, "Camping," beginning on page 217 .

In the following spaces, write down the time and place of five separate troop or patrol activities, and a brief description of each one:

TROOP/PATROL ACTIVITIES RECORD

1. Date _____ Location _____

   What we did _____

2. Date _____ Location _____

   What we did _____

3. Date _____ Location _____

   What we did _____

4. Date _____ Location _____

   What we did _____

5. Date _____ Location _____

   What we did _____

2b. On one of these campouts, select your patrol site and sleep in a tent that you pitched.

In the early days of our country, you could have camped almost anywhere. There were not many people. Towns, roads, and open fields were scarce. The demands on the land were few.

The needs of a growing nation have turned much of that undeveloped territory into farms and cities. Dams have tamed many rivers to provide power, and many forests have been used to produce lumber for construction and pulp for making paper.

The open country that remains is home to a rich variety of animals and plants. It supplies clean water for everyone to drink and it freshens the air we breathe. When we want to get away from the cities, we have the freedom to enjoy parks, forests, and Scout camps across the nation.

With that freedom comes a duty to care for the environment. That means enjoying the outdoors, learning from it, and then leaving it as we found it. Scouts call this *no-trace hiking and camping.* On outings with your patrol and troop, you will discover how to enjoy the outdoors without leaving any signs you were there.

For guidelines on choosing a patrol campsite and sleeping in a tent you have pitched, see chapter 9, "Camping," pages 232–41 ▲. For more on the wise use of the outdoors, see the Outdoor Code, page 219.

2c. On one campout, demonstrate proper care, sharpening, and use of the knife, saw, and ax, and describe when they should be used.

Whether you are splitting firewood, repairing equipment, or clearing a tree that has fallen across a trail, a pocketknife, a saw, and an ax can make your work easier. Take pride in learning the right way to use each of them.

Just as important as knowing how to use woods tools is knowing how **not** to use them. Carving or chopping on live trees can kill them. Hacking at dead trees and logs can leave ugly scars. Don't cut any trees without guidance from a ranger, landowner, or your Scout leader.

POCKETKNIFE

Ever need to cut a rope? Open a can of food? Whittle a tent stake, slice a biscuit, or punch a hole in a belt? Want to tighten a screw on a pack frame, make wood shavings to start a fire, or trim a bandage?

A pocketknife can help you with all those tasks and hundreds more. A good knife for general use has a can opener, a screwdriver, and one or two blades for cutting.

POCKETKNIFE

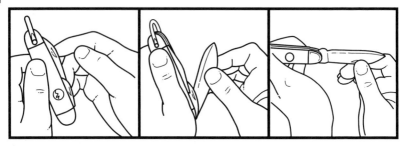

Keep your fingers clear of the sharp edge as you open and close the blade of your pocketknife.

SAFE KNIFE USE

Do keep the blades closed except when you are using them.
Do cut away from yourself.
Do close the blades before you pass a knife to someone else.
Do keep your knife sharp and clean. A sharp blade is easier to control than a dull one.
Do obey any school regulations that prohibit carrying knives on school property.
Don't carry a knife with the blade open.
Don't throw a knife.
Don't cut toward yourself. If the blade slips, you could be injured.
Don't strike a knife with another tool or pry with the point of a cutting blade. The knife could bend or break.
Note: The Boy Scouts of America does not encourage the use of large sheath knives. They are heavy, awkward to carry, and unnecessary for most camp chores.

Taking Care of a Pocketknife

Most modern pocketknives are made of a metal that won't rust. However, dirt and lint can collect inside, and normal use will dull the blades.

Cleaning

Open all of the blades. Twirl a small bit of cloth onto the end of a toothpick, moisten the cloth with light oil, and wipe the inside of the knife. If you have used your pocketknife to cut food or to spread peanut butter and

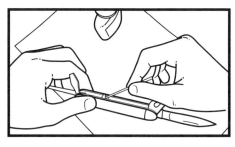

jelly, get rid of bacteria by washing the blade in hot, soapy water along with the rest of your dishes.

Sharpening

Sharpen your knife with a *whetstone.* Most whetstones are made of granite or other materials harder than knife metal. Some experts put water on the stone while they are sharpening, some use light oil, and others keep the stone dry. The choice depends upon the kind of stone as well as individual preference.

For general-use knives, hold the blade against the stone at an angle of about 30 degrees. That means the back of the blade will be tilted off the stone one-third of the way to vertical. The blades of special-use knives, such as those used by whittlers, may be sharpened at angles as small as 10 degrees to produce a keener, though less durable, edge.

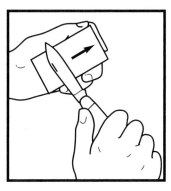

Push the blade along the stone as though you were slicing a layer off the top, or move the blade against the stone in a circular motion. Sharpen the other side of the blade in the same manner.

Wipe the knife with a clean cloth and examine the edge of the blade in the sun or under a bright light. A dull cutting edge reflects light and looks shiny. A sharp edge is so thin that it has no shine at all.

CAMP SAW

A camp saw is the right tool for most outdoor woodcutting. The blades of *folding saws* close into their handles, much like the blades of pocket-knives. *Bow saws* have curved metal frames that hold their blades in place.

When cutting firewood, brace the piece of wood against a chopping block, saw-horse, or other solid support. Use long, smooth strokes and let the weight of the saw pull the blade into the wood.

Clearing branches and brush from a hiking trail is a conservation project you might do with your patrol or troop. To saw a branch from a tree, make an *undercut* first, then saw from the top down. The undercut prevents the falling branch from stripping bark off the trunk. A clean cut close to the trunk won't leave an unsightly "hat rack" that might snag the clothing of hikers. Cut saplings level with the ground so that there are no stumps to trip over.

Treat every saw with the same respect you give your pocketknife. Close folding saws when they aren't in use and store them in a tent or under the dining fly. Protect the blade of a bow saw with a sheath made from a piece of an old garden hose cut to the length of the blade. Cut a slit along the length of the hose, fit it over the blade, and hold it in place with duct tape or cord.

SAFE SAW USE

Do sheathe a saw whenever it is not in use.
Do carry a saw with the blade turned away from your body.
Do replace blades when they become dull. Sharp saws are easier to use and to control.
Do use care when passing a saw to another person.
Do wear gloves and protective eyewear.
Don't cut any trees, alive or dead, without permission.
Don't allow the saw's blade to cut into the ground. Soil and rocks will quickly dull the teeth.
Don't leave a saw lying around camp.

The teeth on saw blades are *set*—bent so that they cut two thin grooves in the wood and then rake out the shavings in between. Even with the best care, the teeth will slowly lose their set and will bind in the wood. Bow saw blades are replaceable and are not very expensive. Take along a spare if you will have a lot of cutting to do.

AX

The ax has a long and colorful history in America's forests. Pioneers used axes to cut trails and roads through the wilderness. Settlers chopped down trees to make way for gardens and fields. With their axes, frontier craftsmen shaped boards and beams for buildings.

Today, axes can be used to split firewood, clear fallen trees from back-country trails, and complete conservation projects on pathways and in campgrounds. As with all woods tools, using an ax safely requires practice and common sense.

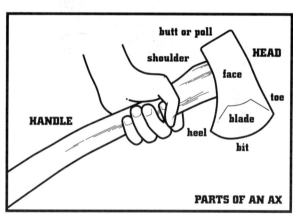

PARTS OF AN AX

Safe Tool

An ax must be in top condition. If the head is loose or the blade is dull, don't use it. Report an unsafe tool to your Scoutmaster and either help repair it or retire it from duty.

Safe Working Area

You must have plenty of room in which to swing an ax. Check your clearance by holding your ax by the head and slowly swinging the handle at arm's length all around you. Select an area that is free of brush and branches. Be certain other people stay at least ten feet away while you are cutting.

In a long-term camp using lots of firewood, rope off an ax yard large enough to provide the space you need to work, and enter the yard only to chop and saw wood. Clean up chips, bark, and other debris of cutting when you are finished.

SAFE AX USE

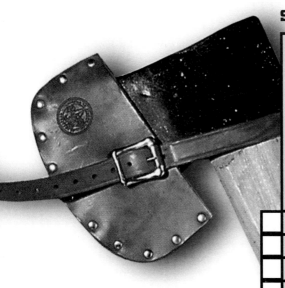

Because of its size and the way in which it is used, an ax can be more dangerous than other woods tools. Remove the sheath only when you are prepared to use the ax correctly, and then follow this checklist:

☐	Safe tool
☐	Safe shoes
☐	Safe working area
☐	Safe technique
☐	Safe carrying
☐	Safe handling
☐	Safe storage

Safe Technique

Chopping branches off a log is called *limbing.* Stand on the side of the log opposite the branch you want to remove. Chop close to the base of the branch, driving the ax into the underside of the limb. Keep the log between you and your cuts. If the ax misses the branch, the blade will hit the log rather than your leg.

Cutting through a log is known as *bucking.* Hold the ax with one hand near the head and the other close to the knob of the handle. Lift the head

above your shoulder, then slide your hands together and swing the *bit* (the cutting edge) into the log. Let the falling weight of the ax head do most of the work. Slide your hand back down the handle to the head, lift the ax, and swing it again. Aim your blows so that you cut a V-shaped notch twice as wide at the top as the log is thick.

Splitting wood is best done on a *chopping block,* a piece of a log that provides a solid, flat surface. A poor swing of the ax will send the bit into the block rather than toward your feet.

To split a large chunk of wood, stand it upright on the chopping block and drive the ax into the end of it. If the wood doesn't split, remove the ax before swinging it again. Do not swing an ax with a piece of wood stuck on the bit.

Split a small stick with the *contact method* by placing the ax bit against the stick. Lift the stick and ax together and bring them down against the block, forcing the bit into the wood. Twist the ax to break apart the pieces.

Safe Carrying

Place a sheath over an ax blade whenever it is not in use. Carry an ax at your side in one hand, with the blade turned out from your body. If you stumble, toss the ax away from you as you fall. Never carry an ax on your shoulder—the ax bit will be too close to your neck and head.

Safe Handling

Hand an ax to another person by holding the handle with the ax head down. Pass it with the bit turned away from both of you. When the other person has a grip on the handle, he should say, "Thank you." That's your signal to release your hold.

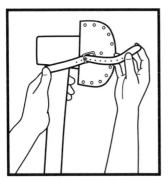

Safe Storage

Sheathe your ax and store it under the dining fly or in a tent to keep it dry, found, and safely out of the way.

Hikers and backpackers seldom need axes on the trail, and usually prefer to leave the weight at home.

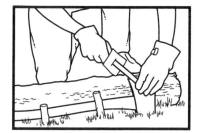

Sharpening an Ax

Keep your ax sharp with an 8- or 10-inch-long *mill bastard file.* The lines across the face of a file are its teeth. They angle away from the point, or *tang.* A sharp file will be drab gray. A silvery shine means a file has broken teeth that won't work very well.

Wear leather gloves to protect your hands as you sharpen with a file. Make a *knuckle guard* by boring a small hole in a 3-inch-square piece of leather, plywood, or an old inner tube, slipping it over the tang of the file, and holding it in place with a *file handle.* You can buy a handle at a hardware store or make one from a piece of wood or a dry corncob.

Brace the ax head on the ground between a log about 6 inches in diameter and two wooden pegs or tent stakes. Another Scout can help hold the ax steady. Place the file on the edge of the blade and push it into the bit. Use enough pressure so that you feel the file cutting the ax metal.

Lift the file as you draw it back for another stroke. A file sharpens only when you are pushing it away from the tang. Dragging the file across the blade in the wrong direction will break the teeth and ruin the file.

Sharpen with firm, even strokes. After you have filed one side of the bit, turn the ax around and sharpen the other side with about the same number of strokes. A dull edge reflects light; continue to file until the edge seems to disappear.

TOTIN' CHIP

Read and understand woods tools use and safety rules from the *Boy Scout Handbook.*	☐
Demonstrate proper handling, care, and use of the pocket-knife, ax, and saw.	☐
Use the knife, ax, and saw as tools, not playthings. Use them only when you are willing to give them your full attention.	☐
Respect all safety rules to protect others.	☐
Respect property. Cut living and dead trees only with permission and with good reason.	☐
Subscribe to the Outdoor Code.	☐
Scout leader _____	☐
Date _____	

CAMP SHOVEL

A small camp shovel or garden trowel is handy for removing and saving earth from a cat hole. You can move hot coals with a metal shovel while cooking with aluminum foil or a Dutch oven.

Don't dig ditches around tents, though. Ditches are unnecessary, and they can start erosion. For guidance on choosing campsites with good drainage, see pages 232–33 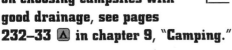 in chapter 9, "Camping."

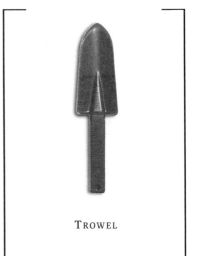

TROWEL

2d. Use the tools listed in requirement 2c to prepare tinder, kindling, and fuel for a cooking fire.

2e. Discuss when it is appropriate to use a cooking fire and a lightweight stove. Discuss the safety procedures for using both.

2f. Demonstrate how to light a fire and a lightweight stove.

2g. On one campout, plan and cook over an open fire one hot breakfast or lunch for yourself, selecting foods from the four basic food groups. Explain the importance of good nutrition. Tell how to transport, store, and prepare the foods you selected.

A fire can warm you, cook your meals, and dry your clothes. Bright flames lift your spirits on a rainy morning. On a starry night, glowing embers stir your imagination. The smell of a campfire and the crackle of burning wood are among the best memories of adventures gone by.

Every good Scout knows how to build a fire. He also knows when he should not build one. Many areas do not permit open fires. Even where fires are allowed, there might be good reasons to use a backpacking stove instead. For guidelines on deciding when to build a fire or light a stove and how to use each one safely, see chapter 10, "Cooking," pages 248–55 ❄. That chapter also contains information on planning menus, pages 260–62 ❄; good nutrition, page 259 ❄; and storing, handling, and cooking foods on a campout, pages 263–80 ❄.

3. Participate in a flag ceremony for your school, religious institution, chartered organization, community, or troop activity.

Scouts have many opportunities to present the flag at BSA meetings and public events.

Throughout the history of the BSA, Scouts have taken part in ceremonies paying respect to the American flag. They have served as honor guards at troop meetings, public gatherings, parades, and patriotic events.

Flag ceremonies offer all of us a time to think about our nation's history, to reflect on what it means to be an American, and to pledge ourselves to do our share to make our country the best it can be.

For information about how to carry and display the flag, turn to chapter 3, "Tenderfoot Scout," page 44 🄣. For more on your role as an American, see chapter 12, "Citizenship," beginning on page 331 🌐.

4. Participate in an approved (minimum of one hour) service project.

A service project is a special Good Turn that allows you to put Scout spirit into action.

Service projects can take many forms—community cleanup; repairing a church, a museum, or the home of an elderly person; improving wildlife habitat; volunteering at a hospital or with a public safety group; organizing a recycling effort; cleaning up a neighborhood lot or park; or any of a thousand other possibilities.

Giving of yourself will improve the lives of those around you. It will also enrich your own life as you discover that your actions make a real difference. The more you give, the more you will get back—in satisfaction, in accomplishment, and in understanding that you have done the right thing.

While this requirement asks for a minimum of only an hour, you don't have to limit yourself. Service to others, to your community, and to the environment can become a habit that you will want to practice often.

In the following space, write a short description of an approved service project you have completed:

SECOND CLASS SERVICE PROJECT

_____

_____

_____

_____

_____

_____

Date completed

"A scout walks through the

woods with silent tread. . . .

He sees tracks and signs

which reveal to him the

nature and habits of the

creatures that made them.

He knows how to stalk

birds and animals and

study them in their natural

haunts. He sees much, but

is little seen."

Handbook for Boys,
2nd edition, c. 1925

5. Identify or show evidence of at least ten kinds of wild animals (birds, mammals, reptiles, fish, mollusks) found in your community.

Scout hikes and campouts are often good times to observe wildlife. You might also find plenty of evidence of animals in your neighborhood. As you study animals, try to figure out where they live and what they eat. What do they need to survive? How do they raise their young? Are they prey to other animals?

Your observations can tell you quite a bit about animals and their environments. Books and Internet sites devoted to nature will also explain much about the complex web of life going on all around you.

KINDS OF WILD ANIMALS

Biologists divide all animals into two large groups—*vertebrates* and *invertebrates*. Vertebrates have backbones; invertebrates do not.

There are five classes of vertebrates, each based on physical similarities:

BIRDS
Warm-blooded animals with wings and feathers are birds. They hatch their young from eggs.

MAMMALS
Deer, bears, foxes, squirrels, moles, and other mammals are warm-blooded vertebrates that have some kind of hair. They nurse their babies with milk.

REPTILES
Snakes, alligators, crocodiles, lizards, and turtles are all reptiles— cold-blooded, air-breathing animals with backbones. Some move on short legs while others crawl on their bellies. Reptiles are covered with scales or bony plates.

FISH
Fish are cold blooded, live in water, and breathe through gills. Their bodies are covered with scales.

AMPHIBIANS
Frogs, toads, newts, salamanders, and other amphibians start life in the water as gilled aquatic larvae hatched from eggs. Adult amphibians breathe air and generally live on land.

Invertebrates greatly outnumber vertebrates on our planet, and can be divided into many more groups. The largest invertebrate group is made up of *arthropods*—insects, arachnids, and crustaceans. The *mollusk* group, second in size to the arthropod group, includes snails, clams, oysters, mussels, and squids.

HOW TO FIND EVIDENCE OF ANIMALS

Looking

Slow down and give your eyes time to notice what is all around you. Rather than glancing around quickly in a forest or in your front yard, carefully examine one tree, or get down on your hands and knees and inspect a square foot of earth. What meets the eye will often be far more than you expected. Watch for animal footprints, tufts of fur caught on twigs, overturned stones,

shells on a shore, or a feather on the ground. Be alert to movement in the brush, in the water, and in the sky.

Listening

Sit quietly for a while, listen carefully, and you will discover that the out-doors is full of sounds. The buzz of insects and the croaking of frogs can be mating calls. Some birds use their songs to claim their territory. The chatter of a squirrel and the slap of a beaver's tail are often warnings. Sometimes it is the absence of sound that is important. When birds suddenly stop singing, it could be because they have noticed a cat nearby, or maybe they've seen you.

The ears of many animals are shaped to scoop up sounds. Increase your own hearing by cupping your hands behind your ears. Turning your head from side to side might help you locate the source of a noise.

Smelling

A keen sense of smell is as important to some animals as hearing and sight are to others. Ants lay down scent trails to lead them back to their nests. Wolves sniff the wind for signs of prey. Elk are startled by the smell of predators nearing them. Mountain lions mark their domains with the scent of their urine.

Even though humans in the outdoors are less dependent on smell, your nose can provide a few clues as to what's going on. Notice the aromas of flowers, trees, earth, and moss. Stagnant water smells different from a fresh stream. The stench of an animal carcass can reveal its location.

Touching

A snake flicking out its tongue is picking up vibrations in the air. Nerves running along the bodies of fish alert them to changes in the water. Moles, opossums, and earthworms rely more upon touch than upon their other senses. Even animals with keen eyesight or finely tuned noses are aware of the feel of things around them.

Building birdhouses can improve wildlife habitat and increase your carpentry skills. Check the Bird Study *merit badge pamphlet for birdhouse plans.*

BIRD STUDY

Birds are among the animals you are most likely to see around your home and on Scout outings. Many Scouts make a hobby of studying birds, keeping lists of those they have watched.

Your troop or your public library might have bird identification books you can use to figure out the names of birds and learn about their range, diet, and behavior. Even better would be a patrol hike with someone who could help you recognize birds by their markings and their calls. Use binoculars, if you have them, to get close-up views of birds and their nests.

A bird's *habitat* is the area in which it finds conditions best for feeding and nesting. Scouts can improve the habitat of many bird species by putting up birdhouses and feeders.

TRACKING

Every animal traveling on land leaves tracks. Footprints, bent grass, broken twigs, chewed leaves, scat, rubbed bark, a shiny strip of slime—following these and other clues can teach you much about animals. With a little luck, the tracks could lead you right to the creatures themselves.

Tracking is a skill you can master by doing lots of it. Practice in your yard, alongside rivers, and in parks, fields, and forests. Here's how to get started:

Find Some Tracks to Follow

Winter snow holds a surprising number of tracks. During other seasons, try the soft soil near ponds and streams. In dry country, scan the dust for prints and look for pebbles and brush that have been disturbed.

Study a Single Track

Examine one footprint and fix its details in your mind. You might even measure it and make a sketch of it. That can help you stay with a trail even if other animals have crossed the tracks you are following.

Track Early or Late

Early in the morning and late in the day, shadows cast in the prints make them easier to see.

SCAT

Droppings, or *scat*, are evidence of an animal's diet. Break scat apart with a stick. Hulls of seeds, skins of berries, and bits of leaves suggest the animal is an *herbivore*—an animal that eats only plants. Small bones, fur, and feathers might appear in the scat of *carnivores*—animals that feed on other animals. Mixed scat indicates an *omnivore*—a species whose diet includes both animal and plant material.

Think Like the Animal

If you lose the track, ask yourself where you would go if you were the animal, then look in that direction. Mark the last print with a stick, then explore all around it until you find more evidence of the animal's route.

(For more on animal tracks, see the *Fieldbook*.)

COLLECTING TRACKS

Perhaps you've heard the no-trace hiking slogan, "Take only photographs, leave only footprints." Here's a way you can bring home some footprints, too.

Notch the ends of a cardboard strip, form it into a collar, and place it around a footprint you want to preserve. Mix up some plaster of paris. (Plaster of paris is available at drug stores. Mixing instructions are on the label.)

Pour the plaster into the collar and wait for it to harden—ten to twenty minutes in warm weather. Remove the cast and brush off the dirt. On the back of the cast, write the date, where you found the track, and the name of the animal that made it.

Casts of prints are fine souvenirs of your adventures. You can also press them into damp sand to recreate the tracks—a valuable study aid for improving the animal-observing skills of everyone in your patrol.

DON'T DISTURB HUMAN ARTIFACTS

While you are tracking, hiking, and camping, you might come across arrowheads, broken pottery, or other items from earlier cultures.

Don't touch or move anything you find. The way artifacts lie on the ground can tell scientists a great deal about the people who made and used them.

Report what you have seen to local authorities. They will know if archaeologists should examine the site. (For more information on protecting and understanding artifacts, see the *Archaeology* merit badge pamphlet.)

TRACKING ANIMALS

Sneaking up close to animals without them knowing you are there is an ancient art. It allows you to find out what animals look like, where they go, and what they do. Tracking animals is an exciting challenge that will test your patience and skill. If you have a camera, it can also put you in position to photograph animals large and small.

Tracking by Waiting

Let the animals come to you. Hide long enough near a well-used animal trail and there's a good chance you'll see them coming by. Take cover in the brush, sit in a blind, or climb up into a tree and wait quietly for animals to appear.

Much of the animal world is active after dark. On a night with a full moon, wait in silence at the edge of a meadow or beside a lake or stream where you might see and hear lots of wildlife activity.

Tracking by Moving

To move closer to animals, make yourself invisible and silent. Hide behind trees, stumps, and clumps of grass. Stay near the ground, looking around the sides of rocks and bushes, not over the top. Your shape will show against the sky, so stay low as you cross ridges.

Move only when animals are looking away, and freeze if they glance in your direction. Place your feet with care; stepping on twigs or dry leaves might make enough noise to send animals running.

Many animals will be able to smell you from long distances. Try to stay downwind as you are tracking. When the wind is coming toward you, it won't carry your scent to the animal.

Observing wild animals is an exciting way to learn more about your world. With knowledge can come a greater desire to care for the environment.

Finally, be kind to wildlife. Respect their boundaries and their needs. If you can quietly move close to an animal, you can just as quietly slip away without disturbing it. Don't chase wild animals or touch nests or burrows. If you come upon a young animal, leave it alone; its parents are very likely hiding nearby, waiting for you to leave.

Why Care About Nature?

Studying animals and plants along with weather, water, sunlight, and everything else that affects them is called *ecology*. It comes from the old Greek words *oikos*, meaning "house," and *ology*, meaning "to study." Ecology is simply the study of the home we share with all species.

We are affected by changes in nature happening everywhere on the globe. Likewise, what we do has effects on the environment that can reach far beyond our neighborhoods. The way we treat the Earth today will leave its mark for years to come.

Each of us has a great responsibility to care for this Earth-house of ours. The better we understand it, the more we can work to keep it clean, repair it where it has been damaged, and do it no harm.

(For more on ecology and nature, see the BSA's *Fieldbook* and the following merit badge pamphlets: *Bird Study, Environmental Science, Fish and Wildlife Management, Forestry, Geology, Insect Study, Mammal Study, Nature, Plant Science, Reptile and Amphibian Study, Soil and Water Conservation,* and *Weather.*)

To become a Tenderfoot Scout you learned about poisonous plants, how to perform the Heimlich maneuver, and ways to treat a few common injuries. The requirements for Second Class will help you understand the bigger picture of first aid as you practice the right way to approach the scene of an accident, figure out what is wrong, and then decide what to do.

Detailed information for each requirement can be found on the pages listed below:

6a. Show what to do for "hurry" cases of stopped breathing, serious bleeding, and internal poisoning. (See chapter 11, "First Aid," pages 293–302 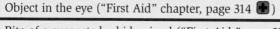.)

6b. Prepare a personal first aid kit to take with you on a hike. (See chapter 11, "First Aid," page 289 .)

6c. Demonstrate first aid for the following:

Object in the eye ("First Aid" chapter, page 314)
Bite of a suspected rabid animal ("First Aid," page 312)
Puncture wounds from a splinter, nail, and fishhook ("First Aid," page 305)
Serious burns (second-degree) ("First Aid," page 306)
Heat exhaustion ("First Aid," page 319)
Shock ("First Aid," page 303)
Heatstroke, dehydration, hypothermia, and hyperventilation ("First Aid," pages 320, 321, 323, 314)

On a hot summer day there's nothing better than having fun in the water, and that means knowing how to swim.

Swimming is an important Scouting skill. In addition to enjoying yourself in pools and lakes, you will be able to take care of yourself if you ever fall out of a boat or tumble into a stream. After training in lifesaving, you will be prepared to help a person in trouble in the water.

7a. Tell what precautions must be taken for a safe swim.

"If some folks wouldn't talk so much about swimming being so hard to do a fellow would find it a whole lot easier to learn."

Handbook for Boys,
5th edition, 1948

BSA SAFE SWIM DEFENSE*

1. **Qualified supervision.** A conscientious and experienced adult leader must supervise all activity in, on, or around the water.

2. **Physical fitness.** Evidence of fitness for swimming activity is required in the form of a complete health history from a physician, parent, or legal guardian. The supervisor must know the physical condition of all participants and must adjust the supervision, discipline, and protection to anticipate any potential risks associated with individual health conditions.

3. **Safe area.** Scouts never swim in an area that has not been carefully inspected and prepared for safe swimming. Depth, bottom and perimeter hazards, water quality and clarity, access control, other use or traffic, and temperature are all important safety factors.

4. **Lifeguards on duty.** Trained and specially equipped lifeguards must be on duty whenever and wherever Scouts go swimming.

5. **Lookout.** The supervisor or someone he or she appoints must be positioned where they can see and hear everything in the swimming area.

6. **Ability groups.** Each participant's swimming ability must be evaluated, and each participant is limited to the swimming area and activity that suits his ability.

7. **Buddy system.** Scouts never swim alone. Each Scout must stay close to a buddy who always knows where he is and what he is doing.

8. **Discipline.** Scouts know and respect the rules, and always follow directions from the lifeguards and supervisor.

*For the complete statement of the BSA Safe Swim Defense standards, see *Swimming* merit badge pamphlet, No. 33352; *Lifesaving* merit badge pamphlet, No. 33297; or *Guide to Safe Scouting*, No. 34416.

7b. Demonstrate your ability to jump feetfirst into water over your head in depth, level off and swim 25 feet on the surface, stop, turn sharply, resume swimming, then return to your starting place.

The best way to learn to swim is by taking courses from qualified instructors. Many Scout camps offer swimming classes. So do the Red Cross, YMCA, and other organizations, and there might be lessons at your neighborhood pool. Your Scout leaders can help you find the instruction you need.

SWIMMING STROKES

The best first swimming strokes for you to learn are the crawl strokes—the *front crawl* and the *back crawl*. These are strong swimming strokes using the *flutter kick* and the familiar rotating arm stroke. Particularly important is the rhythmic breathing used on the front crawl; you will not be a fast, strong, or confident swimmer until you are comfortable exhaling in the water and inhaling in rhythm with your stroke.

Front Crawl

The *front crawl* has three parts: the flutter kick, the rotating arm stroke, and rhythmic breathing. It is the fastest, and one of the most graceful, of all swimming strokes.

The flutter kick relies on relaxed ankles and the use of the entire leg. The movement begins at the hips and flows to the feet. As one foot moves downward, the other comes up in a beating or fluttering rhythm. The kick should be smooth and steady, of even depth (eight to twelve inches), and just below the surface of the water. You can work on the kick by holding the edge of the pool or by supporting yourself on a buoyant kickboard.

Practice the arm stroke in waist-deep water. Bend forward so that the top of your body is in a swimming position. Extend your right arm and swing it down to your hip, then raise that elbow and stretch your arm forward again. Alternate with your left arm. Keep your fingers together and your hands cupped.

Push off into a glide. Use the flutter kick and arm stroke together to move you through the water. Remember to exhale

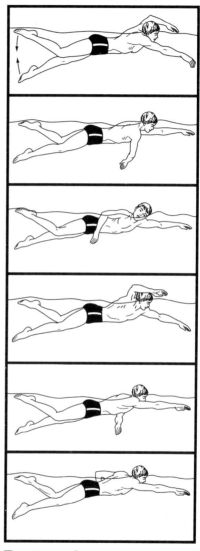

Front crawl

through your mouth and nose while your face is in the water. To inhale, roll your head to one side as the arm on that side is pulling to your hip and the elbow is lifting out of the water. Inhale through your mouth, then turn your face back into the water as your arm is recovering to the extended position in front of you.

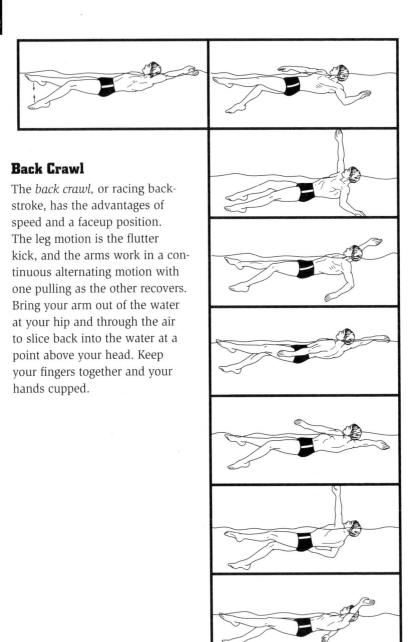

Back Crawl

The *back crawl,* or racing backstroke, has the advantages of
speed and a faceup position.
The leg motion is the flutter
kick, and the arms work in a continuous alternating motion with
one pulling as the other recovers.
Bring your arm out of the water
at your hip and through the air
to slice back into the water at a
point above your head. Keep
your fingers together and your
hands cupped.

Back crawl

Leaping entry

ENTERING DEEP WATER

An important first step in swimming is jumping into deep water. Begin with a simple *jump entry* into chest-deep water. Stand at the pool or dock edge, bend slightly at the knees, and hop forward. Pretend you are going to land with your feet together on the top of the water. Your arms should be extended forward and your body leaning slightly forward from the waist. Once you can do this easily, try standing with one foot back and then leap forward as though you were jumping over a puddle. This *leaping entry* will land you on or near the surface of the water, ready to begin swimming.

Now try taking off on one foot, leaning forward, reaching out and up with both arms, and stretching your front leg far ahead—as if you were hurdling a low fence. Leap far out. When you hit the water, snap your legs together and slap downward with your arms. If you do it well, you won't even get your face wet.

When you are confident of your leaping entry and have mastered the basic crawl strokes, you are almost ready for your first jump and swim in deep water. All you need now are some very useful deep-water maneuvers.

TURNS, REVERSES, STOPS, AND STARTS

Some skills are not particularly significant when swimming in shallow water where footing is always available. But being able to stop and restart swimming, reverse direction, and turn while swimming is very important when swimming in deep water. (Note that Second Class requirement 7b asks you to stop, turn, and resume swimming.)

To stop while swimming the crawl stroke, simply stop kicking and raise your head while pushing down and slightly forward with your arms. A reverse after stopping can be done in one quick motion by sweeping both arms in the same direction across the front of your body while turning your head and shoulders in the opposite direction of your arm movement. Starting your swim stroke in deep water is accomplished by pressing your arms down from the surface of the water and back alongside your body while at the same time leaning forward, putting your face down in the water, and beginning the flutter kick. This planes your body into the prone glide position for the crawl stroke to begin.

To turn while swimming the crawl, simply sweep wide with the arm stroke on the side opposite the turn and reach out in the direction of the turn with the other arm. When down in the prone glide position, your head can serve as a rudder to assist in swimming turns. (A turn when swimming on your back is also accomplished by using your head as a rudder and sweeping wide with the arm stroke opposite the turning side.)

7c. Demonstrate water rescue methods by reaching with your arm or leg, by reaching with a suitable object, and by throwing lines and objects. Explain why swimming rescues should not be attempted when a reaching or throwing rescue is possible, and explain why and how a rescue swimmer should avoid contact with the victim.

WATER RESCUES

Several thousand Americans drown every year. By learning how to swim, you can take care of yourself in the water. To help someone else who is in danger of drowning, you must learn lifesaving techniques **before** you need them. Practice water rescues at Scout camp or take a course at a local pool. Many Scouts learn water rescue skills by earning the Lifesaving merit badge.

The most effective rescue methods are also the easiest and safest—they do not require any swimming. The rescue methods taught in Scout lifesaving are—in order of use—(1) reach, (2) throw, (3) row, and (4) go (with support). But even the most experienced lifesaver will never attempt a swimming rescue when assistance can be given by a safer and easier method. The reaching and throwing methods are what you will learn and practice as a Second Class Scout.

Reaching Rescues

Reaching rescues are safe, simple, and highly effective. Well over half of all drownings occur within twenty feet of safety. If the person is quite close, lie down, extend a hand, and try to grab his wrist. Nothing could be simpler. It could, however, save his life.

When you establish contact with the person, he is likely to stop his own efforts to remain afloat. Such action can topple the unprepared rescuer into the water. This is the reason for lying down or otherwise bracing yourself.

If he is beyond the reach of your hand or leg, use any available object to extend your reach. This might be a pole, paddle, stick, or towel. Again, keep your weight low and well braced.

The tired swimmer or the panicked victim will grab for whatever object you extend. The drowning nonswimmer, however, might not be able to reach for an object. It must therefore be placed in contact with his hands.

The simplest reaching rescues are performed without entering the water, but in some cases you might need to extend your reach by stretching your arm or leg into the water while holding securely to a rigid support such as a pool ladder or dock support. One safe and efficient method for extending a reach is the human chain.

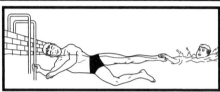

Throwing Rescues

If a person needing assistance is beyond any possible reach, try a *throwing rescue.* Life jackets, picnic coolers, wooden benches, deck chairs, spare tires, or any other items that float and could give support can be thrown, heaved, or shoved to a victim. A floating object with a line attached would be best, but either the object or the line could be used alone. Practice throwing both weighted and unweighted lines accurately for rescue purposes.

Throw floating support

Heaving line (unweighted)

Items for throwing rescues

Get Help!

If you encounter a swimmer in need, take a few seconds to assess the situation and remember your training. Remain calm. Someone else might have already started a rescue. If so, stand out of the way and be ready to help. Pinpoint the victim's position from shore. Make sure medical aid has been summoned if needed. Keep curious bystanders from interfering with the rescue effort. If no one else is attempting a rescue, then you must act quickly.

As a Second Class Scout, you will be prepared to give reaching or throwing assistance. Usually this is all that is needed. If reaching or throwing assistance is impossible, then you should **get help!**

Help might be a boat that could get you or someone else close enough to reach or throw to the victim. First, be sure to put on a life jacket, then row to within throwing or reaching distance of the victim. When you are firmly braced in the boat, extend an oar or paddle or throw a flotation device for the victim to grab. If you cannot reach, throw, or use a boat, yell or go for help.

Only in rare situations will a swimming rescue be the only choice. After you have completed Lifesaving merit badge, you will be prepared to use swimming rescue methods if they are ever needed. But you will also understand the danger of being in the water with a panicky or unconscious drowning victim, and you will continue to make every effort to avoid attempting a swimming rescue. Even when a swimming rescue is attempted, the rescuer should always take with him something that can be used for flotation or extended to the victim in order to avoid direct contact. Getting entangled with a drowning victim is a sure way to get in trouble. Don't put yourself in danger. If reaching and throwing don't work, **get help!**

8. Participate in a school, community, or troop program on the dangers of using drugs, alcohol, and tobacco and other practices that could be harmful to your health. Discuss your participation in the program with your family.

Knowledge is the greatest weapon you can have for protecting yourself from the dangers of drugs, alcohol, and tobacco or of taking part in other practices that could be harmful to your health. The more you know, the greater your ability to make wise decisions.

Many schools, communities, and Scout troops have programs that provide valuable information. You might also want to share with others some facts about the negative effects of drugs, alcohol, and tobacco. Teaching is one of the best ways to research and understand a subject. It also allows you to be of service to your school, community, or troop.

9. Demonstrate Scout spirit by living the Scout Oath (Promise) and Scout Law in your everyday life.

Most requirements for Scout ranks can be measured by other people. When you set out to swim 50 feet for the Second Class swimming requirement, anyone can see that you have covered the distance.

How well you live the Scout Oath and Scout Law in your life, though, is something for you to judge. You know when you are being kind, when you are helpful and a good friend. You know when you are trustworthy and reverent. You alone know how you act when no one is around to witness what you do.

Do the best you can to live each day by the Scout Oath and Law. You might look back on some of the decisions you've made and wish you had acted differently, but you can learn from those moments and promise yourself you will do better in the future.

And don't be surprised that when you use the Scout Oath and Law for guidance, others will recognize those values in you and respect you for it. Set high standards for yourself and strive to reach them. No one can ask anything more of you.

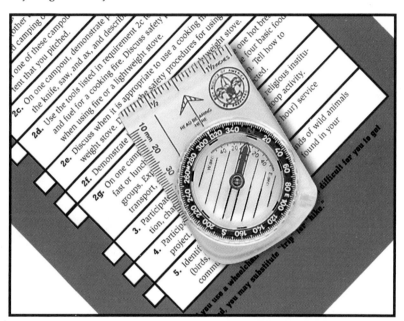

10. Participate in a Scoutmaster conference.

Your Scoutmaster will want to congratulate you on completing the Second Class requirements and discuss your progress with you. What do you like best about Scouting? What are you contributing to your patrol and troop? Are there ways that troop leaders can make the experience even better for you?

As you look toward First Class, your Scoutmaster might remind you that he and the rest of your Scout troop are behind you. They are cheering you on and are always ready to give you a hand whenever you need it.

11. Complete your board of review.

TRAILHEAD

FIRST CLASS SCOUT

READY FOR LOTS MORE HIKING AND CAMPING? Want to cook outdoors, practice first aid, identify native plants, and lash together rustic structures? All of that and more await you on the trail to First Class.

Becoming a First Class Scout also prepares you to be more of a leader in your patrol, your troop, and your community. People will expect more of you, and you will expect more of yourself.

More time in the outdoors, more responsibilities, more knowledge of Scouting's skills—that's what becoming a First Class Scout is all about. A good place to begin is by getting out a map and compass and increasing your knowledge of how to find your way.

The First Class badge joins together the Tenderfoot and the Second Class badges. When you have earned the right to wear it, you will have completed the training you need to take part in most of Scouting's activities and adventures.

FIRST CLASS
RANK REQUIREMENTS

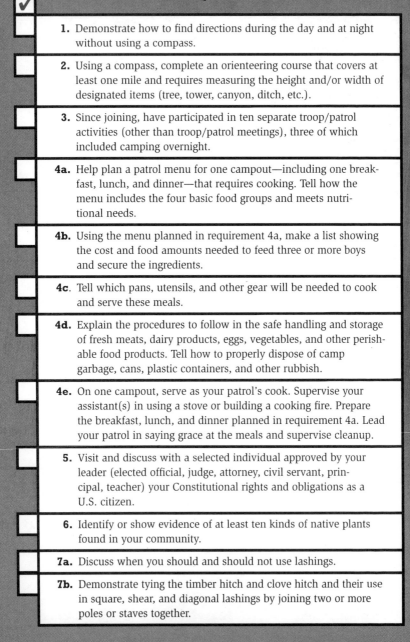

✓

1. Demonstrate how to find directions during the day and at night without using a compass.

2. Using a compass, complete an orienteering course that covers at least one mile and requires measuring the height and/or width of designated items (tree, tower, canyon, ditch, etc.).

3. Since joining, have participated in ten separate troop/patrol activities (other than troop/patrol meetings), three of which included camping overnight.

4a. Help plan a patrol menu for one campout—including one breakfast, lunch, and dinner—that requires cooking. Tell how the menu includes the four basic food groups and meets nutritional needs.

4b. Using the menu planned in requirement 4a, make a list showing the cost and food amounts needed to feed three or more boys and secure the ingredients.

4c. Tell which pans, utensils, and other gear will be needed to cook and serve these meals.

4d. Explain the procedures to follow in the safe handling and storage of fresh meats, dairy products, eggs, vegetables, and other perishable food products. Tell how to properly dispose of camp garbage, cans, plastic containers, and other rubbish.

4e. On one campout, serve as your patrol's cook. Supervise your assistant(s) in using a stove or building a cooking fire. Prepare the breakfast, lunch, and dinner planned in requirement 4a. Lead your patrol in saying grace at the meals and supervise cleanup.

5. Visit and discuss with a selected individual approved by your leader (elected official, judge, attorney, civil servant, principal, teacher) your Constitutional rights and obligations as a U.S. citizen.

6. Identify or show evidence of at least ten kinds of native plants found in your community.

7a. Discuss when you should and should not use lashings.

7b. Demonstrate tying the timber hitch and clove hitch and their use in square, shear, and diagonal lashings by joining two or more poles or staves together.

FIRST CLASS
RANK REQUIREMENTS

7c. Use lashing to make a useful camp gadget.	☐
8a. Demonstrate tying the bowline knot and describe several ways it can be used.	☐
8b. Demonstrate bandages for a sprained ankle and for injuries on the head, the upper arm, and the collarbone.	☐
8c. Show how to transport by yourself, and with one other person, a person • From a smoke-filled room • With a sprained ankle, for at least 25 yards	☐
8d. Tell the five most common signs of a heart attack. Explain the steps (procedures) in cardiopulmonary resuscitation (CPR).	☐
9a. Tell what precautions must be taken for a safe trip afloat.	☐
9b. Successfully complete the BSA swimmer test.*	☐
9c. Demonstrate survival skills by leaping into deep water wearing clothes (shoes, socks, swim trunks, long pants, belt, and long-sleeved shirt). Remove shoes and socks, inflate the shirt, and show that you can float using the shirt for support. Remove and inflate the pants for support. Swim 50 feet using the inflated pants for support, then show how to reinflate the pants while using them for support.*	☐
9d. With a helper and a practice victim, show a line rescue both as tender and as rescuer. (The practice victim should be approximately 30 feet from shore in deep water.)	☐
10. Demonstrate Scout spirit by living the Scout Oath (Promise) and Scout Law in your everyday life.	☐
11. Participate in a Scoutmaster conference.	☐
12. Complete your board of review.	☐

*This requirement may be waived by the troop committee for medical or safety reasons.

NOTE: Alternate requirements for the First Class rank are available for Scouts with physical or mental disabilities if they meet the criteria listed in the *Boy Scout Requirements* book, No. 33215.

As you complete each requirement, ask your Scoutmaster to initial his or her approval on pages 442–43.

1. Demonstrate how to find directions during the day and at night without using a compass.

FINDING DIRECTIONS USING THE STARS

For thousands of years, people have imagined they could see groups of stars forming the shapes of warriors, animals, maidens, and monsters. Many of the names they gave these constellations are still with us today. You can use a *star chart*—a map of the heavens—to find them in the night sky.

With the stars to guide them, sailors of old crossed the seas, and travelers made their way to distant lands. You can use the stars to find directions at night, too. Here's how:

North Star Method

Ursa Major is the ancient name for a constellation known as the Great Bear. It contains the stars that form the Big Dipper. Four bright stars form the dipper's bowl, and three stars make up the handle.

Look closely and you might see that the middle star in the Big Dipper's handle is really two stars, Mizar and Alcor. Some Native Americans thought of the larger star as a horse, the smaller as a rider.

To find the North Star, train your eyes on the *pointer stars* of the Big Dipper—the two stars farthest from the handle. Imagine a line connecting them and extending upward to a point about five times the span between the two pointers. You should see the North Star at that point. The Earth's North Pole lies directly under the North Star.

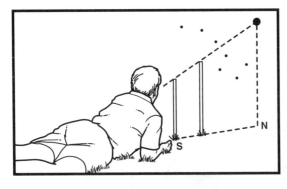

Push a two-foot-long stick into the ground. Place a shorter stick in such a way that when you sight over the tips of both sticks you can see the North Star. A straight line scratched between the sticks is a true north-south line.

Constellation Method

As you become familiar with the constellations, their locations will suggest directions. Scorpius, for example, fills the southern sky in the summer. Orion rises in the southeast on winter evenings. Shaped like a horseshoe, the Northern Crown opens toward the north. Cassiopeia circles the North Star opposite the Big Dipper.

(For more information on stars, see the BSA's *Fieldbook,* No. 33200.)

FINDING DIRECTIONS USING THE SUN

Depending on the season, the sun rises more or less in the east and sets in a westerly direction. At other times of the day, try one of the following methods:

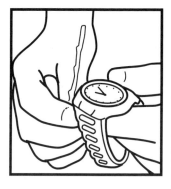

Watch Method

Hold your watch level. Place a short, straight twig upright against the edge of the watch at the point of the hour hand. (If you're wearing a digital watch, note the hour, imagine where the hour hand would be pointing, and place the twig accordingly.) Turn the watch until the shadow of the twig falls along the hour hand's position—that is, until the hour hand points toward the sun.

Notice the angle formed between the numeral 12 (the top of a digital watch) and the shadow lying on the real or imaginary hour hand. A line from the center of the watch that divides that angle in half will point south.

Note: This method requires standard time. If your watch is set on daylight savings time, turn it back one hour.

Shadow-Stick Method

Push a short, straight stick into the ground. Angle it toward the sun so that the stick makes no shadow, then wait until it casts a shadow at least six inches long. The shadow will be pointing east from the stick. A line at right angles across the shadow will be north-south.

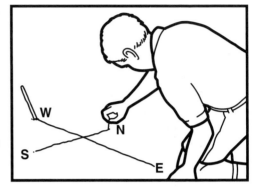

Equal-Length Shadow Method

In the morning, push a straight three-foot-long stick upright into the ground. Tie a string around the base of the stick with a bowline, then extend the string to the end of the stick's shadow. Tie a peg to the string at that point and use it to scratch a circle on the ground around the stick. Push the peg into the ground where the tip of the stick's shadow touches the circle.

In the afternoon, place another peg where the tip of the shadow again touches the circle. A straight line drawn between the pegs is a west-east line, with west at the morning peg. A line drawn at right angles across the west-east line will be north-south.

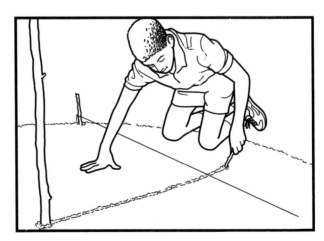

FINDING DIRECTIONS USING THE MOON

The moon comes up in the east and goes down in the west, as does the sun. The *shadow-stick method* described for use with the sun will work just as well on nights when the moon is bright enough to cast a shadow.

"When you are acting as scout to find the way for a party you should move ahead of them and fix your whole atten- tion on what you are doing, because you have to go by the very smallest signs, and if you get talking and thinking of other things you are very apt to miss them."

—*Baden-Powell,* Scouting for Boys, *1917*

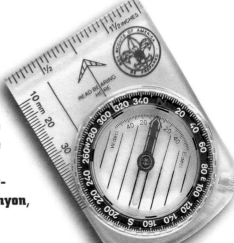

2. Using a compass, complete an orienteering course that covers at least one mile and requires measuring the height and/or width of designated items (tree, tower, canyon, ditch, etc.).

COMPASS GAME

The Second Class Scout chapter explains basic map reading and compass use (see pages 66–74). Try the following challenge to refresh your memory and test your skill as you prepare for the First Class orienteering requirements:

1. Push a stick into the ground beside your foot. Turn the housing on your compass to any bearing (15 degrees, for example). Orient the compass and sight along the direction-of-travel arrow to a landmark. Walk 50 steps toward it.

2. Add 120 degrees to your first bearing, and set your compass again (in this example, 120 degrees plus 15 degrees equals 135 degrees). Take a second bearing and walk 50 steps on the new heading.

3. Finally, add 120 degrees to the second compass setting (120 degrees plus 135 degrees equals 255 degrees) and adjust the compass housing. Take a final bearing and walk 50 steps.

   If your bearings have been accurate and your steps all the same length, you should be standing near the stick where you started.

WHAT IS AN ORIENTEERING COURSE?

Some troops have special orienteering courses set up for patrols to practice and enjoy map and compass skills. Many Scouts also sharpen their orienteering skills in open country, using their maps and compasses to reach destinations chosen by troop leaders.

Whether going cross-country or traveling over a frequently used area, an orienteering course can offer you the following challenges:

1. You will be given a map with five or six points marked on it. Figure out the compass bearings you will follow to go from one point to another.

2. Upon reaching a point marked on the map, you might find a marker (a brightly colored card hanging from a branch, for example) or a landmark (a road intersection, a stream, a hilltop, etc.).

3. After making a note of the landmark or signing the card to prove you were there, you'll set out on a new compass bearing toward the next destination on the course.

Orienteering can be an exciting sport for everyone in a patrol or troop. Teams of Scouts can go together to complete the course quickly and accurately, combining map and compass ability with route finding, observation, and physical fitness.

USING YOUR ORIENTEERING SKILLS
ON SCOUT ADVENTURES

In addition to the fun you can have, knowing how to use a map and compass will make your outdoor adventures better. An orienteering hike might call for a topography map like the one on this page.

Let's say you want to hike from Log Chapel to the road intersection at 179. Study the map and figure out your route before you begin hiking. Here are some possibilities:

Stay on quiet roads to Meadow Knoll Cemetery, then turn north to intersection 179.

You could avoid most of the roads if you walk south of the chapel until you reach a stream, then turn left and follow the stream bank in an easterly direction. From the point where it spills into a second stream, you might be able to see your destination. If not, place your compass on your map, determine the correct bearing to reach intersection 179, then let the compass lead you the rest of the way.

Another route would take you over the tops of the hills in the center of the map. To stay on course, you might need to take compass bearings from your starting point to the top of the first hill, and then from one summit to the next.

For a *bee-line hike*, use the map and compass to figure out the bearing for a straight line from Log Chapel to intersection 179. Follow that bearing as carefully as you can and see how close you come to your goal.

Want to figure out how far you will hike? Try this method:
1. Put one end of a piece of string on the map at your starting point—in this case, Log Chapel.
2. Lay out the string so that it rests on top of your entire route. Pinch the string where it touches your destination (intersection 179) and pick it up.
3. Stretch the string on the bar scale at the bottom of the map and measure it up to the point where you are pinching it. That's the length of your hike.

MEASURING DISTANCES

Your walking *stride* is a good tool for estimating distances. Learn the length of your step this way:

1. Using a tape measure, mark a 100-foot course on the ground.
2. Walk at a normal pace from one end of the course to the other, counting your steps as you go.
3. Divide the total number of steps into 100 and you'll know the length of one step.

For example, if you used 50 steps to go 100 feet, your step length is 2 feet. If it took you 40 steps, figure 2½ feet per step. And if 33 steps got you close, your stride is about a yard per step. (Because you are growing, recheck the length of your step every six months or so.)

Some Scouts find it easier to measure distances by counting every step along the way. Others have better luck counting each time their right foot touches the ground. That's called a *pace*.

MEASURING HEIGHTS

Here are some simple ways to measure a tree's height or to estimate the elevations of towers, waterfalls, cliffs, and walls:

Stick Method

1. Have a friend whose height you know stand beside the object you want to measure; a tree, for example. Step back and hold a straight stick upright at arm's length in front of you.

2. With one eye closed, sight over the stick so that the top of it appears to touch the top of your friend's head. Place your thumbnail on the stick where it seems to touch the base of the tree.

3. Now move the stick up to see how many more times this measurement on the stick will "fit" into the height of the tree. Multiply that number by your friend's height and you will know the approximate height of the tree.

Felling Method

1. Back away from the object you want to measure— a flagpole, for example.

2. Hold a stick upright at arm's length. Adjust the stick so that its tip appears to touch the top of the flagpole while your thumb seems to be at its base.

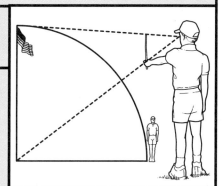

3. Swing the stick 90 degrees to a horizontal position, as if the flagpole were falling.

4. Keep your thumb in line with the base of the pole and notice where the tip of the stick appears to touch the ground. Measure the distance from that point on the ground to the base of the flagpole to get the flagpole's height.

Personal Measurements

You carry a measuring tool with you all the time—yourself. Use a ruler or yardstick to figure out the following measurements, and you'll be ready to size up the diameter of a tree, the next fish you catch, and anything else you want to measure.

Arm span _____   Finger length _____

Arm reach _____   Foot length _____

Hand span _____   Height _____

MEASURING WIDTHS

Imagine that you need to know the width of a stream. There is no bridge, and you can't get your feet wet. What will you do? Here are three methods for figuring out widths:

Salute Method

1. Stand on the shore and hold your hand to your forehead in a salute. Move your hand down until the front edge of it seems to touch the opposite shore.

2. Without changing the position of your head or hand, make a quarter turn. Notice the point at which the edge of your hand seems to touch the ground. Measure the distance to that point, and you will know the width of the stream.

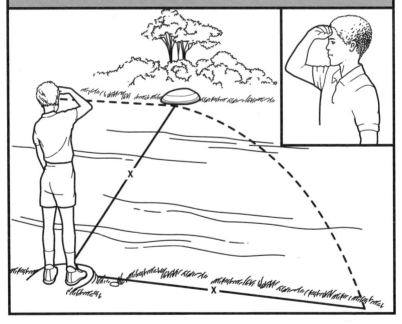

Stick Method

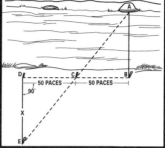

1. Locate an object on the far side of the stream; a rock, for example *(A)*.

2. Push a stick into the ground next to where you are standing, opposite the rock *(B)*.

3. Walk along the shore at a right angle to *AB*. Take any number of paces (twenty, for example), and mark that point with another stick *(C)*.

4. Continue walking along the shore in the same direction for the same number of paces as before (in this case, twenty more). Put a stick there *(D)*.

5. Finally, walk away from the stream at a right angle to *BD*. When you can sight a straight line directly over stick *C* to the rock on the far shore, stop and mark your spot *(E)*.

6. Measure *DE* to get the width of the stream.

Compass Method

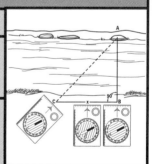

1. Locate an object—a rock, for example—*(A)* on the far shore directly opposite from where you are standing *(B)*.

2. Take a bearing by pointing the direction-of-travel arrow of your compass at the rock and turning the compass housing until the needle lies over the orienting arrow. Read the degrees (in this case, 120).

3. Add 45 degrees (120 degrees plus 45 degrees equals 165 degrees). Set your compass at the new reading (in this case, 165).

4. Walk along the shore, pointing the direction-of-travel arrow toward the rock. When the compass needle again lies over the orienting arrow, stop and mark your spot *(C)*. Distance *BC* is the same as the width of the stream.

3. Since joining, have participated in ten separate troop/patrol activities (other than troop/patrol meetings), three of which included camping overnight.

Troop and patrol activities are the heart of Scouting. On your way to becoming a First Class Scout, there might be many opportunities for you to teach Scouting skills to others, as well as to learn more yourself. You will also discover that you are being given more responsibilities in your troop and patrol. Your chances to be a leader are increasing, too.

In the following spaces, write down the time and place of ten separate troop or patrol activities, and a brief description of each one:

TROOP/PATROL ACTIVITIES RECORD

The first five activities are the ones you completed for Second Class requirement 2a. Copy them over below from page 75.

1. Date _____ Where we went _____
   What we did _____
   _____

2. Date _____ Where we went _____
   What we did _____
   _____

3. Date _____ Where we went _____
   What we did _____
   _____

4. Date _____ Where we went _____
   What we did _____
   _____

5. Date _____ Where we went _____
   What we did _____
   _____

6. Date _____ Where we went _____
   What we did _____
   _____

7. Date _____ Where we went _____
   What we did _____
   _____

8. Date _____ Where we went _____
   What we did _____
   _____

9. Date _____ Where we went _____
   What we did _____
   _____

10. Date _____ Where we went _____
    What we did _____
    _____

4a. Help plan a patrol menu for one campout—including one breakfast, lunch, and dinner—that requires cooking. Tell how the menu includes the four basic food groups and meets nutritional needs.

4b. Using the menu planned in requirement 4a, make a list showing the cost and food amounts needed to feed three or more boys and secure the ingredients.

4c. Tell which pans, utensils, and other gear will be needed to cook and serve these meals.

CAMP COOKING

4d. Explain the procedures to follow in the safe handling and storage of fresh meats, dairy products, eggs, vegetables, and other perishable food products. Tell how to properly dispose of camp garbage, cans, plastic containers, and other rubbish.

4e. On one campout, serve as your patrol's cook. Supervise your assistant(s) in using a stove or building a cooking fire. Prepare the breakfast, lunch, and dinner planned in requirement 4a. Lead your patrol in saying grace at the meals and supervise cleanup.

Rich stews, good desserts, breakfasts that get the day off to a roaring start—there's nothing better than tasty meals outdoors, especially if you cook them yourself. Whether the ingredients are fresh foods for an evening cookout or lightweight dried ingredients for a long backpacking journey, some general skills, a few spices, and a bit of creativity on your part will result in feasts as memorable as the adventure itself.

Chapter 10, "Cooking," (beginning on page 247 ) has the information you need to learn the basics of planning and cooking nutritious outdoor meals, the safe handling of food, and cleaning up afterward.

Take a moment before a meal to share your thanks for the food you have been given, the experiences you are having, and the joy of being with friends. The grace used at Philmont Scout Ranch is one way of expressing that gratitude:

Philmont Grace

For food, for raiment,

For life, for opportunity,

For friendship and fellowship,

We thank Thee, O Lord.

Amen.

Tooth of Time,

Philmont Scout Ranch,

Cimarron, New Mexico

5. Visit and discuss with a selected individual approved by your leader (elected official, judge, attorney, civil servant, principal, teacher) your Constitutional rights and obligations as a U.S. citizen.

Much of Scouting prepares you to explore the outdoors and understand the natural world all around you. Just as important, though, is getting to know your own community—who does what, how people must cooperate to improve their neighborhoods, and what you can do to help make things go.

Many individuals are dedicated to public service. Visiting with them can help you understand the challenges and rewards of their work. You might also discover some of the many ways that you can be of service to your neighborhood and your community. For more on your rights and responsibilities as a citizen, see chapter 12, "Citizenship," beginning on page 331 ⬤.

A Visit with a Community Leader

In the spaces below, write a brief summary of your discussion with an elected official, judge, attorney, civil servant, principal, teacher, or other community leader.

Date _____

Person's name and occupation _____

What you learned about your Constitutional rights and obligations

_____

_____

_____

_____

_____

_____

_____

_____

_____

_____

_____

6. Identify or show evidence of at least ten kinds of native plants found in your community.

From grasses pushing through cracks in a city street to ancient forests covering the sides of a mountain, vegetation is a vital part of our world:

Plants purify the air and pump oxygen into the atmosphere.
Roots keep soil from washing away, and leaves (on branches and on the ground) slow the rain so that it can seep into the earth. Fallen trees, grasses, and leaves enrich the soil as they decay.
Vegetation provides shelter and food for wildlife. Even a dead tree can be important to animals as a roosting site, a place to build nests, and a source of nutrition.
Plants are used in many ways by people, too. Fields feed us and forests give us lumber to use in our buildings. Paper, rubber, many medicines, and thousands of other products are possible only because of plants.
Shaded yards and city parks offer us places close to home where we can relax and play. Forests and wilderness areas provide us varied and challenging settings for hiking, camping, and exploring nature.

"Different sorts of trees look

pretty much alike to many

people; but by observing their

different traits we can learn

to know a large number of

trees just as we have learned

to know our friends. The nat-

ural history of trees can be

learned only by keeping our

eyes open, training ourselves

to observe closely."

Handbook for Boys, 2nd edition, 1915

When you can identify trees, shrubs, and grasses, you can more easily discover all the places they live, the uses they have, and their importance to the environment.

A good way to learn about plants in your community is to spend time with someone who knows a lot about them. Your troop leaders might be acquainted with gardeners, botanists, or other plant experts who enjoy sharing their knowledge with groups of Scouts. They can show you how to recognize the shapes and sizes of different plants, the outlines of their leaves, and other clues that can lead to an identification.

You also can identify plants by using books called *field guides.* Your local and school libraries might have copies, as might your troop. Many field guides include information about the roles plants play in their surroundings.

Photosynthesis
The green pigment,
chlorophyll, in leaves
draws power from sun-
light to convert carbon
dioxide from the air into
nutrients for the tree.
This process, called
photosynthesis, returns
oxygen to the atmos-
phere. It is an important
way that the air we
breathe is cleaned and
refreshed.

Why Leaves Change Color and Fall to the Ground

Each autumn the leaves of many broad-leaved trees turn red, orange, yellow, and brown. Those colors were in the leaves all summer, but were hidden beneath the green of the chlorophyll.

With the approach of colder weather and fewer hours of daylight, a tree's food production drops, and so does the amount of chlorophyll in the leaves. The green fades, and other colors show through.

Next, a layer of cells in the stem cuts the tissues that hold the leaf on its branch, and it falls to the ground. There it decomposes, releasing nutrients into the soil so that they can be used again.

COLLECTING EVIDENCE OF NATIVE PLANTS

Trees are the largest and the oldest living things on Earth. Over a thousand species grow in the United States, each one different from all others. Some thrive in sunlight, others in shade. A few require fire in order to reproduce. Certain trees grow very fast while others, especially those living hundreds of years, gain their height and mass very slowly.

The two large groups of American trees are *conifer trees* and *broad-leaved trees*. Also known as evergreens, *conifers* bear cones and have needlelike or scalelike leaves that usually stay on the trees for several years. Broad-leaved trees have flat leaves that generally fall off in the autumn.

(For more information on trees, see the BSA's *Fieldbook*, No. 33200.)

Deciduous

Evergreen

Conifers

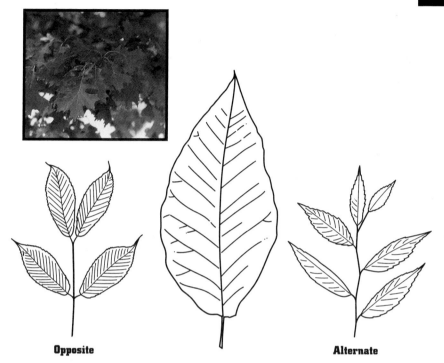

Opposite   Alternate

Broad-leaves

Softwoods and Hardwoods

Woodworkers refer to pine, fir, cedar, spruce, and other conifers as *softwoods* because lumber from them is easy to cut and shape. Experienced campers know that firewood from conifers burns quickly with hot, smoky flames.

Oak, walnut, maple, and most other broad-leaved trees are called *hardwoods.* They are used to build furniture and other structures requiring strength and durability. Hardwood campfires burn down slowly into long-lasting beds of coals.

As you learn to identify trees and other native plants, you can gather evidence of them to help you remember their characteristics. Two forms of evidence are pressed leaves and leaf ink prints:

Pressing Leaves

When you have leaves you would like to preserve, put each one between two sheets of paper, lay the sheets on a board or other flat surface, and then place heavy books or some other flat weight on top. Give the leaves several days to flatten and dry. Mount them in a scrapbook along with the details of where and when you found them, their identities, and any other information you have learned about their individual natural histories.

Making Leaf Ink Prints

Use a rubber roller to spread a dab of printer's ink on a glass plate. Place a leaf on the glass with the veined side against the ink. Run the roller over the leaf several times, then lay the leaf, inked side down, on a clean sheet of paper. Cover the leaf with a piece of newspaper and run the roller over it to make a print. After the ink dries, arrange the pages in a scrapbook.

WHY CARE ABOUT PLANTS?

The world around us is a complicated web of relationships among thousands of types of plants and animals. That diversity helps all species survive. Strong forests, prairies, and other plant communities increase the stability of the environment.

Our actions affect the water, air, vegetation, and wildlife all around us. Recycling, using no-trace methods of hiking and camping, and being thrifty in the use of natural resources are a few of the ways you can help. Learning all you can about the environment will allow you to make choices that are good for the long-term health of the Earth.

Cherish the Earth. Use it in such a way that it sustains life today and makes it possible for future generations to continue to sustain life.

7a. Discuss when you should and should not use lashings.

7b. Demonstrate tying the timber hitch and clove hitch and their use in square, shear, and diagonal lashings by joining two or more poles or staves together.

7c. Use lashing to make a useful camp gadget.

Native Americans had no nails or screws with which to make their tools. Settlers moving into the American frontier built homes with materials they found in the forests. In Indian camps and pioneer settlements, people depended on lashings to bind together structures as simple as tripods and as complex as river crossings.

You will seldom have the time or the need on campouts and backpacking trips to build pioneering projects. However, where they are appropriate, a few structures can make you more comfortable. A table will lift food preparation off the ground. A tripod can hold a washbasin. Lashings can bind together several pack frames to form a stretcher for an emergency evacuation. At Scout camp, you might even have a chance to lash together a tower or a bridge.

Obtain permission before building camp gadgets or other structures—they are prohibited in many backcountry areas as a way of encouraging no-trace camping. Use only the materials that have been approved for the project. **Take everything apart when you are done, and leave no evidence that you were there.**

What Are Staves?

In Scouting's early days, hiking staffs, or *staves*, were almost a part of the uniform. Handbooks explained how staves could be used as parts of pioneering projects and to make stretchers and splints for first aid emergencies. For more on using hiking sticks today, see page 213.

TIMBER HITCH

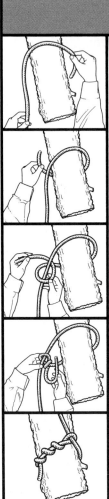

TIMBER HITCH

While working on your Tenderfoot requirements, you learned that a *hitch* is a knot that ties a rope to an object. The *timber hitch* is the knot to use for dragging a log across the ground. It is also the knot that starts a *diagonal lashing.* Here's how to tie a timber hitch:

Pass the end of the rope around the log. Loop the end around the standing part of the rope, then wrap the end around itself three or more times. Tighten the hitch against the log.

CLOVE HITCH

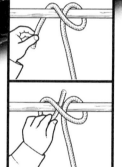

CLOVE HITCH

Clove comes from the word *cleave,* meaning "to hold fast." The *clove hitch* can be used to start most lashings:

Bring the rope end over and under a pole. Take it around a second time, crossing over the first wrap to form the shape of an **X**. Bring the rope end around a third time and tuck it under itself at the center of the **X**. Pull the end of the rope to tighten the hitch.

An alternative way of tying a clove hitch makes it easy to lay the knot over the end of a pole. It is also a good knot for attaching a rope or cord to your *bear bag*—a bag of food hung from a tree out of the reach of animals.

Make a loop near the end of the rope. Make an identical loop next to the first. Without turning over either loop, lay the first loop on top of the second. Place the pair of loops over the end of a pole or over the neck of the bear bag and tighten.

For more on bear bags, see page 263.

Increase the stability of a structure
by including triangles in its design:

A trestle

X trestle

H trestle

SQUARE LASHING

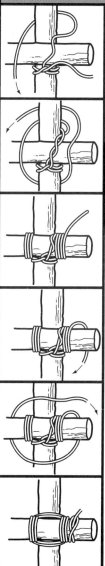

SQUARE LASHING

Use a *square lashing* for binding together two poles that are at right angles, or *square,* with one another:

Place the poles in position. Tie a clove hitch around the bottom pole near the crosspiece. Make three tight *wraps* around both poles. As you form the wraps, lay the rope on the **outside** of each previous turn around the top pole, and on the **inside** of each previous turn around the bottom pole. Wind two *fraps* around the wraps, pulling the rope very tight. Finish with a clove hitch around the top pole.

SHEAR LASHING

SHEAR LASHING

Poles secured with a *shear lashing* can be raised as an A-frame:

Lay two poles side by side and tie a clove hitch to one of them. Make three very loose wraps around the poles, and then put two loose fraps between them. Finish with a clove hitch around the other pole. Spread the ends of the poles to form the shape you need. Redo the lashing if it proves to be too tight or too loose.

DIAGONAL LASHING

DIAGONAL LASHING

To bind poles at an angle other than a right angle, use a *diagonal lashing*:

Tie a timber hitch around both poles and pull it snug. Make three tight wraps around the poles, laying the wraps neatly alongside the timber hitch. Make three more wraps across the first three. Cinch down the wraps with two fraps between the poles. Tie off the rope end with a clove hitch.

A few additional lashings will allow you to build special structures or to put the finishing touches on a table, tower, or other project:

Shear or diagonal lashing

Monkey bridge

Square lashing

Tripod lashing

Desert water bag

Square lashing

Kitchen rack

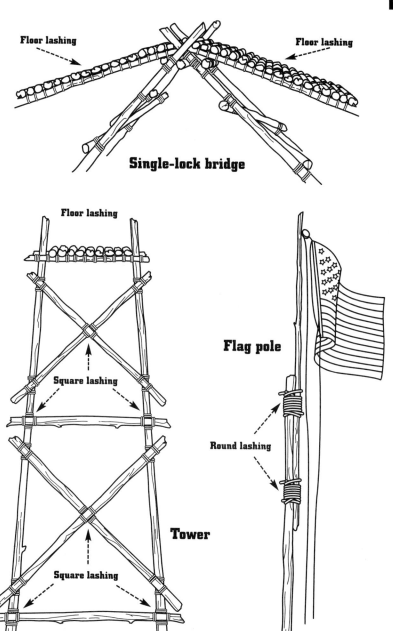

Floor lashing   Floor lashing

Single-lock bridge

Floor lashing

Square lashing

Square lashing

Tower

Flag pole

Round lashing

TRIPOD LASHING

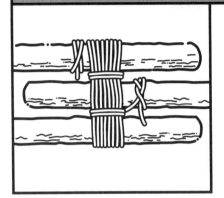

TRIPOD LASHING

A close relative of the shear lashing, a *tripod lashing* is the lashing to use for making a tripod or for joining together the first three poles of a tepee:

Lay three poles alongside each other with the top of the center pole pointing the direction opposite that of the outside poles. Tie a clove hitch around one outside pole. Loosely wrap the poles five or six times, laying the turns of rope neatly alongside one another. Make two very loose fraps on either side of the center pole. End with a clove hitch. Spread the legs of the tripod into position. If you have made the wraps or fraps too tight, you might need to start over.

ROUND LASHING

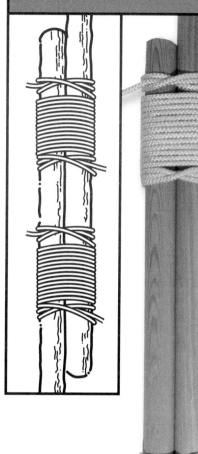

ROUND LASHING

Round lashings bind two poles side by side:

Position the poles beside each other and tie them together with a clove hitch. Make seven or eight very tight, neat wraps around the poles. Finish the lashing with another clove hitch around both poles.

There are no fraps in a round lashing. The wraps must do all the work, so pull them as tight as you can. Make a second round lashing farther along the poles to keep them from twisting out of line.

FLOOR LASHING

The *floor lashing* will secure the top of a table, the deck of a raft, the floor of a signal tower, or the walkway of a bridge:

Lay the poles side by side on top of the *stringers*—the logs or poles on which your platform will rest. Tie a clove hitch around one stringer. Bend the standing part of the rope over the first pole. Pull a loop of rope under the stringer and cast it over the second pole. You might need to lift the end of the pole in order to get the loop over it. Pull the rope tight, then bend it over the third pole. Continue until all the poles are bound to the stringer. Finish with a clove hitch, then repeat the procedure to lash the other ends of the poles to the other stringer.

Scale Models of Pioneering Projects

With straight sticks and strong string you can lash together models of any rustic structure. Use a pocketknife to cut sticks the right length. A signal tower might be only two feet high. A bridge might have a span of just twelve inches.

Make your models as authentic as you can, using the correct knots and lashings. If you ever have a chance to build the real thing, you will know just what to do.

For more on knots, lashings, and pioneering projects, see the *Pioneering* merit badge pamphlet.

8a. Demonstrate tying the bowline knot and describe several ways it can be used.

The *bowline* is among the most useful of knots because it forms a loop that will not slip and it is easy to untie. Use it to attach a cord to a pack frame, to tie a rope through the grommet of a tent, to secure a line to a canoe, in rescue situations, and in a thousand other ways. Learn to tie the bowline around a post and in the free end of a rope. With practice, you can even tie it with one hand.

BOWLINE KNOT

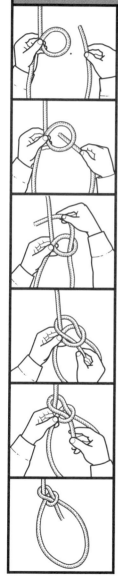

BOWLINE KNOT

Make a small overhand loop in the standing part of a rope. Bring the rope end up through the loop, around behind the standing part, and back down into the loop. Tighten the bowline by pulling the standing part away from the loop.

SHEET BEND

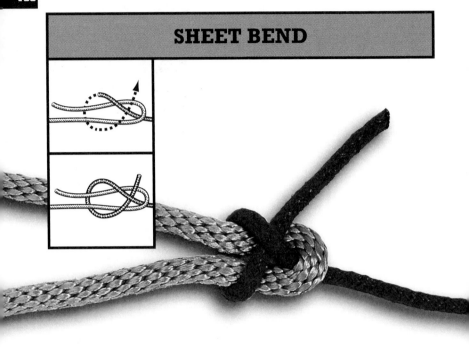

SHEET BEND

The *sheet bend* is a very good knot for tying together two ropes of the same or different diameters. It is a close relative of the bowline, and is untied in the same way.

Put a *bend* in the end of the thicker rope and hold it with one hand. Pass the end of the other rope through the bend, then take that end around behind the bend. Bring the end across the front of the bend and tuck it under its own standing part. Tighten the knot by pulling the standing part of the smaller line.

FIRST AID KIT

By now you should know how to approach the victim of an accident, how to treat hurry cases, and how to plan what to do next. (See chapter 11, "First Aid," beginning on page 287 .) The first aid requirements for First Class will add to your skill in bandaging wounds, transporting injured persons, recognizing signs of heart attack, and understanding cardiopulmonary resuscitation (CPR).

Detailed information for each requirement can be found on the pages listed below:

8b. Demonstrate bandages for a sprained ankle and for injuries on the head, the upper arm, and the collarbone. (See chapter 11, "First Aid," pages 309, 316–17 ⊕.)

8c. Show how to transport by yourself, and with one other person, a person

- **From a smoke-filled room**

- **With a sprained ankle, for at least 25 yards**

(See chapter 11, "First Aid," pages 326–28 ⊕.)

8d. Tell the five most common signs of a heart attack. Explain the steps (procedures) in cardiopulmonary resuscitation (CPR). (For common signs of a heart attack, see chapter 11, "First Aid," page 298 ⊕. For an explanation of cardiopulmonary resuscitation (CPR), see pages 294–98 ⊕.)

"I look upon swimming as an essential qualification for First

Class Scout, and for every man. Also, I don't consider a boy

is a real Scout till he has passed his First Class Scout."

—Lord Baden-Powell

To be a First Class swimmer you must increase your swimming strength and stamina, and learn how to rest while swimming in deep water. You will also learn boating safety, water survival skills, and how to serve as a lifeguard when your troop goes swimming.

9a. Tell what precautions must be taken for a safe trip afloat.

Some of Scouting's most exciting activities happen on the water. Rowing, canoeing, sailing, sailboarding, motorboating, waterskiing, rafting, kayaking, and surfboarding can be highlights of many adventures. Safely take part in them by following the BSA Safety Afloat guidelines.

BSA SAFETY AFLOAT*

1. **Qualified supervision.** A conscientious and experienced adult leader must supervise all activity afloat.

2. **Physical fitness.** Evidence of fitness for swimming activity is required in the form of a complete health history from a physician, parent, or legal guardian. The supervisor must know the physical condition of all participants and must adjust the supervision, discipline, and protection to anticipate any potential risks associated with individual health conditions.

3. **Swimming ability.** You must be classified as a "swimmer" to participate in Scout activity afloat. (A Scout who has not passed the swimmer test may ride as a passenger in a rowboat or motorboat with an adult classified as a swimmer, or in a canoe, raft, or sailboat with an adult certified as a lifeguard or lifesaver by a recognized agency.)

4. **Personal flotation equipment.** Properly fitted U.S. Coast Guard–approved personal flotation devices (PFDs) must be worn by all persons engaged in activity on the open water.

5. **Buddy system.** Scouts never go on the water alone. Every person has a buddy, and every craft on the water has a "buddy boat."

6. **Skill proficiency.** All persons participating in activity afloat must be trained and practiced in craft-handling skills, safety, and emergency procedures.

7. **Planning.** Before Scouts go afloat, they develop a "float plan" detailing their route, time schedule, and contingency plans. The float plan considers all pertinent water and weather conditions and all applicable rules or regulations, and is shared with all who have an interest (parents, local authorities, Scout leaders, and others).

8. **Equipment.** All equipment must be suited to the craft, to the water conditions, and to the individual. Equipment must be in good

repair and meet all applicable standards. Appropriate rescue equipment must be available.

9. **Discipline.** Scouts know and respect the rules, and always follow directions from the adult supervising the activity afloat.

*For the complete statement of the BSA Safety Afloat standards, see *Canoeing* merit badge pamphlet, No. 33305; *Rowing* merit badge pamphlet, No. 33404; or *Guide to Safe Scouting*, No. 34416.

9b. Successfully complete the BSA swimmer test.

As a Second Class Scout, you have already learned to jump into deep water and begin swimming. You also know how to stop and start, and how to turn while swimming. These skills are all part of the BSA swimmer test. Now you need to develop sufficient strength and stamina to swim 75 yards with one of your crawl strokes, or with one of several new strokes. Additionally, you need to master the elementary backstroke and floating so that you can rest while swimming, working, or playing in deep water.

BSA Swimmer Test

Jump feetfirst into water over the head in depth, level off, and begin swimming. Swim 75 yards in a strong manner using one or more of the following strokes: sidestroke, breaststroke, trudgen, or crawl; then swim 25 yards using an easy, resting backstroke. The 100 yards must be completed in one swim without stops and must include at least one sharp turn. After completing the swim, rest by floating.

FLOATING

Floating faceup is probably the best way to rest in deep water. This simple skill requires buoyancy and balance. Buoyancy comes mainly from the air you hold in your lungs, and the balance is achieved by distributing your body mass above and below your chest. Think of your lungs as balloons supporting the center of a seesaw. You want to spread the weight so the seesaw balances and holds steady in the water. You add weight above your chest by extending your arms above your shoulders and bending

your head as far back as your neck will stretch.

Practice in chest-deep water. Start from a standing position. Take a deep breath and hold it. Bend your knees slightly and lean backward, arching your back and stretching your neck backward until your ears are in the water and your chin is your highest point. Slowly extend your arms above the shoulders, palms up. Do not try to armstroke or kick yourself into a higher position, because this will throw you off balance. Relax and let your body settle into its natural floating level and position on the water. The natural floating position for many people is with their legs and feet hanging down almost vertically under the water. Others float high on the water with their hips and legs near the surface.

Begin by holding the float position as long as you can hold your breath. When it is necessary to breathe, quickly blow out a short puff and suck in new air through your nose. As your floating experience and confidence increase, you will be able to breathe in a more relaxed and natural rhythm.

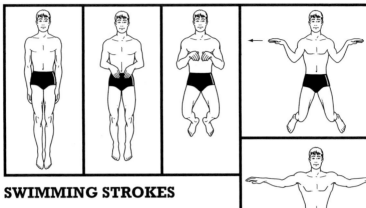

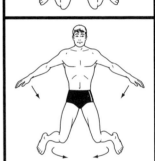

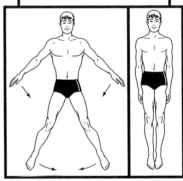

SWIMMING STROKES

Elementary Backstroke

This is the resting stroke for the last 25 yards of your test, and you should be less exhausted at the end of the distance compared to when you began the stroke. Use this stroke for long-distance swimming, or for when you are tiring and want to rest while continuing to make progress.

Start on your back in the glide position, legs extended, arms at your sides, hands at your thighs, and toes pointed. Move your hands up and at the same time begin to drop your heels. As you extend your hands outward, turn your toes outward. Now complete the "power" part of the stroke by sweeping your hands downs toward your feet and whipping your feet back together in a circular motion. To avoid getting water in your mouth and nose, bring your chin to your chest as your arms push toward your feet.

Make your movements continuous, resting only at the end of the stroke to permit a long glide. As you finish your glide, repeat the process. Keep your head in line with your body. Don't be in a hurry. Remember, this is a resting stroke, so be sure to relax and glide for three or four counts.

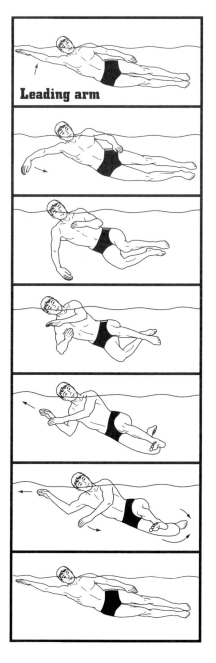

Leading arm

Sidestroke

This is another good long-distance stroke with a long, restful glide. It also introduces the scissors kick which is used in swimming rescues.

Start in the extended glide position on your side with one ear in the water, your nose and mouth turned to the shoulder out of the water, and your eyes looking toward your feet. Begin moving the leading arm into a catch motion, then start the trailing arm and leg action. The leading arm pulls as the trailing arm slices through toward the upper chest; the legs bend as the trailing arm moves forward. Pull the leading arm to a point just below your chest. As your arms begin to change directions, extend your top leg forward and your lower leg back. Without stopping, continue to move your arms and snap your feet together in a scissoring motion. The stroke is complete when you arrive back at the glide position. Hold the glide position for three or four counts and repeat the stroke.

Breaststroke

This is one of the oldest strokes used in Scouting, and variations range from a restful distance stroke to a competitive racing stroke. With an extended glide as taught in Scouting, the breast-stroke is a powerful, long-distance stroke that conserves energy and has certain applications in life-saving. The stroke uses a whip kick and shallow arm pull.

Start in the prone glide position with your face in the water. As you drop and pull your hands, lift your face out to breathe and draw your feet toward your hips. When your arms are at the level of your shoulders, your legs should be under your hips with your feet drawn up. Breathe in and have your face ready to go back in the water. Rotate your hands until they meet under your chin and thrust them through the water to the extended position. Your legs push out and back in a circular motion, your face returns to the water, ankles touch, and legs extend. Hold the glide for a count of three or four while exhaling into the water. Then begin the stroke again.

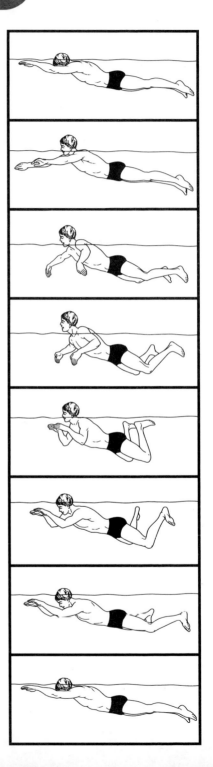

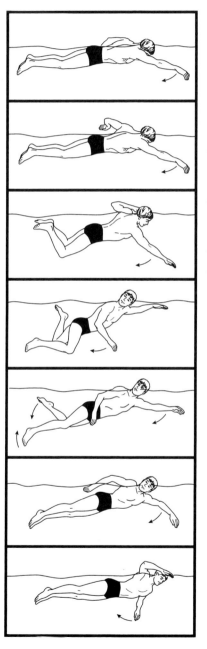

Trudgen

This interesting stroke, named for Englishman John Trudgen who first introduced the stroke in competition in 1868, combines the arm movements and breathing of the front crawl stroke with the scissors kick. The kick is completed with the hips turned up on the breathing side just as the arm on that side completes its pull. The legs trail in the extended position as the other arm pull is performed. Mature swimmers frequently prefer the trudgen as a strong, energy-conserving all-purpose stroke.

9c. Demonstrate survival skills by leaping into deep water wearing clothes (shoes, socks, swim trunks, long pants, belt, and long-sleeved shirt). Remove shoes and socks, inflate the shirt, and show that you can float using the shirt for support. Remove and inflate the pants for support. Swim 50 feet using the inflated pants for support, then show how to reinflate the pants while using them for support.

Shirt inflation

If you ever fall into deep water far from shore, inflating your shirt and pants are survival skills that can keep you afloat until you are rescued or can make your way to safety.

Perhaps even more importantly, fulfilling this requirement will involve maintaining yourself in deep water for several minutes while you complete a manual task. You will have to develop

Shirt floation

your scissors kick or "rotor" for treading water, learn to rest by floating occasionally, and learn to relax in a facedown float while you tie a square knot and prepare the clothing for inflation.

If you fall into the water wearing a button-up shirt made of cotton or other tightly woven fabric, you can stay afloat by trapping air in the shirt's back and shoulders. Button the top collar button. Open a space between the shirt's second and third buttons, roll forward so that your mouth is below the opening, and then blow into it. Hold the collar tight and keep your elbows down to prevent air leakage.

Pants of closely woven fabric can be turned into an effective life jacket. While wearing the inflated shirt, remove the pants carefully. Do not turn them inside out. Next, inflate a pocket with a puff of air. (The pocket will support the pants should you lose contact.) Now tie the pant legs

Inflating a pocket

together as near to the ends as you can. Pull the knot tight and close the fly.

Splashing air into the pants is the quickest and easiest means of inflation, but it might take some practice before you can do it well. Hold the waistband open just below the surface, cup your hand in the air, and strike the water just in front of the pants. Follow through so that the air pulled down by your hand enters the opening of the pants. You should move the air just below the surface and then

sideways so that it bubbles upward into the pants. The method will not work if you fail to lift your hand clear of the water or if you strike directly downward. If you have difficulty with this method, you can fill the pants by blowing air into them from beneath.

When the pants are inflated, grasp the waist with the fly toward you and place your head

Inflating pants

through the opening between the legs. Rest your head on the knot, lie back, and relax. If you have a belt, bunch the belt loops, run the belt around one of your legs, and refasten. Your hands are now free for

Pants flotation

signaling or slowly swimming a backstroke toward shore.

Air will escape from your pants if you allow the material to dry. Splash water over them occasionally. When needed, air can be added simply by loosening the waist and splashing in air; the pants need not be removed.

9d. With a helper and a practice victim, show a line rescue both as tender and as rescuer. (The practice victim should be approximately 30 feet from shore in deep water.)

The fourth point of Safe Swim Defense requires lifeguards on duty, and as a First Class Scout you will be prepared to serve in this role using the procedure specified in the full statement of the Safe Swim Defense standards. This procedure requires two strong swimmers, one as a line tender and the other as a rescuer. It is a reaching rescue method; the line is taken out to the victim instead of being thrown. The risks are minimal even if the rescuer and victim become entangled, because the line tender will simply pull both in rapidly to safety.

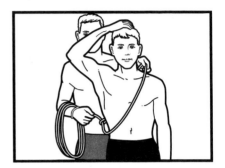

Be sure you prepare your line before you go on duty. Tie a bowline to make a large loop in the end of a 100-foot length of ¼-inch line. Place the loop over the shoulder and under the opposite arm of the rescuer. Tie a small loop on the other end and make a slip noose to secure to the line tender's wrist. The line tender and rescuer guard the swim by standing together watching the activity, ready to respond if any assistance is needed.

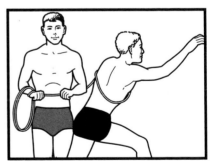

In the event of an emergency, the rescuer leaps in and swims rapidly toward the victim while the tender stays on shore where he feeds out the line, prevents it from becoming tangled, and keeps a sharp eye on the rescuer and the victim.

The rescuer swims past the victim and then turns so that the line is pulled within the victim's grasp. The rescuer then signals for the tender to pull them to shore. The tender must be well braced as he pulls them in hand over hand.

An unconscious victim or injured person might not be able to hold onto the line. When that's the case, the rescuer can grasp the victim and hold his head out of the water while the line tender pulls them in.

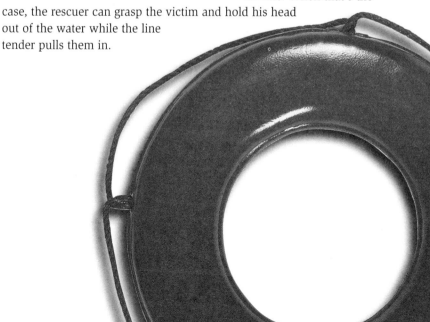

10. Demonstrate Scout spirit by living the Scout Oath (Promise) and Scout Law in your everyday life.

At troop and patrol gatherings you've recited the Scout Oath and the Scout Law dozens of times. The words come easily to you, but do you know what those words mean?

The Scout Oath and Scout Law are not just for reciting at meetings. They are not just to be obeyed while you are wearing a uniform. The spirit of Scouting that they represent is every bit as important when you are at home, at school, and in your community.

> A SCOUT IS:
>
> **TRUSTWORTHY**
>
> **LOYAL**
>
> **HELPFUL**
>
> **FRIENDLY**
>
> **COURTEOUS**
>
> **KIND**
>
> **OBEDIENT**
>
> **CHEERFUL**
>
> **THRIFTY**
>
> **BRAVE**
>
> **CLEAN**
>
> **REVERENT**

The Scout Oath begins with the words, "On my honor . . ." Your honor is your word. By giving your word, you are promising to be of good character and to keep your reputation untarnished.

Be trustworthy in all you say and do. Extend friendship to others. Be thrifty with your time and resources. Be tolerant of others, regardless of their differences, and celebrate the great diversity that enriches our nation and the world. Express reverence in accordance with your beliefs. Offer a helping hand because you want to, not because you expect a reward.

The standards set by the Scout Oath and Scout Law are very high. Strive to reach them every day, and you will find that they become as natural for you to live by as they are for you to say.

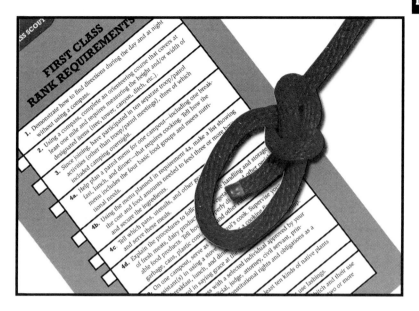

11. Participate in a Scoutmaster conference.

By completing the First Class requirements, you will have proven to yourself and others that you can meet the challenge of Scouting. Your Scoutmaster will want to express his pride in all that you have accomplished and encourage you to give yourself a pat on the back for your achievements.

He might also point out that some of the greatest opportunities of Scouting lie ahead. You might soon find yourself taking on greater leadership roles in your troop. Adult Scouters will rely on you even more to help plan and carry out service projects, camping trips, and unit meetings.

As a First Class Scout, you'll be surprised to discover how much the younger Scouts are looking up to you, and how effectively you can teach them many of the Scouting skills you have mastered. You can also set your sights on earning the Star and Life ranks, and perhaps even the Eagle Scout Award—the highest rank in Scouting.

12. Complete your board of review.

STAR, LIFE, AND EAGLE SCOUT

STAR, LIFE, AND EAGLE SCOUT

"The Star, Life, and Eagle Ranks are respectively the highest steps in Scout advancement. Those who attain these honors, of necessity, should be real Scouts, representative Scouts—Scouts on the inside as well as on the outside."

Handbook for Boys, 3rd edition, 1927

The trail to Eagle leads through the ranks of Star Scout and Life Scout—an exciting pathway that will challenge you, test you, and open many doors to new ideas and opportunities. Building on the knowledge and experience you gained in becoming a First Class Scout, the requirements for Star and Life offer plenty of freedom in choosing the direction your interests take you, and many options for achieving each higher rank. The requirements also emphasize the roles that the Scout Oath and Law play in your life, and the importance of service to your Scout troop and to others.

A community clothing drive to help the homeless reflects the spirit of Scouting.

To earn the Star, Life, and Eagle Scout awards, you must

Be active in your troop and patrol.

Demonstrate Scout spirit by living the Scout Oath and Scout Law.

Earn a certain number of merit badges.

Serve actively in a position of responsibility in your troop.

Take part in service projects.

Participate in a Scoutmaster conference.

Complete your board of review.

BE ACTIVE IN YOUR TROOP AND PATROL

TO GAIN FULL ADVANTAGE of all that Scouting has to offer, you need to be present when things are happening. Take part in meetings, in planning activities, and in the fun of adventures. If you're there, you can do your part to make your patrol and troop a success.

- A First Class Scout must hold that rank for at least 4 months before becoming a Star Scout.

- A Star Scout should be active in his troop and patrol for no less than 6 months before becoming a Life Scout.

- A Life Scout must serve for at least 6 months before rising to the rank of Eagle.

The required minimum of time served between ranks encourages you to enjoy Scout opportunities through-out the year and to learn and appreciate all that is available to you. Of course, you may take longer if you wish, and many Scouts do. The speed at which you advance through Scouting's ranks is up to you. Begin counting your time for a new rank from the day you pass a board of review.

DEMONSTRATE SCOUT SPIRIT

BY NOW, DOING GOOD TURNS should be a regular part of your day. You are always on the lookout for ways to help others.

By now, *Be Prepared* should describe your efforts to make the most of educational opportunities, get along with others, and take part in outdoor adventures.

By now, the Scout Oath and the twelve points of the Scout Law should be the guidelines by which you direct your actions in your family, community, church, school, and nation.

Living by these high standards is always a personal choice and something only you can fully measure. But by now, many other people should be seeing qualities in you that make it clear you are choosing wisely.

"Your standing as a Scout does not depend so much on the skills of your hands or the badges on your merit badge sash, as on the spirit in your heart—on what you are willing to do for others, on whether you are doing your very best to live the Scout Oath and Law."

Boy Scout Handbook, 6th edition, 1959

EARN MERIT BADGES

THE REQUIREMENTS FOR the Star, Life, and Eagle ranks ask that you earn merit badges. Some, including First Aid, Family Life, and Camping, come from a list of required badges that round out the skills expected of every Eagle Scout. The others may be chosen from more than a hundred merit badges that allow you to explore subjects from Astronomy to Woodwork, and from Backpacking to Canoeing. For more information on merit badges, turn to chapter 7, "Merit Badges," beginning on page 185 **M**.

Completing Scouting's higher ranks will introduce you to a world of exciting subjects and skills both indoors and out.

SERVE IN A POSITION OF RESPONSIBILITY

THE LONGER YOU ARE IN SCOUTING, the more your troop will recognize your experience and knowledge by offering you positions of leadership. Being a good leader is a skill that can be learned only by doing it. Troop leadership opportunities will allow you to speak in front of people, guide discussions, make decisions, and encourage others toward greater achievements.

The badges of office shown here represent the leadership positions of a Boy Scout troop. In addition, your Scoutmaster might offer you leadership positions for special projects or events.

BE OF SERVICE

SERVICE TO OTHERS has been a hallmark of the Boy Scouts of America since its beginnings. Good Turns and projects involving your patrol and troop have encouraged you to seek ways to help others. The Star, Life, and Eagle service projects allow you to expand the scope of your good works.

STAR AND LIFE SERVICE PROJECTS

The requirements for the ranks of Star and Life call upon you to give at least 6 hours of service to others. You may complete this requirement on your own or do it along with other members of your patrol, squad, troop, or team. The project must be approved by your Scoutmaster.

EAGLE SCOUT SERVICE PROJECT

There is a major difference between the service projects for Star and Life, and the one you will complete for Eagle. In the first two, you can be a follower. The Eagle Scout service project requires that you be a leader. You must plan, develop, and provide leadership to others in a service project of real value benefiting the environment, your community, or a religious group, school, or other worthy group. Ideas for service projects may come from visits with school administrators, civic officials, clergy, law enforcement officers, and park department or land management personnel.

Your idea for a project must be approved by your troop leader, troop committee, district or council advancement committee, and the recipient of the project *before you begin.* Upon completion, the project must be reviewed by your district or council advancement committee.

An Eagle Scout project requires more hours of planning and effort than do projects for Star and Life. Here are a few service projects Scouts have done to fulfill this Eagle requirement:

- Worked with local law enforcement officials to organize and carry out a bicycle safety campaign. Trained fellow Scouts as inspectors and judges, then ran a bike rodeo that included a bicycle safety check and contests promoting safe riding.

- Organized a used-toy collection. Supervised fellow Scouts in repairing the toys and delivering them to organizations serving disadvantaged children.

- Planned and built a lawn sprinkling system at a church. Figured out the details of the construction, encouraged church members to donate the materials, then organized Scouts to dig the trenches and install the system.

- Worked with rangers to learn the skills necessary to build a footbridge in a national forest. Gathered materials and tools, and then, with ranger guidance, directed a Scout work group doing the construction.

All these projects required the assistance of other Scouts. In each case, the Eagle Scout candidate planned the project, lined up the materials and the help he needed, and led the effort to get the work done.

A trail maintenance or building project at your local Scout camp is an example of a conservation project.

The Life to Eagle Packet, BSA publication No. 18-927, can help you plan your service project, receive the necessary approvals for it, carry it out, and then provide a report upon completion.

PARTICIPATE IN A SCOUTMASTER CONFERENCE

BY THE TIME YOU complete the requirements to become a Star Scout and a Life Scout, you should know the BSA program well. You and your Scoutmaster will have enjoyed many adventures together, and your Scoutmaster will have come to rely upon you as a leader in your troop and patrol. The conferences you have with your Scoutmaster before achieving the ranks of Star and Life can be worthwhile discussions about your increasing responsibilities and ways the troop can enhance the experience for you.

At the conference that takes place when you have become a candidate for the rank of Eagle Scout, you and your Scoutmaster will want to look back over all of your Scouting career. Your troop leader might remind you that completing the BSA's highest rank is not the end of your involvement with Scouting. There will be many ways for you to offer continued leadership to Scout units and to keep living the Scout ideals in your home, church, community, and all other parts of your life.

For more on Scoutmaster conferences, see page 11. For more on Scout program involvement for Eagle Scouts, see chapter **18**, "Opportunities for Older Scouts," beginning on page 419 ▟.

COMPLETE A BOARD OF REVIEW

STAR AND LIFE BOARDS OF REVIEW

The Star Scout and Life Scout boards of review are made up of adults associated with your troop who want to learn more about you and better understand what Scouting is doing for you. Their purpose is not to retest you, but rather to be certain you have passed the requirements for a higher rank, to get a sense of the value Scouting has for you, and to clear the way for your further advancement. They will be interested in discussing your service to others, what you have learned from the merit badges you have completed, and ways in which you are acting as a leader in your patrol and troop.

EAGLE SCOUT BOARD OF REVIEW

The board of review that will convene after you have completed the Eagle Scout requirements will include at least one advancement representative from your district or council. The board will review your full Scouting experience—what you have done, where you have gone, and what you have learned. Board members will be interested in hearing about your Eagle Scout service project, your leadership experiences, and your future Scouting plans. Most of all, they will want to explore how the spirit of Scouting has become part of your daily life. For more on boards of review, see page 61.

COURTS OF HONOR

A COURT OF HONOR is an impressive formal ceremony to recognize you and your fellow Scouts for rank advancement and other Scouting achievements. This event is held with an audience of family, friends, chartered organization officials, and troop leaders.

The Eagle Scout rank is such a high achievement that the award will be presented to you at a special Eagle Scout court of honor.

STAR SCOUT RANK REQUIREMENTS

1. Be active in your troop and patrol for at least 4 months as a First Class Scout.

2. Demonstrate Scout spirit by living the Scout Oath (Promise) and Scout Law in your everyday life.

3. Earn 6 merit badges, including any 4 from the required list for Eagle.

   Name of Merit Badge

   _____ (required for Eagle)*

   _____ (required for Eagle)*

   _____ (required for Eagle)*

   _____ (required for Eagle)*

   _____

   _____

4. While a First Class Scout, take part in service projects totaling at least 6 hours of work. These projects must be approved by your Scoutmaster.

5. While a First Class Scout, serve actively for 4 months in one or more of the following positions of responsibility (or carry out a Scoutmaster-assigned leadership project to help the troop):

   Boy Scout troop. Patrol leader, assistant senior patrol leader, senior patrol leader, troop guide, den chief, scribe, librarian, historian, quartermaster, bugler, junior assistant Scoutmaster, chaplain aide, or instructor.

   Varsity Scout team. Captain, cocaptain, program manager, squad leader, team secretary, librarian, historian, quartermaster, chaplain aide, instructor, or den chief.

6. Take part in a Scoutmaster conference.

7. Complete your board of review.

*A Scout may choose any of the 15 required merit badges in the 12 categories to fulfill requirement 3. See page 180 of this book for a complete list of required badges for Eagle.

NOTE: As you complete each requirement, ask your Scoutmaster to initial his or her approval on page 444.

LIFE SCOUT RANK REQUIREMENTS

✓

1. Be active in your troop and patrol for at least 6 months as a Star Scout.

2. Demonstrate Scout spirit by living the Scout Oath (Promise) and Scout Law in your everyday life.

3. Earn 5 more merit badges (so that you have 11 in all), including any 3 more from the required list for Eagle.

Name of Merit Badge

_____ (required for Eagle)*

_____ (required for Eagle)*

_____ (required for Eagle)*

_____

_____

4. While a Star Scout, take part in service projects totaling at least 6 hours of work. These projects must be approved by your Scoutmaster.

5. While a Star Scout, serve actively for 6 months in one or more of the positions of responsibility listed in requirement 5 for Star Scout (or carry out a Scoutmaster-assigned leadership project to help the troop).

6. Take part in a Scoutmaster conference.

7. Complete your board of review.

*A Scout may choose any of the 15 required merit badges in the 12 categories to fulfill requirement 3. See page 180 of this book for a complete list of required badges for Eagle.

NOTE: As you complete each requirement, ask your Scoutmaster to initial his or her approval on page 445.

BECOMING AN EAGLE SCOUT

THE FIRST *Boy Scout Handbook* described anyone worthy of the Eagle Scout Award as "the all-round perfect scout." That is a very demanding standard indeed, and a worthy goal. Striving to become an Eagle Scout will require your best efforts to master the skills of leadership, service, and outdoor know-how, and to practice good citizenship and ethical behavior of the highest order. The long trail to Eagle is full of opportunities for you to learn, to lead, to listen, and to teach. Along the way and throughout your life, the rewards from earning the Eagle Scout Award will be great.

Fewer than 4 percent of all Scouts earn the Eagle rank— a testament to its high standards. Among those who have worn the Eagle Scout badge are some of America's finest athletes, physicians, politicians, scientists, writers, astronauts, business leaders, film directors, and even a president of the United States.

EAGLE SCOUT RANK REQUIREMENTS

☑

1. Be active in your troop and patrol for at least 6 months as a Life Scout.

2. Demonstrate Scout spirit by living the Scout Oath (Promise) and Scout Law in your everyday life.

3. Earn a total of 21 merit badges (10 more than you already have), including the following: (a) First Aid, (b) Citizenship in the Community, (c) Citizenship in the Nation, (d) Citizenship in the World, (e) Communications, (f) Personal Fitness, (g) Emergency Preparedness OR Lifesaving, (h) Environmental Science, (i) Personal Management, (j) Swimming OR Hiking OR Cycling, (k) Camping, and (l) Family Life.*

Name of Merit Badge

_____

_____

_____

_____

_____

_____

_____

_____

_____

_____

4. While a Life Scout, serve actively for a period of 6 months in one or more of the following positions of responsibility:

Boy Scout troop. Patrol leader, assistant senior patrol leader, senior patrol leader, troop guide, den chief, scribe, librarian, historian, quartermaster, junior assistant Scoutmaster, chaplain aide, or instructor.

Varsity Scout team. Captain, cocaptain, program manager, squad leader, team secretary, librarian, quartermaster, chaplain aide, instructor, or den chief.

EAGLE SCOUT RANK REQUIREMENTS

5. While a Life Scout, plan, develop, and give leadership to others in a service project helpful to any religious institution, any school, or your community. (The project should benefit an organization other than Boy Scouting.) The project idea must be approved by the organization benefiting from the effort, your Scoutmaster and troop committee, and the council or district before you start. You must use the Life to Eagle Packet, BSA publication No. 18-927, in meeting this requirement.

6. Take part in a Scoutmaster conference.

7. Successfully complete an Eagle Scout board of review.

*You must choose only one merit badge listed in items *g* and *j*. If you have earned more than one of the badges listed in items *g* and *j*, choose one and list the remaining badges to make your total of 21.

NOTE: All requirements for Eagle Scout must be completed before a candidate's 18th birthday. The Eagle Scout board of review can be held after the candidate's 18th birthday. For more information, see *National BSA Advancement Policies and Procedures*, publication No. 33088.

If you have a permanent physical or mental disability you may become an Eagle Scout by qualifying for as many required merit badges as you can and qualifying for alternative merit badges for the rest. If you seek to become an Eagle Scout under this procedure, you must submit a special application to your local council service center. Your application must be approved by your council advancement committee *before you can work on alternative merit badges*.

As you complete each requirement, ask your Scoutmaster to initial his or her approval on pages 446–47.

EAGLE PALMS

AFTER BECOMING AN EAGLE SCOUT, you will certainly want to continue taking part in activities with your troop, and you may continue earning merit badges. The BSA recognizes achievements beyond the Eagle Scout rank by awarding Eagle Palms.

EAGLE PALM REQUIREMENTS

✓

Bronze Palm

1. Be active in your troop and patrol for at least 3 months after becoming an Eagle Scout or after the award of your last Palm.

2. Demonstrate Scout spirit by living the Scout Oath (Promise) and Scout Law in your everyday life.

3. Make a satisfactory effort to develop and demonstrate leadership ability.

4. Earn 5 additional merit badges beyond those required for the Eagle rank.*

_____ merit badge

_____ merit badge

_____ merit badge

_____ merit badge

_____ merit badge

5. Take part in a Scoutmaster conference.

6. Complete your board of review.

Gold Palm

1. Be active in your troop and patrol for at least 3 months after becoming an Eagle Scout or after the award of your last Palm.

2. Demonstrate Scout spirit by living the Scout Oath (Promise) and Scout Law in your everyday life.

3. Make a satisfactory effort to develop and demonstrate leadership ability.

4. Earn 5 additional merit badges beyond those required for the Bronze Palm.*

_____ merit badge

_____ merit badge

_____ merit badge

_____ merit badge

_____ merit badge

EAGLE PALM
REQUIREMENTS

5. Take part in a Scoutmaster conference.

6. Complete your board of review.

Silver Palm

1. Be active in your troop and patrol for at least 3 months after becoming an Eagle Scout or after the award of your last Palm.

2. Demonstrate Scout spirit by living the Scout Oath (Promise) and Scout Law in your everyday life.

3. Make a satisfactory effort to develop and demonstrate leadership ability.

4. Earn 5 additional merit badges beyond those required for the Gold Palm.*

_____ merit badge

_____ merit badge

_____ merit badge

_____ merit badge

_____ merit badge

5. Take part in a Scoutmaster conference.

6. Complete your board of review.

You may wear only the proper combination of Palms for the number of merit badges you earned beyond the rank of Eagle. The Bronze Palm represents 5 merit badges, the Gold Palm 10, and the Silver Palm 15.

*Merit badges earned anytime since becoming a Boy Scout may be used to meet this requirement.

NOTE: Scouts who earn three Palms may continue to earn additional Palms in the same order—bronze, gold, and silver. All requirements for Eagle Palms must be completed before a candidate's 18th birthday.

As you complete each requirement, ask your Scoutmaster to initial his or her approval on pages 448–49.

MERIT BADGES

"Two of the reasons for the Scout Merit Badge Plan are

(1) to give you more skill in things you like to do; (2) to

give you a chance to try out new activities, so that you can

find new things which you really like."

Handbook for Boys, 5th edition, 1948

When Baden-Powell started the Scouting movement, he felt that any Scout who mastered a set of skills should be recognized for the effort. He gave to each Scout who passed certain tests a badge to wear on his uniform. The emblem recognized the importance of what the Scout had done and let others know of his achievement. That is how the badge system became a part of Scouting.

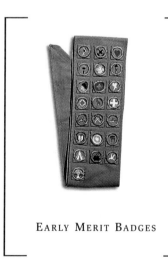

EARLY MERIT BADGES

A merit badge is an invitation to explore an exciting subject. With more than a hundred to choose from, some merit badges encourage you to increase your skill in subjects you already like, while others challenge you to learn about new areas of knowledge. Many of the merit badges are designed to help you increase your ability to be of service to others, to take part in outdoor adventures, to better understand the environment, and to play a valuable role in your family and community. Earning a merit badge can even lead you toward a lifelong hobby or set you on the way to a rewarding career.

"Many men who were once Scouts feel that their entire lives were influenced by their merit badge work. . . . Hundreds of doctors, engineers, forest rangers, and naturalists had their ambitions kindled while earning merit badges as Scouts. You, too, may start on your lifework by working on a merit badge."

Boy Scout Handbook, 6th edition, 1959

EARNING A MERIT BADGE

WORKING ON MERIT BADGES is especially enjoyable when you do it with another Scout. The BSA encourages this by making the buddy system a part of the merit badge program. Together, you can meet with merit badge counselors, plan projects, and keep your enthusiasm high.

The requirements for each merit badge appear in the current BSA merit badge pamphlet for that award, and in the book *Boy Scout Requirements*, available at Scout shops and council service centers. When you have decided on a merit badge you would like to earn, follow these steps:

Obtain from your Scoutmaster a signed merit badge application and the name of a qualified counselor for that merit badge. (A counselor must know a subject well, have the ability to work effectively with Scouts, and be currently registered as a merit badge counselor by the Boy Scouts of America.)

Along with another Scout, a relative, or a friend, set up and attend your first appointment with the merit badge counselor. The counselor will explain the requirements for the badge and help you plan ways to fulfill them so that you can get the most out of the experience.

Complete the requirements, meeting with your counselor whenever necessary until you have finished working on the badge.

Scout advancement lets you move ahead in your own way and at your own speed. Rather than competing against others, you challenge yourself to go as far as your ambition will carry you. Your rate of advancement depends upon your interest, effort, and ability.

HOW TO WEAR MERIT BADGES

MERIT BADGES may be worn on a merit badge sash with the BSA uniform. Up to six merit badges may be worn in rows of two on the right sleeve of a long-sleeved uniform shirt, starting 3 inches from the bottom edge of the cuff. No merit badges may be worn on a short-sleeved shirt.

MERIT BADGES REQUIRED FOR EAGLE

Camping

Citizenship in the Community

Citizenship in the Nation

Citizenship in the World

Communications

Environmental Science

Family Life

First Aid

Personal Fitness

**Personal
Management**

Lifesaving

OR

**Emergency
Preparedness**

Cycling

OR

Hiking

Swimming

OR

ELECTIVE
MERIT BADGES

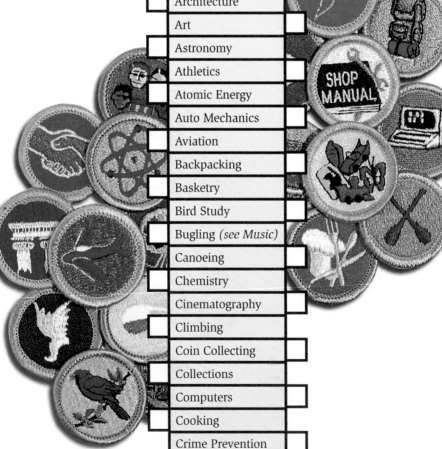

- American Business
- American Cultures
- American Heritage
- American Labor
- Animal Science
- Archaeology
- Archery
- Architecture
- Art
- Astronomy
- Athletics
- Atomic Energy
- Auto Mechanics
- Aviation
- Backpacking
- Basketry
- Bird Study
- Bugling (see Music)
- Canoeing
- Chemistry
- Cinematography
- Climbing
- Coin Collecting
- Collections
- Computers
- Cooking
- Crime Prevention

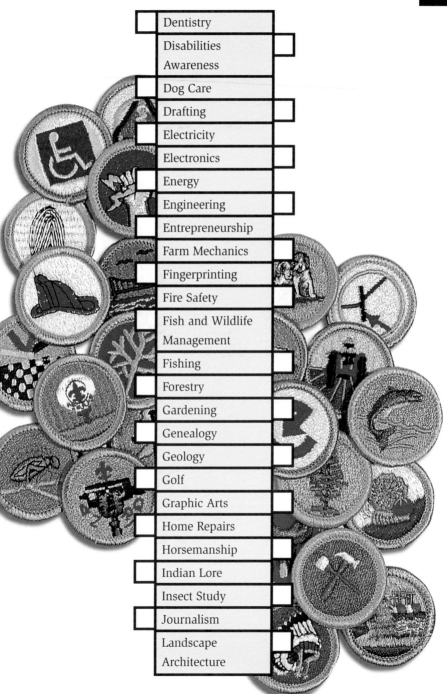

- Dentistry
- Disabilities Awareness
- Dog Care
- Drafting
- Electricity
- Electronics
- Energy
- Engineering
- Entrepreneurship
- Farm Mechanics
- Fingerprinting
- Fire Safety
- Fish and Wildlife Management
- Fishing
- Forestry
- Gardening
- Genealogy
- Geology
- Golf
- Graphic Arts
- Home Repairs
- Horsemanship
- Indian Lore
- Insect Study
- Journalism
- Landscape Architecture

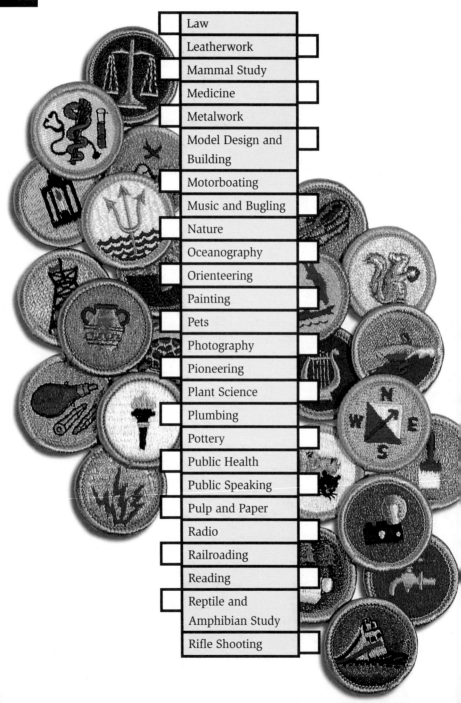

	Law	
	Leatherwork	
	Mammal Study	
	Medicine	
	Metalwork	
	Model Design and Building	
	Motorboating	
	Music and Bugling	
	Nature	
	Oceanography	
	Orienteering	
	Painting	
	Pets	
	Photography	
	Pioneering	
	Plant Science	
	Plumbing	
	Pottery	
	Public Health	
	Public Speaking	
	Pulp and Paper	
	Radio	
	Railroading	
	Reading	
	Reptile and Amphibian Study	
	Rifle Shooting	

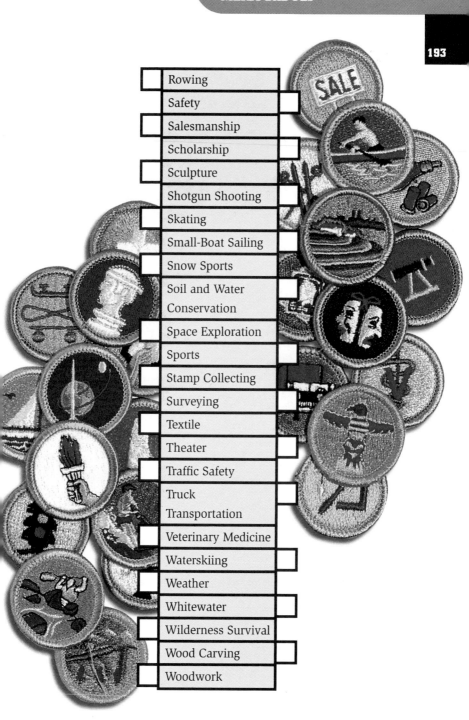

- [ ] Rowing
- [ ] Safety
- [ ] Salesmanship
- [ ] Scholarship
- [ ] Sculpture
- [ ] Shotgun Shooting
- [ ] Skating
- [ ] Small-Boat Sailing
- [ ] Snow Sports
- [ ] Soil and Water Conservation
- [ ] Space Exploration
- [ ] Sports
- [ ] Stamp Collecting
- [ ] Surveying
- [ ] Textile
- [ ] Theater
- [ ] Traffic Safety
- [ ] Truck Transportation
- [ ] Veterinary Medicine
- [ ] Waterskiing
- [ ] Weather
- [ ] Whitewater
- [ ] Wilderness Survival
- [ ] Wood Carving
- [ ] Woodwork

SCOUTING'S SKILLS

READY

FOR THE GREAT OUTDOORS

HIKING

TRAILHEAD

8

HIKING

HIKING IS ONE of Scouting's great activities. Whether on trails, across open country, or along city streets, traveling on foot is a terrific way to get out and see the world.

Every season is special when you are hiking, and so is every place you go. Set out to walk through neighborhoods and parks in a city, or to a museum or zoo. Roam the backcountry, using your map and compass to guide you. On camping trips your hikes might take you to the top of a mountain, the edge of a lake, or some other natural setting in which to watch wildlife.

Rain will sometimes fall while you are hiking, and maybe even a little snow. Your route might be rocky and steep, and there will be times when you are weary to the bone. But overcoming hardships can be part of hiking, too. Keep at it, and your hiking experiences will help you become a seasoned outdoor traveler with dozens of stories to tell about plenty of memorable journeys.

The skills you learn on even the shortest hike can help you on journeys of any length:

- **The clothing you use for hiking is the same you'll need for camping and backpacking.**

- **The Scout Outdoor Essentials you carry are the items you'll also take each time you set out for the backcountry.**

- **No-trace methods you use to protect the trails will allow you to care for campsites, too.**

- **A trip plan is important for an afternoon walk, and also for a weeklong wilderness trek.**

MAKING A TRIP PLAN

A TRIP PLAN prepares you for the challenges of a hike, a campout, or any other outdoor activity. Write down the following five *W*'s of a trip plan:

THE FIVE *W*'S

Where are you going? Decide on your destination and the route you will use to reach it and to return. For backcountry trips, leave a copy of a map with your route marked in pencil.

When will you return? If you are not back reasonably close to the return time you wrote on your trip plan, Scout leaders and your family can take steps to locate you and, if necessary, provide assistance.

Who is going with you? List the names of your hiking partners. If you need a ride to or from a trailhead, write down who will be driving.

Why are you going? To fish in a lake? Climb a peak? Explore a new area? Write a sentence or two about the purpose of your journey.

What are you taking? You'll always want to carry the Scout Outdoor Essentials (see page 207). If you are camping out, you might need additional food, gear, and shelter. (For a camping equipment checklist, see chapter 9, "Camping," pages 224–27 🔺.)

Add one more item to the list:

How you will respect the land by using no-trace hiking skills.

FOOTGEAR FOR HIKING

"A hiker is only as good as his feet. Take good care of them."

Scout Field Book, 1st edition, 1948

If your feet feel good, chances are you'll have a great time hiking. Taking care of your feet begins when you choose what to wear on them.

SHOES AND BOOTS

Almost any shoes will do for short walks on easy terrain. Lightweight boots with fabric uppers are fine for most hiking in good weather. Most leather boots are heavier, but they will give your feet and ankles the most protection and support. They can also keep snow and rain from soaking your socks. Choose leather if you will do a lot of hiking and backpacking on rugged trails. Boots made for mountaineering or hard winter travel are probably more than you need.

New boots must fit well. At the store, try on different boots while wearing the socks you will use on hikes. Your heels should not slip much when you walk, and your toes should have a little wiggle room. Before using new boots on a hike, wear them around home for a few days until they adjust to the shape of your feet.

Many hikers and campers carry a pair of lightweight shoes in their packs so that they can get out of their boots at the end of the day. A pair of running shoes might be just right. If you must wade across a stream, you can keep your socks and hiking boots dry by taking them off and wearing your extra shoes through the water.

CARING FOR YOUR BOOTS

Hiking boots will last a long time if you take care of them. When they get wet, let them dry in the sun. High heat can melt nylon and harm leather, so don't put your boots too close to a fire.

Remove mud and dirt from your boots with a pocketknife or a stiff brush. Fabric boots shouldn't require any other care. Treat leather with a boot dressing meant for outdoor footwear. Oils and waxes in the dressing will keep the leather flexible and help the boots repel water.

SOCKS

Hiking socks made of wool or a wool/nylon blend cushion your soles as you walk and draw sweat away from your feet. Wear a pair of thin wool or synthetic-blend socks underneath your hiking socks. The inner socks will slide against heavier outer socks and take moisture away from your skin, reducing friction and lessening your chances of getting a blister.

Carry spare socks on your hikes. If your feet begin to tire, change into fresh socks and hang the used ones on your pack to air out and dry.

CLOTHING FOR HIKING

DRESS FOR THE OUTDOORS by wearing layers so that you can adjust your clothing to match changing weather conditions.

Imagine setting out on a snowy trail. The sky is clear and there is no wind. You're wearing a T-shirt, a wool shirt, and a sweater. Because the day is chilly, you also have on mittens and a warm hat.

Hiking burns energy, and soon you are too warm. Stop for a moment to peel off your sweater and mittens, and stuff them into your pack.

As the miles pass, clouds fill the sky and the air becomes colder. Put your mittens and sweater back on. If the wind begins to blow, you can take a parka out of your pack and pull it on, too.

WARM-WEATHER CLOTHING CHECKLIST FOR HIKING, CAMPING, AND BACKPACKING

Short-sleeved shirt	
T-shirt	
Hiking shorts	
Long pants	
Sweater or warm jacket*	
Hiking boots or sturdy shoes	
Socks	
Hat with a brim for shade	
Bandanna	
Rain gear	
Extra underwear (for longer trips)	

(Items marked with an asterisk [*] should be made of wool or a warm synthetic fabric.)

COLD-WEATHER CLOTHING CHECKLIST FOR HIKING, CAMPING, AND BACKPACKING

- [ ] Long-sleeved shirt*
- [ ] Long pants*
- [ ] Sweater*
- [ ] Long underwear*
- [ ] Hiking boots or sturdy shoes
- [ ] Socks
- [ ] Insulated parka or coat with hood
- [ ] Warm hat*
- [ ] Mittens*
- [ ] Rain gear
- [ ] Extra underwear (for longer trips)

(Items marked with an asterisk [*] should be made of wool or a warm synthetic fabric.)

FABRICS FOR HIKING WEAR

Wool

Wool can keep you warm even when it is damp from rain. If wool feels scratchy against your skin, wear long underwear or a T-shirt beneath it.

Cotton

Cotton is good for warm, dry weather. Once wet, though, cotton will not keep you warm. That can make it dangerous to wear on trips when conditions might turn chilly, rainy, or snowy.

Synthetic

Many synthetic fabrics offer the comfort of cotton and the warmth of wool. Clothing made of polypropylene, polar fleece, and other modern materials can insulate you whether it is wet or dry. Look for these fabrics in long underwear, sweaters, vests, parkas, mittens, and hats.

RAIN GEAR

Poncho

A poncho is a waterproof cape that protects you and your gear from summer rains. Because it is loose and can flap in the wind, a poncho is not the best choice for severe weather.

Rain Parka

A parka is a long jacket that repels sleet, rain, and snow. It should have large pockets for carrying the Scout Outdoor Essentials, and a hood you can pull over your head.

Rain Pants

Rain pants extend the protection of a poncho or parka down to your ankles.

Gaiters

Gaiters shield your feet and lower legs from rain, and during winter hikes, they'll keep snow out of your boots.

Hat

A broad-brimmed hat or baseball cap will protect your face from sun and storm. If you wear glasses, the brim of a hat will keep them clear of rain.

RAIN GEAR FABRICS

Nonbreathable

Coated nylon and plastic are used to make many ponchos, rain parkas, rain pants, and gaiters. The advantages are that this gear is waterproof and often inexpensive. The disadvantage is that moisture given off by your body can be trapped inside, causing you to feel damp and chilled.

Breathable

Some fabrics will keep rain out but let body moisture escape—the ideal combination. The disadvantage of breathable rain gear is that it is expensive.

EQUIPMENT FOR HIKING

CARRYING THE SCOUT OUTDOOR ESSENTIALS with you can make a pleasant journey even better. In an emergency, they might get you out of a jam.

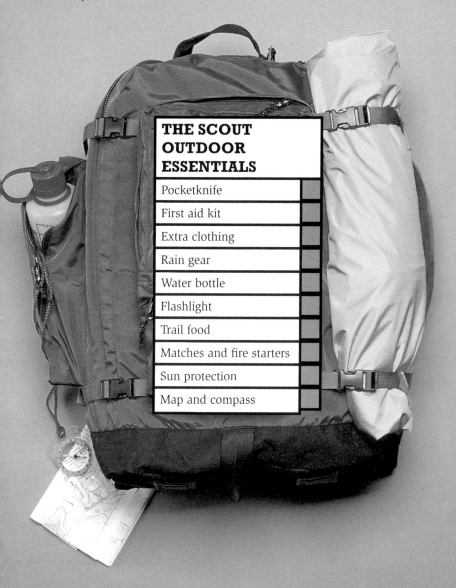

THE SCOUT OUTDOOR ESSENTIALS

Pocketknife	
First aid kit	
Extra clothing	
Rain gear	
Water bottle	
Flashlight	
Trail food	
Matches and fire starters	
Sun protection	
Map and compass	

Pocketknife

A pocketknife is the most useful tool you can own. Keep yours clean and sharp. (For more on pocketknives, see pages 77–79.)

First Aid Kit

Besides the complete first aid kit carried by your patrol or troop leader, bring along your own supplies to treat minor injuries. (For more on first aid kits, see page 289.)

Extra Clothing

With layers of clothing, you can adjust what you wear to match the weather. (For more on clothing for outdoor adventures, see pages 202–5.)

Rain Gear

A rain parka or poncho will shield you from showers and storms. In warm weather you can turn a large plastic trash bag into a poncho by cutting holes in it for your head and arms. (For more on rain gear, see page 206.)

Flashlight

Finding your way in the dark can be tough without a flashlight. A sturdy one that uses a couple of AA-cell batteries doesn't weigh much, and it gives out a strong beam. Reverse the batteries during the day or put duct tape over the switch to prevent the light from coming on in your pack and draining the power.

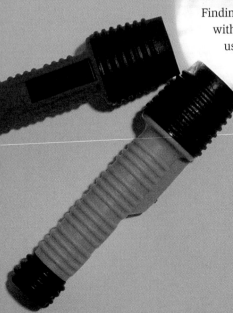

Trail Food

The most important meal for hiking is the breakfast you eat before you hit the trail. Whether in camp or at home, a hearty breakfast starts the day right.

Carry a lunch in your pack. Sandwiches, fruit, nuts, and raisins are tasty. Or try crackers with peanut butter or cheese.

A small bag of granola, dried fruit, or a couple of energy bars can give you a nutritional boost between meals, especially if you are out longer than you had expected. (For more on food for the outdoors, see pages 265–80.)

Water Bottle

Fill your water bottle before you start out, and sip from it whenever you are thirsty. In hot weather, you might need to carry several containers of water. Purify any water taken from streams, lakes, or springs before you drink it. (For ways to purify water, see page 256.)

Matches and Fire Starters

With wooden strike-anywhere matches or a butane lighter, you can kindle a fire in any weather. (For more on when and how to build fires, see pages 248–52.)

Sun Protection

Too much exposure to the sun's rays can be harmful, especially if you have a fair complexion. Guard your skin with a sunscreen that has a sun protection factor (SPF) of 15 or higher. A broad-brimmed hat, lip balm, and sunglasses will give added protection.

Map and Compass

Carry a compass and a map whenever you travel in areas unfamiliar to you. Of course, they won't do much good unless you know how to use them, so take the time to learn. (For more on maps and compasses, see pages 66–74 **2** and pages 118–25 **1**.)

OTHER HIKING GEAR

Day Pack

A small pack will hold everything you need for a day of hiking. You might already use this kind of pack to carry your books to school.

Fanny Pack

Zip your hiking gear into a fanny pack and strap it around your waist. Fanny packs ride comfortably against your lower back as you walk, and won't throw you off balance when your adventures include cross-country skiing or mountain biking. Many troops stow their first aid supplies in a fanny pack that goes on every outing.

CROSS-COUNTRY HIKING

CROSS-COUNTRY HIKING TAKES you away from everything man-made, including trails. Of course, you must be able to find your way so that you don't become lost. That might mean using a map and compass.

Staying with your patrol is as important in cross-country hiking as for any other outdoor adventure. You can share the fun, and you will be there if your patrol needs your assistance.

Away from the smooth tread of a trail, footing can be uncertain. Underbrush and rugged terrain make for slow going. Watch where you put your hands if you are scrambling on rocks—you don't want to end up with a snakebite or an insect sting. Avoid trampling vegetation by walking on bare ground, rocks, and snow.

By charting your course on a map before you start a cross-country hike, you shouldn't be surprised by rivers, cliffs, and other barriers. If you do run into terrain that you aren't sure you can cross safely, detour around it or go back the way you came. A smart hiker always knows when to turn his back on a dangerous route.

NO-TRACE HIKING

HIKING SO THAT you leave no trace shows you care about the land and know how to travel through it wisely.

When your route takes you along a trail, stay on the pathway. Hikers cutting across switchbacks or taking other shortcuts often trample vegetation that holds topsoil in place. The resulting erosion can damage or even destroy the trail.

Some sections of parks and forests are managed as wilderness areas. Regulations protecting those areas might limit group size, forbid campfires, and restrict other activities. Find out what the guidelines are before you start a hike, then obey them.

Keep trails clean by picking up litter. See if your patrol or troop can pitch in to help repair and maintain the hiking trails you enjoy using.

HIKING TIPS

"It is an excellent plan when on a hike to take off shoes and socks at least at mid-day, so that feet, socks, and shoes may cool. Turn your socks inside out to cool, and when you replace them put the one you had on the right foot on the left, and vice versa."

—*Edward Cave,* The Boy Scout's Hike Book, *1916*

Hiking Stick

Baden-Powell's first drawing of a Scout shows a boy with a hiking stick in his hand. Try one yourself, and you might find that the miles glide by.

Use a hiking stick to push back branches and to poke behind rocks. When you wade a stream, a hiking stick will give you the stability of a tripod.

You can keep a record of your adventures by whittling a small notch on your hiking stick for every five miles you walk. Elsewhere on the staff, cut a notch for each night you camp out under the stars.

Pace

Walking quickly is often not very important during a hike. Take time to enjoy the sights and sounds around you. The journey really is as important as reaching your destination.

Hike at a pace that is comfortable for the slowest member of your patrol. Even though you might feel that you could race along forever, the safety and good fellowship of the whole group staying together is more important than speed.

Resting

When you're taking it easy on a hike and stopping often to look at plants, animals, and scenery, you might not need any rest stops at all. However if you are pushing steadily along the trail, a five-minute break every half hour or so is a good idea. It will give you a chance to adjust your clothing, check your feet for signs of hot spots or blisters, sip some water, and have a bite of food.

Each patrol leader takes responsibility for keeping the members of his patrol together on the trail. In addition, every Scout hikes with a buddy. This will ensure that the patrol stays together and that everyone is safe.

Conditioning

Hiking is good for your body. It hardens your muscles and strengthens your heart and lungs. It is also good for your mind. It fills you with confidence, energy, and respect for the outdoors.

To enjoy hiking to the fullest, start out with short trips. As your legs become accustomed to hiking, you can increase the length of your journeys. You can also train for hiking by exercising regularly, jogging, and eating a healthy diet.

Trail Manners

Travel single file on most trails, leaving some space between you and the Scout ahead of you. You can see where you are going, and you won't run into him if he suddenly stops. Be courteous to other hikers by stepping to the side of the trail so that they can pass.

Horses and mules can be spooked by hikers. If you meet people on horseback, stop where you are and ask the riders what you should do. They will usually ask you to step a few paces downhill from the trail and stand quietly while the animals pass.

For more on safe hiking and on what to do if lost, see pages 38–41.

Overcoming hardships is an important challenge for hikers, but there might be times when you discover you are not prepared for the conditions you are facing. The weather might be worse than you expected, or the bugs especially bad. No matter how hard you try, you might simply be having a miserable time.

If that's the case, sometimes the best thing you can do is turn around and go home. The trail will always be there; you can come back and try again when you are really ready for it.

CAMPING

TRAILHEAD

9

CAMPING

FROM YOUR FIRST TENDERFOOT CAMPOUT to the rugged journeys you might already have taken deep into the backcountry, camping is
Scouting at its best. Learn how to make yourself comfortable outdoors for
a night or more, and you'll be ready for all kinds of BSA adventures.

The long, warm days of summer are perfect for campouts, but don't
put away your tent and camp stove just because cold weather has
arrived. Snow can turn familiar countryside into a wintry wilderness just
right for overnight trips that might include snowshoeing, skiing, building
igloos, and tracking animals.

Master the skills needed for camping and you'll have the knowledge to
take care of yourself in the outdoors and to take care of the outdoors, too.

THE OUTDOOR CODE

As an American, I will do
my best to—

BE CLEAN in my outdoor manners,

BE CAREFUL with fire,

BE CONSIDERATE in the outdoors,

and

BE CONSERVATION-MINDED.

The Outdoor Code reminds Scouts of the importance of caring for the environment. The code's ideals have special meaning whenever you are camping, hiking, and taking part in other outdoor events.

Being clean in your outdoor manners, careful with fire, and considerate means you can enjoy the outdoors to the fullest, but in ways that do the environment no harm. This handbook and your Scout leaders will help you learn how.

Being conservation-minded encourages the protection and the thoughtful use of natural resources. You can also roll up your sleeves and do your part in service projects that improve the condition of wildlife, water, air, forests, and the land itself.

The wisdom you gain about the outdoors through your Scouting experiences can direct your actions wherever you are, whatever you do, and at every stage of your life. Your commitment to the Outdoor Code and your efforts to leave no trace will make a positive difference in the quality of the environment today and for generations to come. Read carefully the "Principles of Leave No Trace" at the end of this chapter so you can do your part in protecting our Earth.

PLANNING A CAMPING TRIP

PLAN AHEAD and you will be prepared for anything you might meet along the way. See page 199 for the five *W*'s of planning a hiking trip. Use the same method to figure out the where, when, who, why, and what of planning a camping trip.

In 1803 the explorers Lewis and Clark set out on a three-year journey across America. They secured the food they needed by hunting and by trading with Native Americans. But they had to carry everything else with them—tools, blankets, medicine, and pots and pans.

Planning the gear, clothing, and food to take on a camping trip is important for Scouts, too. Pack just what you need, and leave everything else at home. Camping will quickly show you the joys of living simply and well, just like those explorers of old.

Where Do You Want to Go?

Every part of the United States has terrific places to camp. Your Scoutmaster will know of some. So will officials at federal, state, and local land management agencies. Look for their numbers in the telephone directory.

Camping equipment stores often have guidebooks that describe camping areas of interest, and a search of the Internet might turn up information on outdoor opportunities near you. If you obtain permission, private lands might also offer good camping. Many Scout camps can be used year-round.

When Are You Leaving and How Long Will You Be Gone?

Know the length of a camping trip so that you can take along enough food, clothing, fuel, and gear. Based on their duration, three kinds of Scout camping are *short-term, long-term,* and *high adventure:*

- *Short-term camping* includes one-night outings and weekend trips. Many troops and patrols try to go camping once a month or more, often in local parks or at BSA campgrounds.

- *Long-term camping* allows you to spend at least six days and five nights with your troop at Scout camp or on expeditions into the back-country, along rivers and lakes, or over the open road. These longer trips often occur in the summer, but you might have opportunities for winter outings, too.

- *High-adventure treks* begin at adventure bases operated by the BSA National Council or a BSA local council. Some troops also plan and embark on their own high-adventure treks. On journeys of a week or longer, you can push toward a mountaintop, paddle your canoe across wilderness lakes, or even sail a ship on the open sea. (For more information, see *Passport to High Adventure,* BSA publication No. 4310.)

Who Is Going with You?

Most Scout camping trips will include your patrol or troop and several adult leaders. Group sites in Scout camps and public campgrounds are laid out so that the reasonable activities of large groups will not bother other campers or harm the environment.

In many areas, though, a big group can be hard on the land by trampling vegetation and requiring a lot of space for tents and cooking. The noise and visual impact of a large group might disturb other hikers and campers who are trying to get away from crowds.

Be considerate of other people and limit your impact on the environment by learning about any local guidelines on group size and then obeying them. Do not exceed the group size established by landowners or land management agencies—often set at no more than eight to eleven campers, including at least two adult leaders.

In highly restricted areas, each patrol should plan its own itinerary that is different from that of any other patrol. Each patrol should also hike, camp, and cook on its own as a separate and distinct group.

By following area regulations on group size, Scouts show that they can protect the land and be courteous to others. Breaking those rules sends the wrong message about Scouting to everyone.

Why Are You Going?

To have fun, of course. To learn about the outdoors. To be with your friends, see new sights, and explore the backcountry. You will come up with plenty of reasons to go camping.

How Much Does Scout Camping Cost?

Camping can be simple and inexpensive. Much of the clothing you need for the outdoors is probably in your closet right now. Many troops have tents, cook pots, and other group overnight gear. Some of your personal camping gear can be made from things around the house or purchased at surplus stores, garage sales, or from the BSA's national Supply Division.

You might be asked to cover your share of meal costs, but there are probably ways you can earn a few dollars for camp. Ask your Scoutmaster. No Scout should ever be left behind because of lack of money.

What Should You Take with You?

Carry your Scout Outdoor Essentials on every Scout outing. When you want to camp out under the stars, add personal and group overnight gear. Use the following check-lists to gather what you'll need:

PERSONAL OVERNIGHT CAMPING GEAR
✓ **Scout Outdoor Essentials**
☐ Pocketknife
☐ First aid kit
☐ Extra clothing
☐ Rain gear
☐ Water bottle
☐ Flashlight
☐ Trail food
☐ Matches and fire starters
☐ Sun protection
☐ Map and compass
(For descriptions of the Scout Outdoor Essentials, turn to pages 208–10 .)
Clothing for the season ✓
(For clothing checklists, turn to pages 203–4 .)
✓ **Backpack**
✓ **Rain cover for backpack**

✓	**Sleeping bag, or two or three blankets**	
✓	**Sleeping pad**	
✓	**Ground cloth**	
	Eating kit	✓
	Spoon	
	Plate	
	Bowl	
	Cup	
	(For more on eating kits, see page 264 ✳.)	
✓	**Cleanup kit**	
	Soap	
	Toothbrush	
	Toothpaste	
	Dental floss	
	Comb	
	Washcloth	
	Towel	
	Personal extras (optional)	✓
	Watch	
	Camera and film	
	Notebook	
	Pencil or pen	
	Sunglasses	
	Small musical instrument	
	Swimsuit	
	Gloves	

PATROL OR GROUP OVERNIGHT CAMPING GEAR

- ✓ **Tents with poles, stakes, ground cloths, and lines**
- ✓ **Dining fly**
- ✓ **Nylon cord, 50 feet**
- ✓ **Backpacking stoves and fuel**
- ✓ **Cook kit**
  - Pots and pans
  - Spatula, large spoon and/or ladle, depending on menus
  - Plastic sheets, two 4-by-4-foot
  - Matches and/or butane lighters in waterproof containers

  (For more on cook kits, see page 264 ❅.)
- ✓ **Cleanup kit**
  - Sponge or dishcloth
  - Biodegradable soap
  - Sanitizing rinse agent (bleach)
  - Scouring pads (no-soap type)
  - Plastic trash bags
  - Toilet paper in plastic bag

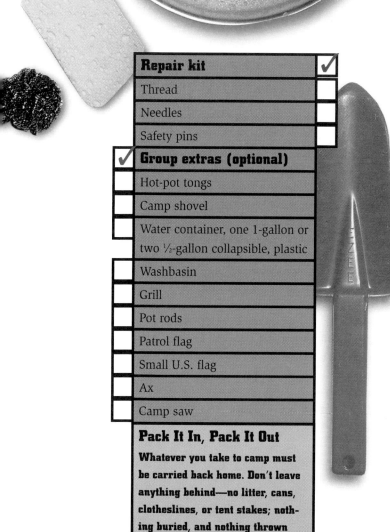

Repair kit	✓
Thread	
Needles	
Safety pins	

✓	Group extras (optional)
	Hot-pot tongs
	Camp shovel
	Water container, one 1-gallon or two ½-gallon collapsible, plastic
	Washbasin
	Grill
	Pot rods
	Patrol flag
	Small U.S. flag
	Ax
	Camp saw

Pack It In, Pack It Out

Whatever you take to camp must be carried back home. Don't leave anything behind—no litter, cans, clotheslines, or tent stakes; nothing buried, and nothing thrown into the woods, lakes, or streams.

BACKPACK

A backpack gives you a place to stow your camping gear and food. Fully loaded, it should be comfortable to carry for a short hike to a campground or a long day on the trail.

Most backpacks have an external metal frame or a stiff internal frame that gives the pack its shape and stability. A hip belt shifts the weight from your shoulders to the strong muscles of your legs. Your pack might also have outside pockets for water bottles, maps, and other gear that you might want to reach quickly.

Backpacks with external frames are great for general backpacking, especially hiking on open trails.

Different backpacks will fit differently. If you will be choosing from among several models, try each one on with plenty of weight packed inside. Adjust the straps and hip belt for a better fit.

Because it is snug against your back, an internal-frame pack is a good choice for skiing and mountaineering as well as backpacking.

Packing Up Long Ago

In BSA's early years, many Scouts made *bedroll packs* by rolling their equipment and supplies inside their blankets. They bent the loaded blankets into a horseshoe shape, tied the ends together, and slung the bundle over one shoulder. Bedroll packs weren't as roomy or as easy to carry as today's backpacks, but they got the job done.

Packing Up

Stuff Sacks

A handy way to organize your gear is by putting clothing into one stuff sack, cooking utensils into another, and so on. Bread wrappers can be used as stuff sacks. Even better are 1-gallon self-sealing plastic bags. Sturdy nylon stuff sacks can be purchased at camp supply stores.

Loading a Pack

In addition to your own gear, you might carry some patrol or group equipment. Your share might include several pots, part of a tent, a camp stove, and some food. Arrange soft items in your pack so that they will cushion your back. Keep your rain gear, flashlight, first aid kit, and water bottle near the top or in the outside pockets where you can reach them easily.

If there is room, you can put your sleeping bag inside your pack. Otherwise, wrap it with a ground cloth or stuff it in a plastic trash bag to protect it from the elements, and tuck it under the pack's top flap or strap it to the frame.

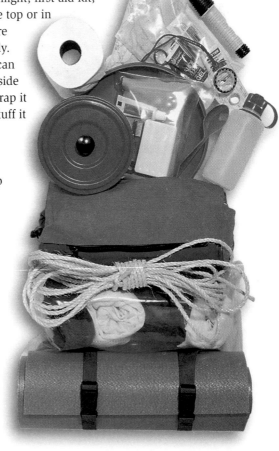

Stowing items of gear in the same place in your pack each time you get ready for the trail helps you quickly find what you need when you need it.

Rain Cover

Most backpacks will protect your gear from a light shower, but heavy rains can leak through the fabric. If you leave your pack outside during the night, you can fit a large plastic trash bag over it to keep it dry. On rainy hikes, cut a slit in the bag so that you can cover the pack and still leave the straps free. Tuck the loose ends of the bag behind the straps or under the frame.

Cook pot too big to fit inside your pack? Try slipping it over one end of your sleeping bag before you strap the bag to the frame.

SELECTING A CAMPSITE

MUCH OF THE SUCCESS of a campout depends upon the campsite you choose. A good site offers plenty to see and do. It is also easy on the land, allowing you to camp without leaving a trace.

Here are some pointers for deciding where to make camp:

Environmental Impact

Protect the environment by using established campsites whenever you can, or by camping on durable surfaces that will not be harmed by your presence. If fires are allowed, build them in existing fire rings. Try not to put fresh marks on the land.

Carelessness in choosing a campsite can harm the land in several ways. Tents will mat down vegetation and cut it off from water, air, and sunlight. Campers walking to and from cooking areas, water sources, and their tents will trample vegetation and form unwanted pathways. The weight of many footsteps in the same area will compact the soil, making it difficult for new plants to take root and sometimes leading to erosion.

A trail is an example of a strip of soil that has become so compacted that nothing will grow in it. The same is true of many campsites. We accept them because they concentrate human activities to limited areas, leaving the rest of the landscape untouched. However, it is important to do all you can to recognize and bypass places that might not withstand the impact of camping and hiking.

Safety

Don't pitch your tents under dead trees or limbs that might fall in a storm. Stay out of gullies or other low spots that could flood. Choose a site away from lone trees, mountaintops, high ridges, and other likely targets of lightning. Camp some distance from game trails, especially in bear country.

Size

A site must be large enough for patrol members to pitch their tents and cook their meals. When hanging food to keep it away from animals, find the trees you need at least two hundred feet (seventy-five steps) away from where you will be sleeping.

Water

Your patrol will require water for drinking, cooking, and cleanup—several gallons a day for each Scout. Public water supplies are safest. Water taken from streams, rivers, or lakes must be purified before use. Camping in dry regions can be rewarding, though you might have to carry water to your site. (For information on purifying water, see page 256 ❄ .)

Terrain

Does the site slope gently for good drainage? Leaves, pine needles, and other natural cover can keep the ground from becoming muddy. An area open to the east and south will catch sunlight early in the day and perhaps be drier than slopes facing north.

CAMP STOVE

Stoves and Campfires

Where fires are permitted, look for a site with an existing fire ring and a good supply of dead twigs and fallen branches. If fires are not allowed, wood is scarce, or you don't want to spend much time preparing meals, use a lightweight camp stove to heat your water and cook your food. (For more on stoves and campfires, see pages 248–55 ❄ .)

Privacy

Respect the privacy of others. Trees, bushes, and some forms of terrain can screen your camp from trails and neighboring campsites. When other campers are staying nearby, keep the noise down.

Permission

Get permission from owners before camping on private property. Check well ahead of time with land managers of public parks, forests, and reserves. They can issue any permits you need, and might suggest how you can make the most of your campout.

BE EASY ON THE LAND

SEVERAL TYPES of terrain demand special care in campsite selection:

Meadows

Whenever possible, camp in the forest away from meadows and the trees at their edge. Meadows can be important feeding areas for animals that could be frightened away by your activities. Deeper in the woods you will be sheltered from sun and wind, and your camp will blend into its surroundings. You are also less likely to beat down meadow grasses and create erosion.

Lakes and Streams

Bodies of water might be heavily used by wildlife. Pitch your tents at least two hundred feet (seventy-five steps) away from streams and lakes. That will allow the animals to reach the water and will reduce your impact on shorelines.

Alpine Areas

Winters in the high mountains are often long and harsh, leaving plants just a few warm months in which to grow. Camping on top of alpine vegetation can cause it serious harm. Make your high mountain camps in established campsites, on bare ground, or on snowfields.

TARPS AND TENTS

TARPS

A *tarp* is a large waterproof sheet often used on Scout camping trips as a dining fly to cover the camp kitchen. When the bugs and the weather aren't too bad, tarps also make fine lightweight sleeping shelters.

Some tarps have metal rings called *grommets* spaced along the edges so you can tie cords through them with bowline knots. If there are no grommets, you can still attach lines to a tarp. Start with plenty of ⅛-inch cord and a handful of smooth stones the size of golf balls.

Form a loop by tying two half hitches in the end of a piece of cord, or make the loops for a clove hitch. Hold a stone under the corner of the sheet. Work the knot over the tarp fabric and the stone, then draw it tight. (To tie a bowline knot, see page 149. For two half hitches, see page 36; for a clove hitch, see page139.)

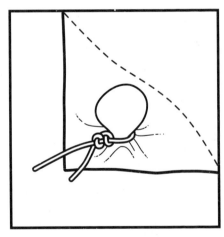

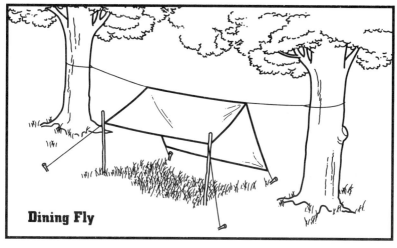

Dining Fly

Experiment with different ways to set up a tarp. For a dining fly over your cooking area, try tying a rope between two trees with taut-line hitches and tightening the rope so it is six to eight feet above the ground. Drape the tarp over the rope, pull out the corners, and use taut-line hitches to tie *guylines* (ropes attached to the corners) to trees or stakes. (To tie a taut-line hitch, see page 37.)

Set the tarp closer to the ground if you want to sleep under it. Lowering the edges will give you extra protection from the wind.

A Homemade Tarp or Ground Cloth

Make inexpensive tarps and ground cloths from a sheet of *polyethylene plastic* like that used by carpenters to cover stored lumber. The best thickness for camp use is *4-mil,* which means four one-thousandths of an inch.

Polyethylene plastic is sold in hardware stores in 10- to 12-foot-wide rolls. To make a tarp, ask a clerk to cut a piece that is as long as it is wide. A ground cloth should be about the size of your tent's floor.

TENTS

Most tents have the shape of an A-frame or a dome, and are roomy enough for two to four campers. Many are made of breathable nylon that allows moisture to escape. A waterproof nylon fly pitched over the body of the tent shields it from rain, snow, and wind.

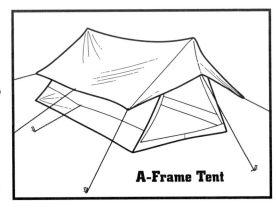

A-Frame Tent

Tents that are shades of green, brown, gray, or dark blue can reduce the visual impact of a campsite by blending in with their surroundings. Each tent should also have its own metal or plastic stakes and strong, lightweight poles made of aluminum or fiberglass. The poles come apart into sections that will fit into your pack. One Scout can take the tent body and poles while another carries the rain fly and stakes.

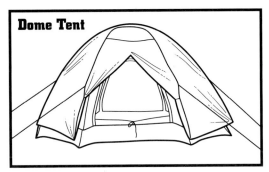

Dome Tent

When you are ready to pitch your tent, first you must choose a level site. Remove stones and large sticks, but don't disturb pine needles or grasses. Spread out a ground cloth to protect the tent floor from dirt, sharp objects, and moisture.

Unfold the tent on top of the ground cloth. Pull out the corners of the floor and stake them to the ground, then assemble the poles and put them in place. Use taut-line hitches to tie the free ends of guylines around stakes you've pushed into the ground, and pull the lines tight.

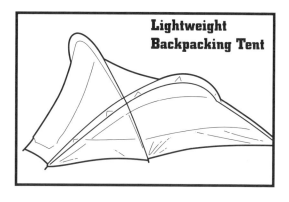

Lightweight Backpacking Tent

Finish by putting the rain fly over the tent and staking it down. Never dig ditches around your tent; they leave scars on the ground that can take a long time to heal. Select a site that drains well, and you will stay dry without disturbing the land.

Whenever possible, let your tent dry in the sun before you take it down. When that's not possible and you have to pack a wet tent, set it up again as soon as you get home, or hang it indoors and be sure it dries completely before putting it away. That will prevent mildew from ruining the fabric.

No Flames in Tents

Keep *all* flames away from tents. Never use candles, matches, stoves, heaters, or lanterns in or near tents. No tent is fireproof. All of them can burn or melt when exposed to heat. *Flashlights only!*

GROUND BEDS

AT HOME, a mattress beneath you and blankets on top trap your body heat and keep you warm. Outdoors, a couple of blankets will do the same on summer campouts in mild weather. You might want to fold the blankets into the shape of an envelope.

If you have a choice, though, use a sleeping bag. Because it is snug around your body, a bag will often be warmer than blankets. It will also be easier to pack and to keep clean.

Sleeping Bag

The cloth part of a sleeping bag is called the *shell*. Inside the shell is *fill material* of synthetic fibers or the down and feathers of ducks and geese. The fill traps your body heat and holds it close to you. For more warmth, zip the bag closed and pull the drawstring snug around your face. To keep its *loft,* or thickness, evenly distrib-uted, shake your sleeping bag each time you use it.

Sleeping Pad

Increase your comfort and warmth with a *sleeping pad*, a piece of foam that will give you a soft surface on which to sleep and will prevent the cold ground from drawing away your body heat. Pads are often lighter and more durable than air mattresses, and they insulate better. You can find them at camping supply stores.

Ground Cloth

Keep moisture away from your bedding with a *ground cloth*—a plastic sheet cut to the size of your sleeping bag or tent floor. If you will be using a tent, tuck the edges of the ground cloth beneath the tent floor so that rainwater will not collect on the cloth and run under the tent.

HOW TO PREPARE A GROUND BED

To sleep beneath the open sky in good weather, you will want to know how to make a warm ground bed. First, find a fairly level spot. Toss aside stones and sticks that might poke you, but don't rake away pine needles or leaves. They will cushion your bed and reduce your impact on the land.

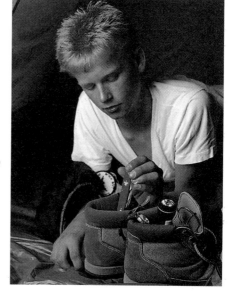

Spread out your ground cloth, lay the sleeping pad on top of it, then arrange your sleeping bag or blankets on the pad. For a pillow, stuff extra clothing inside a sweater or sleeping bag sack. It's a good idea to leave your bag rolled up until you are ready to sleep so that your bedding won't be dampened by humidity or dew.

Making a ground bed in a tent is not much different from making one in the open. You won't need a ground cloth inside the tent—there should already be one spread under the floor.

When you crawl into bed, keep your shoes or hiking boots close. Stow your watch, glasses, and other small items in one of them. Drop your flashlight into the other so you can find it in the dark. Have a water bottle nearby, too, in case you get thirsty before dawn. In the morning, shake out your boots before you put them on; small creatures sometimes creep inside in search of shelter and warmth.

You might discover that you are warmer in a tent because it blocks the wind. Wearing a warm cap to bed also helps prevent heat loss. Changing into dry clothes before crawling into your sleeping bag will help you stay warm, too. You can pull on a warm shirt during the night, and a sweater, extra socks, and even mittens. Finally, don't go to bed hungry. Your body can produce plenty of heat, but only if it has calories to burn.

KEEPING CLEAN

HARD WORK AND PLAY can leave you dusty. Always wash your hands with soap and water before handling food. On a one-night camp-out, you won't need to do much more than brush and floss your teeth before bed. You can clean up when you get home.

During longer adventures, you and those around you will be much happier if you wash your body once in a while. Doing it the right way will prevent any harm to the environment.

Many kinds of soap can be harmful to aquatic plants and animals. *Biodegradable* soaps are safer because they can be reduced to a harmless substance by organisms in the ground, but keep **all** soap at least two hundred feet (seventy-five steps) away from any stream, lake, or spring.

Fill a basin or pot with water, carry it away from the source, then use it to bathe. Scatter the water when you are finished.

PERSONAL CLEANUP KIT

Soap

A little goes a long way. A bar that's nearly used up will be plenty, or a small plastic bottle of biodegrad-able soap. Store your soap in a plastic bag.

Small Towel and Washcloth

It's usually best to take a dark-colored towel and washcloth; also, don't choose from your family's best set of towels.

Toothbrush and Toothpaste

You won't need much. Get the smallest tube you can find, or save a family tube when it's almost empty.

Dental Floss

Flossing every day helps keep your gums and teeth in good shape. Floss can also be used as a strong sewing thread for emergency repairs.

CAT HOLES AND LATRINES

Getting rid of human waste outdoors requires special care. If the campground has rest rooms or outhouses, be sure to use them. If it doesn't, dig a cat hole or a latrine. Completely bury used toilet paper. Always wash your hands with soap and water when you are finished.

Cat Hole

Find a private spot at least two hundred feet (seventy-five steps) from water, campsites, and trails. Dig a hole six to eight inches deep with your heel, a stick, or a shovel. Organisms in the top layers of earth will break down human waste.

Fill the cat hole with soil when you are finished, and replace any ground cover. Push a stick into the earth to warn others against digging in the same area.

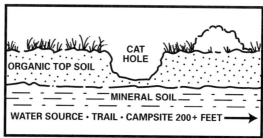

CAT HOLE

ORGANIC TOP SOIL

MINERAL SOIL

WATER SOURCE · TRAIL · CAMPSITE 200+ FEET ➡️

Latrine

A patrol, troop, or other large group camping in the same place for two nights or more can help lessen its impact on the land by digging a single latrine rather than making dozens of cat holes. Check with a ranger or other local expert for guidance.

With a shovel, dig a shallow trench a foot wide and three to four feet long. Remove and save any ground cover. As with a cat hole, dig no deeper than the topsoil so that the waste will be buried in organic earth where it will turn into soil nutrients. Sprinkle a layer of dirt in the latrine after each use to keep away flies and hold down odors. Return all the soil to the latrine when you break camp, and put back the ground cover.

PRINCIPLES OF LEAVE NO TRACE

1. PLAN AHEAD AND PREPARE

Proper trip planning and preparation helps hikers and campers accomplish trip goals safely and enjoyably while minimizing damage to natural and cultural resources. Campers who plan ahead can avoid unexpected situations, and minimize their impact by complying with area regulations such as observing limitations on group size.

2. CAMP AND TRAVEL ON DURABLE SURFACES

Damage to land occurs when visitors trample vegetation or communities of organisms beyond recovery. The resulting barren areas develop into undesirable trails, campsites, and soil erosion.

3. PACK IT IN, PACK IT OUT

This simple yet effective saying motivates backcountry visitors to take their trash home with them. It makes sense to carry out of the backcountry the extra materials taken there by your group or others. Minimize the need to pack out food scraps by carefully planning meals. Accept the challenge of packing out everything you bring.

4. LEAVE WHAT YOU FIND

Allow others a sense of discovery: Leave rocks, plants, animals, archaeological artifacts, and other objects as you find them. It may be illegal to remove artifacts.

5. MINIMIZE CAMPFIRE USE

Some people would not think of camping without a campfire. Yet the naturalness of many areas has been degraded by overuse of fires and increasing demand for firewood.

6. RESPECT WILDLIFE

Quick movements and loud noises are stressful to animals. Considerate campers observe wildlife from afar, give animals a wide berth, store food securely, and keep garbage and food scraps away from animals. Help keep wildlife wild.

7. RESPECT OTHERS

Thoughtful campers travel and camp in small groups, keep the noise down, select campsites away from other groups, always travel and camp quietly, wear clothing and use gear that blend with the environment, respect private property, and leave gates (open or closed) as found. Be considerate of other campers and respect their privacy.

For more on camping, see the *Fieldbook,* BSA publication No. 33200. For information on the Order of the Arrow, the BSA's national brotherhood of honor campers, see page 426–27.

COOKING

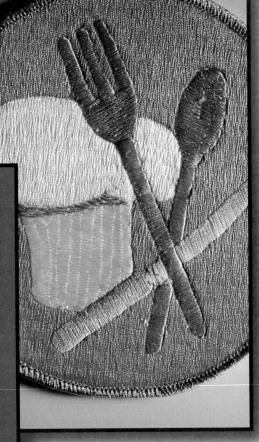

TRAILHEAD

10

COOKING

"A Patrol cooking its own meals is playing one of the most fascinating games in Scouting."

Handbook for Boys,
5th edition, 1948

As dawn breaks over the mountains, the first sound you hear might be the sizzle of bacon and eggs over a backpacking stove. At night under a dining fly rattling with rain, the smell of baking bread can make your mouth water.

At the end of a long day on the trail, how about digging into a big helping of stew, a couple of fresh, hot biscuits, and a bowl of wild blueberries? In the middle of a winter hike, why not pour yourself a steaming mug of cocoa or a cup of rich, thick soup?

Food in the outdoors is more than just a way to cut your hunger. It powers your body through days packed with action. It helps you stay warm at night. When the sky turns stormy or when you are tired and feeling low, a hearty meal will cheer you up and energize you to do whatever needs doing.

Get a feel for mixing ingredients, handling pots and pans, and judging when a dish is done by helping to prepare family meals at home. Learn to cook in your own kitchen, and you will find it's easy to cook on the trail.

A key to no-trace camping is knowing when it's all right to light a fire and when it is better to use a stove.

USING CAMPFIRES AND LIGHTWEIGHT STOVES

MANY SCOUTS use lightweight stoves on all their camping trips. Stoves are clean, quick to heat water and food, and easy to light in any weather. Best of all, they leave no marks on the land. A stove in your pack can make it simpler for you to camp without leaving a trace.

Fires have their place, too. A fire can warm you, cook your food, and dry your clothes. Bright flames can lift your spirits on a rainy morning. At night, glowing embers can stir your imagination.

A good Scout knows how to build a fire, especially in an emergency. He also knows there are often reasons why he should not light one:

- Campfires can char the ground, blacken rocks, and sterilize soil. Vegetation can have a hard time growing again where a fire has been.
- Fires consume dead branches, bark, and other organic material that would have provided shelter and food for animals and plants.
- Where hiking and camping are popular, fire sites can spoil the appearance of the land.
- Campfires must be closely watched to prevent them from spreading into surrounding grasses, brush, and trees.

Find out ahead of time if the area where you want to camp permits the use of fires. Even where fires are allowed, a lightweight stove might be a better choice.

HOW TO BUILD A CAMPFIRE

Make a Safe Fire Site

A safe fire site is one on which nothing will burn except the fuel you feed the flames. It's a spot from which fire cannot spread. Many camping areas have metal fire rings, grills, or stone fireplaces. Use those existing fire sites whenever you can.

Otherwise, select a spot on gravel, sand, or bare earth well away from trees, brush, and dry grasses. Look overhead for branches that sparks could ignite. Stay clear of boulders that could be blackened by smoke, or large tree roots that could be harmed by too much heat.

Rake away pine needles, leaves, twigs, and anything else that might burn. Save the ground cover so you can put it back when you are done with your fire. Keep a pot of water close by to douse the flames should they begin to spread.

Bare-Ground Fire Site

When the ground is bare, haul enough mineral soil to the center of the cleared circle to make an earthen pad about two feet square and three inches thick. Kindle the fire on top of the pad,

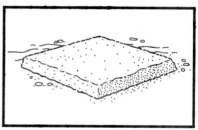

and the mineral soil will protect the ground from the heat. After you have properly extinguished the blaze and disposed of any unburned wood, crush the remaining ashes, mix them with the mineral soil, and return it to the sites from which you borrowed it.

Gather Tinder, Kindling, and Fuelwood

Patience is the key ingredient for successfully building a fire. You will also need *tinder, kindling,* and *fuelwood.*

Tinder

Tinder catches fire easily and burns fast. Dry pine needles, grasses, shredded bark, and the fluff from some seed pods all make good tinder. So do wood shavings cut with a pocketknife from a dead stick. Gather enough tinder to fill your hat once.

Kindling

Dead twigs that are no thicker than a pencil are called kindling. Find enough to fill your hat twice.

Fuel

Fuelwood can be as thin as your finger or as thick as your wrist. Use sticks you find on the ground and gather them from a wide area rather than removing all the downed wood from one spot.

Lay the Fire

There are many ways to arrange tinder, kindling, and fuel so that the heat of a single match can grow into the flames of a campfire. A *tepee fire lay* is a good all-around method:

1. Place a big, loose handful of tinder in the middle of your fire site.

2. Mound plenty of small kindling over the tinder.

3. Arrange small and medium-sized sticks of fuelwood around the kindling as if they were the poles of a tepee. Leave an opening in the "tepee" on the side the wind is blowing against so that air can reach the middle of the fire.

4. Ease a burning match under the tinder. The flame should rise through the tinder and crackle up into the kindling and the fuelwood above.

Fuzz sticks **can help get a fire going. Cut shavings into each stick, but leave them attached. Prop the fuzz sticks upright in among the kindling.**

Fireplaces

A fireplace holds your cook pots above the flames and allows air to reach the fire.

Three-Point Fireplace

For a single pot or pan, stick three metal tent stakes into the embers.

Wet-Weather Fire Tips
• Before the rain begins, gather tinder and kindling for several fires and store it under your dining fly.
• Keep a supply of dry tinder in a plastic bag.
• Split wet sticks and logs with an ax. The wood inside should be dry.
• Keep matches safe from dampness by carrying them in a plastic container with a tight lid.
• A butane lighter will give you a flame in even the wettest weather. Store it away from heat.

PUTTING OUT A CAMPFIRE

Extinguish every fire when you no longer need it. Make sure it is **cold out**—cold enough so that you can run your hands through the ashes.

Pour water on the embers. Stir the wet ashes with a stick and wet them again. Repeat until you can touch every part of the fire site with your bare hands.

CLEANING A FIRE SITE

Clean a permanent fire site by picking out any bits of paper, foil, and unburned food. Pack them home with the rest of your trash.

If you made a new fire site, erase all evidence it was ever there. Scatter any rocks, turning their blackened sides toward the ground. Spread cold ashes over a wide area and toss away extra firewood. Replace any ground cover. When you're finished, the site should look just as it did when you found it.

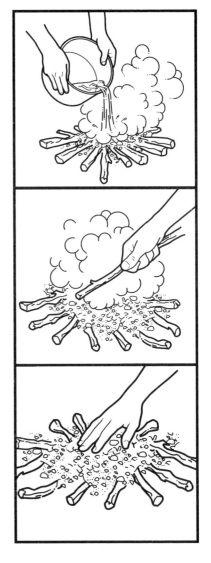

HOW TO USE LIGHTWEIGHT STOVES

A camp stove gives you a fast, easy way to do your cooking. It produces heat just right for warming a small cup of soup or cooking a big pot of pasta. A stove won't blacken rocks and cooking gear or scorch the soil. With a stove, you can camp where there is no firewood or where camp-fires are not allowed. Stoves work equally well in deserts, high mountains, and deep forests, and are ideal for use in storms and on snow.

Many camping stoves burn commercial stove fuel or kerosene. Store these fuels in special metal bottles with lids that screw on tightly. Choose bright red bottles or mark them with colorful tape so there is no chance of mistaking them for water bottles.

Butane and propane stoves burn gas from small cans called *cartridges*. Carry cartridges and fuel bottles in the outside pockets of your pack where gas fumes can't get near your food.

When you are ready to cook, place your stove on a level surface free of leaves, sticks, or other burnable material. A patch of bare ground or a flat rock is all you need.

During winter campouts, put your stove on a piece of plywood about eight inches square. The plywood will hold your stove on top of the snow and prevent the cold ground from chilling the stove.

Different kinds of stoves burn different fuels and operate in different ways. Read your stove's instructions carefully and follow them exactly.

Stove Safety Rules

- Use, refuel, and store stoves and lanterns only with the supervision of a knowledgeable adult and only where allowed.

- Operate and maintain stoves and lanterns according to the manufacturer's instructions.

- Store fuel in approved containers. Keep fuel containers well away from campfires, burning stoves, and all other sources of heat.

- Allow hot stoves and lanterns to cool completely before changing compressed-gas cartridges or refilling from containers of liquid fuel.

- Refill stoves and lanterns outdoors and a safe distance from any sources of heat, including other stoves or campfires. Use cartridges or fuel expressly recommended for your stoves by the manufacturer. Use a funnel to pour liquid fuel into a stove or lantern. Recap the fuel container and the stove or lantern. Before lighting the device, wait until any spilled fuel has evaporated.

- Do not operate stoves or lanterns inside buildings with poor ventilation. Never fuel, light, or operate a gas stove or lantern inside a tent, snow cave, or igloo.

- Place a stove on a level, secure surface before lighting. On snow, place the stove on a six-inch-square piece of plywood to insulate it from the cold and lessen its tendency to tip.

- Have stoves and lanterns checked periodically by knowledgeable adults to make sure they are in top working condition.

- Follow the manufacturer's instructions for lighting a stove. Keep fuel containers and extra canisters well away. Keep your head and body to one side in case the stove flares up.

- Never leave a lighted stove or lantern unattended.

- Do not overload a stove with a heavy pot or large frying pan. When cooking requires a pot capacity of more than two quarts, set up a separate grill with legs to hold the pot, then place the stove under the grill.

- Carry empty fuel containers home for proper disposal. Do not place them in or near fires, or in trash that will be burned.

WATER

DRINK PLENTY OF FLUID each day, in cold weather as well as warm. Drink enough so that your urine remains clear—at least two quarts a day in normal conditions and up to eight quarts during hard exertion in hot, dry climates. Bring the water from home or use the water from public supplies. Water collected from springs, lakes, or streams must be purified before use.

Public Supplies

Water from faucets and drinking fountains in campgrounds and Scout camps usually has been tested by public health officials. It is almost always safe to use.

Open Water

Water taken from streams, lakes, and springs could contain bacteria and parasites too small for you to see. Disinfect **any** water that does not come from a tested source.

Water from Snow

On winter trips and hikes in high mountains, you can get your water from melting clean snow. Each time you sip from your water bottle, replace it with a handful of loose snow. Water remaining in the bottle will help melt the snow.

In camp, gently heat a pot of snow over a stove or fire. A cup of water in the bottom of the pot will speed the process.

HOW TO PURIFY WATER

Boiling

Bringing water to a rolling boil for a full minute or more will kill most organisms.

Purification Tablets

Water purification tablets are sold in small bottles just the right size for hikers and campers. The instructions on the label usually are to drop one or two tablets into a quart of water and then wait thirty minutes before drinking—longer if the water is cold.

Purification tablets can lose their effectiveness after the bottle has been opened. Check the expiration date on the label and use only fresh tablets. The tablets might also leave a chemical taste in the water. To improve the flavor, add some flavored mix **after** the tablets have had enough time to do their work.

Filters

Camping stores and catalogs offer water purification filters that are effective and easy to operate. Some operate by pumping water through pores small enough to strain out bacteria. Others contain chemicals or carbon. Follow the instructions that come with the filter you plan to use. It's a good idea to carry a small bottle of water purification tablets, too, in case your filter malfunctions.

Using a water filter is one way to be sure back-country water is safe to drink. Other methods include boiling it or treating it with tablets.

Keep a Cooking Notebook

Camp cooking is a skill you can master by doing a lot of it. Write your food lists and recipes in a notebook each time you prepare for a campout. At the end of every trip, make notes about what worked well and what didn't. Perhaps you needed a larger frying pan or more oatmeal, or maybe you took too much cocoa. As you plan your next outing, your notebook will remind you of changes you want to make.

PLANNING YOUR MEALS

CAREFUL PLANNING allows you to take enough food so that everyone in your patrol eats well, but there aren't many leftovers. You'll also know which pots, pans, and utensils to take along. Consider the following as you plan your outdoor meals:

- **How many Scouts are going and how long will you be away from home?** Fresh foods are fine for short outings. For trips longer than a day or two, carry supplies that won't spoil.

- **What are you going to do?** If your days will be packed with action, choose recipes that won't take long to prepare. When cooking will be a high point of a campout, take the ingredients and gear needed to make a real feast.

- **How will you reach camp?** Backpackers will want to keep their loads light with simple meals of nonperishable ingredients. If you will be traveling by car to your campsite, you might want to take griddles, Dutch ovens, fresh and canned foods, and plenty of utensils.

- **What weather do you expect?** Winter menus should contain more of the fats your body burns for heat. Take along soup mixes and hot drinks to warm you up. Summer meals can be lighter and should include plenty of fluids.

Forms of Camping Food

Fresh

Fresh foods have the most flavor and nutrition of any camping menu ingredients. They can also be the heaviest. Some, such as fresh meats, must be kept cool until you are ready to cook them. While carrots, apples, hard sausage, and some cheeses might last longer, most fresh foods are best used on trips no longer than one-night campouts.

Nonperishable

Pasta, beans, oatmeal, rice, flour, grains, and other foods that won't spoil are common ingredients for both short-term and long-term camping. The amount of nutrition they provide is high. When stored in plastic bags, they take up a small amount of pack space.

Dried/Dehydrated

Much of the weight of many foods is water. Remove it, and the result is a selection of lightweight ingredients just right for campers. Most grocery stores carry powdered milk, instant cocoa, dehydrated potatoes and other vegetables, soup mixes, and many other dried foods. Some camping stores sell entire camp meals that require only the addition of boiling water.

Canned

Almost any food can be purchased in cans. The primary drawback to canned food is its heaviness—at least as much as fresh food, plus the weight of the cans. Campers must also carry empty cans home with them for recycling or proper disposal. Even so, sometimes a special ingredient, such as a can of peaches for a cobbler, can be worth every bit of effort it takes to get it to your camp. (Avoid carrying glass containers. They are heavier than cans and might break.)

Retort Pouches

Retort pouches are flexible packages of any of a wide variety of foods, and they require no refrigeration. The pouches are convenient for winter camping because they can be heated simply by dropping them in a pot of boiling water, and the contents can be eaten straight out of the pouch.

THE IMPORTANCE OF GOOD NUTRITION

The food you eat should do three things:

- *Build up your body and keep it in good repair.* Protein and minerals are the body's building blocks. They are found in meat, fish, eggs, milk products, and in combinations of grains.

- *Provide the vitamins, minerals, fiber, and bulk that your body must have in order to stay healthy.* You'll find plenty of nutrition in fruits and vegetables, and essential bulk and fiber in these and other foods.

- *Serve as a source of energy for everything you do.* There is fuel in everything you eat, especially breads, grains, fats, and oils.

Many people choose not to eat certain foods because of family background, religious beliefs, or medical restrictions. Vegetarians, for example, avoid meat, but combinations of grains give them diets with plenty of protein.

Don't pass up chances to try different kinds of meals. Eating new dishes is a fun way to learn about other parts of the country and about foreign customs.

The Four Basic Food Groups

The following food groups are the foundation of a balanced diet that provides nutrition essential for good health:

Milk Group
Milk, cheese, ice cream, yogurt (one or more servings a day)

Protein Group
Meat, fish, poultry, lentils, beans, dried peas (two or more servings a day)

Vegetable-Fruit Group
Citrus fruits and tomatoes (at least one serving a day)
Leafy green and yellow vegetables (at least one serving a day)
Other vegetables and fruits (two or more servings a day)

Cereal-Grains Group
Bread, pasta, rice, oatmeal, granola (at every meal)

MENUS

Once you know how many meals you need, write down what you want to prepare and eat for each of those meals. The recipes in this chapter will give you some ideas. Other ideas might come from Scouts in your patrol who have favorite family recipes that are different from the ones you are accustomed to eating at home.

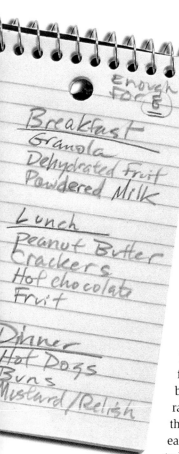

enough for 6

Breakfast
Granola
Dehydrated Fruit
Powdered Milk

Lunch
Peanut Butter
Crackers
Hot chocolate
Fruit

Dinner
Hot Dogs
Buns
Mustard/Relish

Shopping List

List every ingredient for each dish. Use the chart on page 261 to determine the amounts you will need for the number of people in your patrol. Don't forget such items as cooking oil, honey or sugar, and spices.

Cost per Person

Take your shopping list to a grocery store and write down the prices of the ingredients you plan to buy. Figure out each Scout's share by adding up the costs, then dividing the sum by the number of Scouts going on the outing.

Size of Servings

Food packages often list the amounts required for one or more servings. Outdoor activities build up big appetites, so lean toward more rather than less. The following chart lists the amount needed for one serving of each type of food; use the chart to help you figure out how much of each food you will need:

Single Serving Sizes

Vegetables and Fruits

Orange	1
Apple	1
Tomato	1
Juice, canned	4 ounces
Cabbage, fresh	¼ head
Carrots, fresh	1 or 2 medium
Vegetables, canned	4 ounces
Vegetables, dehydrated	½ ounce
Potatoes, fresh	1 or 2 medium
Potatoes, dehydrated	2 ounces
Corn, fresh	1 or 2 ears
String beans	½ cup
Shelled peas	½ cup
Onion, fresh	1 small
Soup, canned	5 ounces
Soup mix	1 individual packet
Fruit, fresh	1 or 2 pieces
Fruit, canned	5 or 6 ounces
Fruit, dried	2 ounces

Breads, Rice, and Pasta

Bread	2 to 4 slices
Cookies	2 to 4 ounces
Cakes	2 ounces
Cereal—oatmeal	2 ounces
Cereal—cold	2 ounces
Pancake mix	3 to 4 ounces
Biscuit mix	½ cup unprepared
Brown rice	½ cup uncooked
White rice	½ cup uncooked
Instant rice	1½ ounces
Spaghetti	3 to 4 ounces
Macaroni	3 to 4 ounces
Noodles	3 to 4 ounces
Ramen-style noodle	1 packet (3 ounces)
Pudding mix	1½ ounces
Tortilla	1

Milk and Cheese

Milk, fresh	1 pint
Milk, powdered	2 ounces
Cocoa, instant	1 individual packet
Cheese	2 ounces

Meat, Poultry, and Fish

Steak	6 to 8 ounces
Chops	4 ounces
Stew meat	4 ounces
Hamburger	4 ounces (1 patty)
Hot dogs	4 ounces (2 hot dogs)
Chicken, fresh	12 ounces
Ham, precooked	3 ounces
Bacon	2 ounces (3 or 4 slices)
Beef, canned	3 ounces
Chicken, canned	3 to 5 ounces
Fish, canned	3 ounces
Tuna fish, canned	3 to 4 ounces
Eggs, fresh	2
Eggs, dried	½ ounce

Condiments and Staples for Camp Cooking

Salt and pepper
Catsup, mustard
Relishes
Salad dressing
Flour
Honey or sugar
Butter, margarine, and cooking fats
Jam, jelly, syrup
Peanut butter

Spice Kit

Spices bring out the flavor of your cooking. Useful spices for camp cooking include salt, pepper, chili powder, thyme, oregano, garlic flakes, bay leaves, and cinnamon.

Carry spices in small plastic containers or bags, then stow in a stuff sack. Use spices lightly. You can always add more, but you can't remove a spice if you use too much.

REPACKAGING FOOD

Lighten your load and save space by getting rid of excess store packaging. Measure only as much of each ingredient as you will need for one meal and put it in a plastic bag. Tape a label on each bag and write on it the name and amount of the ingredient inside.

Place all the repackaged ingredients for each meal in a larger bag. Include the recipes, too. When you reach camp, you will have in one place all the ingredients and instructions for every meal.

FOOD STORAGE

PROTECT YOUR FOOD from mice, raccoons, bears, and other animals by making a *bear bag* to hang from a tree. Put the food in a stuff sack or clean trash bag and tie a rope or nylon cord to it with a clove hitch. Hoist the bag up out of the reach of animals—at least twelve feet off the ground in bear country, and eight or more feet away from the trunks of trees. (To tie a clove hitch, see page 139.)

Menus with a minimum of perishable foods will reduce the challenges of storing and protecting provisions. Plan a meal with fresh meats, cheese, eggs, dairy products, and other perishable foods only if you can keep them properly chilled and out of the reach of animals.

COOK KIT

**BEFORE A CAMP-
OUT,** think about the
meals you have planned
and then figure out what
pots, pans, and utensils you
will need for cooking and serving your
food. By carrying only the kitchen gear
you need, you can keep your load light and
your camp simple.

Many troops have cook kits made just for camping. The
handles of frying pans might be removable, and the pots
might nest together for easy packing. While special cook kits
are convenient, you can also find the cooking gear you need at
garage sales and surplus stores.

Cooking gear used over campfires will be blackened by soot. Some
troops scrub off the soot after every use. Others clean the insides of their
pots and pans, but don't worry about the blackened outside surfaces.
Stowing a pot or pan in a plastic trash bag as you are breaking camp will
keep the soot from rubbing onto anything else in your pack.

PERSONAL EATING KIT

MOST CAMP MEALS can be eaten with simple, lightweight utensils.
Take an unbreakable plate and bowl, a spoon, and a sturdy drinking cup.
An insulated plastic mug keeps drinks and soup warm, and you won't
burn your lips on the rim.

**For an easy way to keep your knife, fork, and spoon
together, drill a hole in the handle of each one.
Run a string through and tie. It also makes
it easier to wash and dry them.**

BREAKFAST IN CAMP

GET YOUR DAY off to a strong start with a real stick-to-your-ribs breakfast. Healthy foods won't take long to prepare. Here are some suggestions. (All recipes are for **one** serving.)

FRUIT

Fresh Fruit

Apples, oranges, and bananas are available all year. Fresh peaches, melons, and berries are in the stores in the summer and fall.

Dried Fruit

Dried fruits, raisins, and banana chips are delicious just as they are. Or, you can soak them overnight or cook them with hot cereal.

Canned Fruit

Many kinds of fruit are available in small and medium-sized cans.

CEREAL

Hot cereal tastes great on chilly mornings. In the summer you might prefer cold cereal or granola with milk. Avoid flakes and other forms of cereal that will be crushed in your pack.

Oatmeal

For each serving, bring 1 cup of water to a boil. Add a pinch of salt. Stir in ½ cup of rolled oats, cover, and cook until ready. For extra flavor, drop some raisins or chopped fruit into the boiling water. Serve oatmeal with milk, brown sugar, butter, cinnamon, or a spoonful of jam.

Granola

Made of toasted oats, granola is terrific as an outdoor breakfast that doesn't require cooking. Different brands come mixed with nuts, raisins, dried fruit, and other good things. Try a bowl of granola with milk. By itself, granola also makes a tasty trail snack.

EGGS

Boiled Eggs

Gently lower eggs into boiling water with a spoon. Cook 5 minutes for soft-boiled, 10 minutes for hard-boiled. Cooling the eggs in cold water makes them easy to peel.

Fried Eggs

Heat a teaspoon of butter, margarine, or cooking oil in a pan. Carefully crack in 2 eggs. For "sunny-side up," fry them over low heat until the white becomes firm. Flip them and cook a while longer if you like your eggs "over easy."

Scrambled Eggs

Beat 2 eggs in a bowl. Add a pinch of salt and pepper. Heat a little butter, margarine, or cooking oil in a pan, then pour in the eggs and cook over low heat. Stir occasionally, scraping the bottom of the pan with a spatula. For variety, add shredded cheese and chopped vegetables such as onion, tomato, green pepper, and mushrooms to the eggs before you cook them.

BACON AND HAM

Fried Bacon

Put bacon slices in a pan and cook over low heat, turning as needed.

Fried Ham

Heat a little cooking oil, butter, or margarine in a pan. Put in slices of precooked ham and fry over low heat until the meat is lightly browned. Turn and fry the other side.

Many breakfast foods can be cooked on a griddle over a camp stove.

BREAKFASTS FROM THE GRIDDLE

Pancakes

Flapjacks are a favorite treat on mornings when you aren't in a hurry to break camp. They are best cooked in a heavy frying pan or on a griddle.

Follow the instructions on a box of pancake mix. For variety, add fresh berries, chopped fruit, or nuts to the batter.

Heat the griddle or pan and grease it with a little cooking oil, butter, or margarine. The griddle is hot enough when a drop of water will dance on the surface. Pour in just enough batter to form each cake and fry over medium heat. When the edges begin to brown and bubbles break in the center of the pancake, turn it and fry the other side. Serve with butter, syrup, or jam.

> **Homemade Pancake Mix**
>
> You can make your own pancake mix before leaving home by combining ½ cup white flour, ¼ cup powdered milk, ½ teaspoon baking powder, a pinch of salt, and ½ teaspoon sugar. In camp, prepare the batter by stirring in 1 egg, 2 tablespoons of cooking oil, and ¼ to ½ cup of water.

French Toast

Beat together 2 eggs, a pinch of salt, and ½ cup of milk. Add a dash of cinnamon. Dip both sides of a slice of bread in the egg mix and fry the bread as if it were a pancake. Two eggs are enough for 4 to 6 slices of French toast. Serve with butter and syrup or jam.

BREAKFAST DRINKS

Milk, cocoa, and fruit juices all go well with breakfast. Use fresh drinks, dried milk, cocoa mixes, or fruit juice powder.

LUNCH IN CAMP

AFTER A BUSY MORNING, you'll be more than ready for some lunch. You can make lunch right after breakfast and pack it along with you, or, if you'll be near the camp kitchen, you might want to cook a hot meal at lunchtime.

SANDWICHES

An easy way to serve sandwiches is to lay out the bread and fillings on a sheet of plastic and let each Scout build his own. Choose from peanut butter and jelly, cheese, luncheon meats, canned tuna or salmon, sliced tomatoes, hard-boiled eggs, pickles, and lettuce. Round out the meal with a glass of milk, a piece of fruit, and a few cookies.

HOT DISHES

A cup of soup will warm you on a chilly day. Make it from a can or a mix by following the instructions on the label. Try grilling a cheese sandwich by frying it on both sides in a little butter or margarine. If you have fresh foods, light a stove and fry a hamburger or boil some hot dogs.

BACKCOUNTRY LUNCH

On longer trips or when you don't want to carry fresh foods, rely on crackers, jelly or jam, hard cheese, salami, summer sausage, fruit, and small cans of chicken or tuna. Add powdered drink mix and a dessert for a lightweight meal that's full of nourishment.

SUPPER IN CAMP

A ONE-POT STEW makes an easy evening meal. Or you can prepare a main dish of meat, poultry, or fish; add some vegetables; and bake some biscuits. A dessert and something to drink will round out a feast to remember.

Many good recipes for camp supper follow. To make your planning easier, most of them are for one serving.

QUICK ONE-POT CAMP STEW

It's hard to beat a one-pot stew for speedy outdoor cooking and hearty dining. With a few ingredients and a little imagination, you can make it in dozens of different ways. Just prepare and combine one item from each of the following lists. Where amounts are not listed below, use the "Single Serving Sizes" chart on page 261.

Spaghetti	Tuna fish	Gravy mix, 1 packet (chicken, mushroom, onion)	Cooked vegetables
Macaroni	Canned chicken		Chopped cheese
Noodles	*or*	Spaghetti sauce, 4 to 8 ounces	Chopped nuts, 1 handful
Ramen noodles	Tofu, 3 ounces	Stroganoff sauce, 4 to 8 ounces	
	or		
	Textured vegetable protein, 3 ounces	Tomato sauce, 8-ounce can	

The vegetables can be eaten separately from the stew or drained and stirred right into the pot. Season to taste. Add a beverage, some bread, and a dessert to round out the meal.

MEAT

Grilling

Kindle a fire and let the flames die down. Place a wire grill over the coals. Lay the meat on the grill and adjust it to hold the meat close enough to the coals for moderate cooking. Grill hamburgers 3 to 4 minutes on each side. A 1-inch-thick steak needs about 8 to 10 minutes on each side. Cut into the center and be sure the meat is fully cooked.

Frying

Heat a spoonful of cooking oil in a fry pan. Ease in hamburger patties, pork chops, or steak, and cook over coals or a stove. Be sure that the meat is fully cooked. Pork must always be very well done.

Stew

For one serving use ¼-pound of beef cut into ¾-inch cubes. Rub flour into them and fry until brown in a pot with a few spoonfuls of cooking oil. Add enough water to cover the meat, put a lid on the pot, and simmer for 30 minutes. Add a chopped onion, carrot, and potato, and simmer 30 minutes more. Season with salt and pepper.

CHICKEN

Frying

Roll chicken pieces in flour. Fry in a few tablespoons of cooking oil until golden brown. Slowly add ½ cup of water, cover with a lid, and steam over low heat for about 20 minutes.

Broiling

Lay pieces of chicken on a wire grill. Cook over coals for 15 minutes on each side. Keep the chicken moist as it broils by brushing it with butter, margarine, or barbecue sauce.

FISH

When you've had some luck with your fishing pole, there are plenty of ways to turn your catch into dinner. First, clean each fish by slitting open the belly and pulling out the guts. If you want to remove the scales, scrape the skin with a knife from the tail toward the head. Burn the entrails or carry them home in a trash bag. Rinse the fish with water inside and out.

Frying

Roll each piece of fish in flour or cornmeal. Fry in a few spoonfuls of cooking oil until golden brown, turning the fish once. It won't take long.

Poaching

Drop fish into salted, boiling water. Simmer gently until the flesh can be picked from the bones.

SIDE DISHES

Vegetables

Boiled Vegetables

For fresh vegetables, choose from
among these single servings: 1 or
2 medium carrots, 2 ears of corn,
¼ head cabbage, or ½ cup of string
beans or shelled peas. Cover with
water and simmer over low heat.
Carrots cook in 25 minutes, corn
on the cob in 6 to 10 minutes, cab-

bage in 7 minutes, string beans in 30 minutes, and peas in 10 minutes. At
high elevations, add a few minutes to each cooking time.

Canned vegetables are already cooked. Pour them into a pan and heat
them in their own liquid.

Boiled Potatoes

Wash a couple of medium-sized potatoes, then peel them or leave the
skins on for the vitamins and minerals they contain. Cut the potatoes into
cubes and boil gently in a pot of water for about 20 minutes. Test with a
fork. If it goes in easily, the potatoes are done. Drain, season with salt
and pepper, and serve with a little butter or margarine.

Fried Potatoes

Boil several potatoes for about 10 minutes and then let them cool. Slice
the cold potatoes and fry in hot oil until they are brown. For extra flavor,
fry a chopped onion with the potatoes. Season with salt and pepper.

Mashed Potatoes

Boil 2 or 3 potatoes. Drain off the water and mash the potatoes. Add a
spoonful of butter or margarine and a dash of salt. For smoother potatoes, stir in 2 tablespoons of milk.

Pasta and Rice

Spaghetti

Bring a large pot of water to a boil. Add a tablespoon of cooking oil, butter, or margarine if you have it, then drop in 4 ounces of spaghetti. Boil for 5 to 10 minutes until tender. Drain and serve with spaghetti sauce.

How to Drain Pasta
Draining boiling water from a patrol's pot of pasta can be awkward in the field. Here are several ways to get the job done:
• **Use a slotted spoon to dip the pasta out of the water.**
• **Bring a colander from home. Hold the colander over the camp sump hole. Carefully pour the water through so that the colander catches the pasta but allows the water to go into the sump hole. (For more on sump holes, see page 283.)**
• **Protecting your hands with hot pads, place the pot on the ground beside the camp sump hole. As one Scout tips the pot, the other holds the lid in such a way that the water spills out but the pasta stays behind. Keep your face and hands away from steam rising from the pot, and don't rush.**

Macaroni

For each serving, stir 4 ounces of macaroni into a pot of boiling water. Boil for 10 to 15 minutes until done, then drain the water. Stir 2 ounces of cut-up cheese, 1 teaspoon of powdered milk, and a spoonful of margarine, butter, or olive oil into the cooked macaroni to make macaroni and cheese. Salt to taste.

Ramen Noodles

Ramen-style noodles come in a 3-ounce package just right for a single serving. Before you open the package, crush the noodles into small pieces. Tear open the wrapper and pour the noodles into 1½ cups of boiling water. Remove from heat and let stand 5 minutes until done.

Rice

Both white and brown rice are rich in minerals and fiber. For one serving, pour ½ cup of uncooked rice and 1 cup of cold water into a pot. Cover with a lid and bring to a boil. Reduce heat and simmer until done—about 10 minutes for white rice, 30 minutes or more for brown rice. There's no need to stir rice while it is cooking.

BREAD

Biscuits

Follow the directions on the package for mixing ½ cup of biscuit mix. Snape the dough into 3 or 4 biscuits about ½ inch thick. Place them on a greased pan and bake for 10 to 15 minutes in a stove-top oven or a reflector oven. Test by pushing a matchstick or wood shaving into a biscuit. The biscuits are done when the wood comes out clean.

> **Homemade Biscuit Mix**
>
> Prepare your own biscuit mix at home by stirring together 1 cup flour, ¼ teaspoon salt, and 1 teaspoon of baking powder. When you're ready to make biscuits, add 2 tablespoons of cooking oil and just enough water or milk to keep the dough together but not make it too sticky.

Dutch Oven Bread

Prepare enough mix for 8 biscuits. Use a shovel to move a scoop of coals to the side of the fire, then place the empty oven on them and let it warm. Arrange the unbaked biscuits in the oven. Replace the lid and shovel coals on top—three times as many coals on the lid as underneath the oven. Check after about 10 minutes, when the biscuits should be ready. Gloves and hot-pot tongs make it easier to handle a hot oven.

DUTCH OVEN

Dutch Ovens

A Dutch oven is a heavy, lidded pot that's perfect for baking bread, cobblers, and pies as well as cooking stews and beans. When made of iron, the oven must be "seasoned" before its first use.

Warm the oven and drop in a dab of butter or grease, then use a paper towel to spread it all over the inside of the oven. Treat the inside of the lid in the same way. The metal will be protected from rust, and foods you prepare are less likely to stick. Soap strips away the grease, so it is best to wash a Dutch oven in hot water only. Reseason your oven whenever it has been scrubbed with soap.

Stove-Top Oven Bread

Ovens for use with backpacking stoves are available at camp supply stores. Use them as you would an oven at home, keeping your stove flame low to allow for gentle baking.

Frying Pan Bread

Almost any bread or biscuit recipe can be cooked in a greased frying pan. Flatten the dough into a large pancake and fry it over the fire. A lid will hold in the heat. Turn the bread with a spatula to allow both sides to brown. The trick is to cook the dough slowly enough for the center to become done before the crust is too brown.

Dumplings

Another speedy way to fix bread is to drop small spoonfuls of biscuit dough right onto the top of a one-pot stew. Cover and let steam for about 10 minutes to make mouth-watering dumplings. Don't lift the lid until the dumplings are done.

Philmont Ranger Cobbler

The Dutch oven peach cobbler often baked by rangers at Philmont Scout Ranch makes enough hot, tasty dessert for an entire patrol. You will need the following ingredients:

2 16-ounce cans of sliced peaches in heavy syrup

2 cups biscuit mix

½ cup sugar

½ teaspoon cinnamon

Preheat a Dutch oven over a bed of coals. Gently pour into the oven one can of peaches and syrup. Drain the syrup from the second can into the first and save it. Place the peaches from the second can into the oven. Sprinkle ¼ teaspoon of cinnamon over the fruit.

Combine the biscuit mix with the sugar, ¼ teaspoon of cinnamon, and enough of the reserved syrup to make a soft dough. Layer the dough mixture over the fruit in the oven.

Place the lid on the oven, cover it with coals, and bake until the dough is golden brown.

DESSERTS

Fruit or cookies finish off a meal nicely. Pudding mixes come in many flavors, and instant pudding requires no cooking. Cobbler, brownies, and other baked desserts are always a treat in camp.

COOKING IN ALUMINUM FOIL

WANT TO LEAVE the pots and pans at home? Then give aluminum foil cooking a try. Simply wrap food in a piece of heavy-duty foil and fold over the edges so the steam can't escape. Place the foil package on a bed of coals and turn it several times during the cooking. When you unwrap your dinner, you can eat right out of the foil.

Foil cooking is possible because aluminum doesn't burn. That also means you will want to carry used foil home for recycling or disposal. Since most ingredients are fresh, foil meals are most appropriate for Scout cookouts or the first meal of a campout.

Hamburger

Shape 4 ounces of hamburger into a patty. Cut a medium-sized potato and carrot into thin strips. Peel and slice a small onion. Arrange all the ingredients on a square of foil and sprinkle lightly with salt. Close the foil, lay the package on the coals, and cook for about 15 minutes.

Stew

Cut 4 ounces of beef or lamb into cubes. Thinly slice a potato, carrot, and small onion, and arrange the slices on the foil. Sprinkle with salt. Add several tablespoons of water and fold up the foil. Cook on the coals for about 20 minutes.

Chicken

Smear chicken pieces with butter or margarine. Salt lightly and wrap each in a separate piece of foil. Turn them several times as they cook over the coals for about 20 minutes.

Potato

Pierce the skin of a potato in several places, then wrap in foil. Bury it in the coals for about 30 or 40 minutes.

Corn on the Cob

Dab butter or margarine on an ear of corn, wrap it in foil, and roast for 10 minutes on the coals.

Fish

Wrap fresh fish by itself in foil, or along with some finely chopped onion and lemon. Bake on the coals about 3 minutes per side for a small fish, 10 minutes or more on each side for a whopper.

Fruit

Cut the core out of a raw apple and replace it with a pat of butter, a few raisins, some cinnamon, and a teaspoon of brown sugar. Wrap in foil and bake for 30 minutes.

COOKING WITHOUT UTENSILS

THE SECRET to cooking a meal without pots, pans, *or* foil is a good bed of hot coals.

Roast Potatoes

Coat the potato with a thick layer of mud and bury it in the coals. Bake 30 to 40 minutes. The mud will become caked and hard, but the potato inside should come out just right.

Roast Corn

Open the husks and remove the thread-like silk. Reclose the husks, dip the ears in water, then place them on the coals. Roast about 8 minutes, turning them often as they cook.

Broiled Steak

Find a long, green, forked stick. Trim off any leaves and twigs. Bend the branches of the fork into the shape of a tennis racquet and twist the branches around each other to hold them in place, forming the frame of your broiler. Weave green sticks across the broiler frame. Lay a steak on them and hold it down with more sticks anchored to the broiler. You can also use the broiler to toast slices of bread.

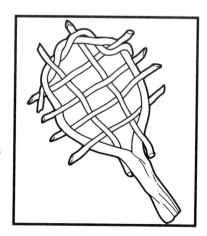

Kabob

Start with 1-inch cubes of beef, lamb, or ham. Add mushrooms and chunks of tomato, onion, green pepper, pineapple, or zucchini. Slide the pieces onto a thin green stick and broil them a few inches above the coals for 10 to 15 minutes, turning slowly. (Marinating the meat in Italian dressing for several hours before cooking will tenderize the meat and add flavor.)

Fish

Run a sharp kabob stick into the flesh along the length of the spine of a small trout. Or, tie the fish to the stick with several wraps of sturdy string. Hold it over the coals and cook for a few minutes. The fins and skin will pull off, leaving the tender meat beneath.

Chicken

Skewer a small whole chicken onto a sturdy green stick about 3 feet long. Tie the legs together with cord and rub the skin with butter or margarine. Rest the ends of the stick on rocks or logs on either side of the coals. Turn the stick occasionally so that the chicken will brown evenly. Allow about 1 hour of cooking time.

Bread Twist

Roll stiff biscuit dough into the shape of a long sausage. Find a clean stick as thick as an ax handle and twist the dough around it. Lean the stick over a bed of coals and turn occasionally until the baking is done.

Bread Cup

Instead of twisting the dough around the stick, mold it onto the end of the stick, then bake it over the coals. Slip it off for a bread cup you can stuff with sandwich fillings.

SHARING KITCHEN DUTIES

WHEN YOU'RE USING the buddy system, both of you can pitch in and help with all the cooking and cleanup. Or one can act as cook while the other cares for the stove or fire, brings in water, and washes the pots. Switch jobs at each meal so you each have a chance to do everything.

In larger groups, write down a duty roster. A third of the group cooks, a third gathers water and firewood or tends to the stoves or fire, and the rest do the cleanup. During a one-night campout, each Scout can have the same job for all the meals and then move to a new spot on the roster for the next outing.

CLEANING UP AFTER MEALS

DEALING WITH LEFTOVERS

Carry food scraps home in a trash bag or burn them in a hot campfire by adding them to the flames a little at a time. You can burn wastepaper, too, but don't put plastic bags into a fire; burning plastic can release toxic gases into the air.

Don't bury leftover food or scatter it in the woods. Animals will almost always find it, and it is not healthy for them to eat. Food scraps can also draw animals close to campsites where they might lose their fear of humans. That can be dangerous for them and for you.

Wash out jars and cans, and carry them home for recycling. Save space by cutting out the ends of cans and then flattening them.

DISHWASHING

Whether you cook with a stove or over an open fire, put on a pot of water before you serve a meal. That way you'll have hot dishwater by the time you finish eating.

Begin cleanup by setting out three pots:

- *Wash pot*—contains hot water with a few drops of biodegradable soap
- *Cold-rinse pot*—cold water with a sanitizing tablet or a few drops of bleach to kill bacteria
- *Hot-rinse pot*—clear, hot water

Each Scout can wash his own eating gear. If each Scout also does one pot, pan, or cooking utensil, the work will be finished in no time at all. Wipe plates first to keep the dishwater as clean as possible. Use hot-pot tongs to dip utensils in the hot rinse. When you're sure no soap is left on them, lay the washed items on a plastic ground cloth and let them air dry.

Before cooking over a wood fire, smear a film of liquid biodegradable soap on the outside of your pots. Soot will wash off more easily.

HOT

COLD

HOT

DISHWATER DISPOSAL

During campouts lasting no more than a couple of days, strain any food bits out of your dishwater and put them in your trash. Carry the wash and rinse water away from camp and at least seventy-five steps from any streams or lakes. Give it a good fling, spreading it over a wide area.

For longer stays at one site, dig a *sump hole* at the edge of camp and at least seventy-five steps from streams, lakes, or other open water. It should be about one foot across and two feet deep. Place a piece of window screen across it and pour wash and rinse water into the sump through the screen. The screen will catch food particles so that you can shake them into a fire or trash bag. Fill the sump hole when you break camp, and replace any ground cover.

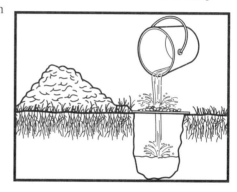

You can also make a strainer by punching small holes in a plastic bag and filling it with pine needles. Pour dirty dishwater through the bag and the needles will strain out food particles. Carry the bag of needles out of the backcountry with the rest of your trash.

Keep Soap and Detergent Away from Open Water

Many soaps, detergents, and shampoos contain chemicals that encourage algae to grow. Algae can crowd out the native plants, making it harder for fish and other animals to survive. Soap and detergent can also leave an oily film in the water that can harm tiny aquatic life.

Never put anything into the water that you wouldn't be willing to drink as it floats away.

SCOUT SERVICE

DOING YOUR PART

FIRST AID

TRAILHEAD

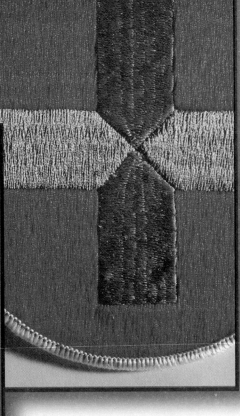

FIRST AID

A baseball hits your teammate in the face and his nose begins to bleed. *What do you do?*

An automobile knocks a woman to the ground. Blood spurts from a gash in her arm, and her leg looks broken. *What do you do?*

A child feels sick. There's a box of poison spilled on the floor. *What do you do?*

A hiker in a T-shirt and shorts is wet and cold. He begins shivering and stumbles. *What do you do?*

What you do is give first aid.

"**First Aid must be both expert and friendly. You must know what has to be done and how to do it quickly and neatly.**

No bungling!"

First Aid merit badge pamphlet, 1939

WHAT IS FIRST AID?

FIRST AID is the first help given the victim of an accident or other health emergency. If more attention is needed, first aid treatment keeps an injured or ill person as safe as possible until trained medical personnel arrive.

FIRST AID
MERIT BADGE

The first aid you learn while earning the Tenderfoot, Second Class, and First Class badges and the First Aid merit badge is a good introduction to basic ways of sizing up an emergency and providing treatment. In years to come, you might want to enroll in more advanced first aid courses taught by the Red Cross and by other safety and outdoors-related organizations. There is always more to learn, and keeping your skills sharp will require regular practice and review.

WHAT FIRST AID SHOULD DO

• **Stop life-threatening dangers.**

• **Protect an injured or ill person from further harm.**

• **Get proper medical help for the victim.**

PERSONAL FIRST AID KIT

Carrying a few first aid items on hikes and campouts will allow you to treat scratches, blisters, and
other minor injuries, and to provide initial care
for more serious emergencies. Everything will fit
in a self-sealing plastic bag. Get in the habit of
taking along your personal first aid kit whenever
you set out on a Scout adventure:

PERSONAL FIRST AID KIT		
Adhesive bandages	6	
Sterile gauze pads, 3-by-3-inch	2	
Adhesive tape	1 small roll	
Moleskin, 3-by-6-inch	1	
Soap	1 small bar	
Antiseptic	1 small tube	
Scissors	1 pair	
Latex gloves	1 pair	
Mouth-barrier device for rescue breathing or CPR	1	
Plastic goggles or other eye protection	1	
Pencil and paper	1 each	

PATROL/TROOP FIRST AID KIT

A complete first aid kit will provide a patrol or troop with supplies to treat a wide range of injuries. Items can be carried by one Scout in a fanny pack that is easy for everyone to recognize. At a minimum, the kit should contain the following:

PATROL/TROOP FIRST AID KIT		
Roller bandage, 2-inch	1	
Roller bandage, 1-inch	2	
Adhesive tape, 1-inch	1 roll	
Alcohol swabs	24	
Assorted adhesive bandages	1 box	
Elastic bandages, 3-inch-wide	2	
Sterile gauze pads, 3-by-3-inch	12	
Moleskin, 3-by-6-inch	4	
Gel pads for blisters and burns	2 packets	
Antiseptic	1 tube	
Triangular bandages	4	
Soap	1 small bar	
Scissors	1 pair	
Tweezers	1 pair	
Safety pins	12	
Splint	1	
Latex gloves	6 pairs	
Plastic goggles/safety glasses	1 pair	
Mouth-barrier device for rescue breathing or CPR	1	
Pencil and paper	1 each	

ACCIDENT SCENES

THE SCENE OF A BAD ACCIDENT can be scary. Injured persons might be screaming. Witnesses might be too stunned to help. Try to stay calm and use the skills you have in the best way you can.

If more experienced first-aiders take charge, tell them you are a Scout and are ready to help. They might ask you to gather first aid supplies, look after persons who are not injured, go for help, or simply stay out of the way. Whatever your role, be positive. Your confidence could help others lose their fear.

FIRST THINGS FIRST
Treat accident victims by performing these steps in this order:
1. Approach with care. Is the scene safe? Guard against being injured yourself.
2. Treat *hurry cases.* Hurry cases are conditions that threaten a victim's life:
• Stopped breathing
• No heartbeat
• Severe bleeding
• Internal poisoning
As you begin, send someone to call for help.
3. Treat every accident victim for shock.
4. Examine every victim for other injuries that might require first aid.
5. Plan what to do next. If help is coming, keep the victim comfortable. Watch for any changes in his or her condition and treat accordingly.

APPROACH CAREFULLY

Look around to see what caused the accident, then be sure you don't get hurt as you approach the victim. Be aware of slippery footing, steep slopes, electrical wires, traffic, and any other hazards.

GET HELP

Help is usually just a telephone call away. In most parts of the United States you can reach emergency services by calling 911, or by dialing 0 for an operator. Take a few minutes now to look in the front pages of your telephone book for information on contacting emergency services in your area.

**DIAL
911**
EMERGENCY

**DIAL
1-800-764-7661**
POISON CENTER

Backcountry adventures can take you far from telephones. An injured person who can walk alone or with some support might be able to hike to a road. A large group of Scouts might be able to build a stretcher and carry an accident victim. If injuries are serious, though, it might be best to treat the victim where he is and send two or more Scouts for help. Write down the following information, and send the note with the messengers:

- Location of the victim

- Description of the injuries or illness

- What time the injury or illness occurred

- Any treatment the victim has received

- Number of people with the victim and their general skill level

- What special assistance and equipment might be needed, including food, shelter, or care for nonvictims

HURRY CASES

MOST FIRST AID YOU USE will be for minor injuries—a scrape, a bruise, a sore ankle. You will have plenty of time to decide what to do and then to do it.

However, stopped breathing, no heartbeat, severe bleeding, and internal poisoning are called *hurry cases* because they pose an immediate threat to a victim's life. They require quick action on the part of a first-aider.

Whenever you come upon an injured person, make a quick assessment of his condition. The assessment should take no more than fifteen to twenty seconds:

Is he breathing? If he seems to be unconscious, pat him on the shoulder and ask him if he is all right. Place your ear near his mouth and nose where you can hear and feel the movement of air. Watch for his chest to rise and fall.

Is his heart beating? Feel for a pulse in the neck artery beneath his ear and just under his jawbone.

Is there severe bleeding? Open rain gear or any outer clothing that might be hiding wounds from your view.

Is there evidence of poisoning? Consider the victim's appearance and behavior and any clues suggesting what he might have swallowed.

Once you have completed the quick assessment, begin treatment and have someone telephone or go for help. Several people working together can treat different symptoms. When you are the only person providing first aid, start by treating the conditions that pose the greatest threat to life.

STOPPED BREATHING

A human brain will survive without oxygen no more than about five minutes before suffering serious damage. At normal temperatures, a person cannot live without air for more than ten minutes. Rescue breathing can keep someone alive until he recovers or help arrives.

FIRST AID FOR STOPPED BREATHING

1. Open the airway:

a. The *airway* is the passage that allows air entering the mouth or nose to reach the lungs. A person cannot breathe if his airway is blocked by the back of the tongue, a chunk of food, or anything else.

b. If a victim is unconscious, place him on his back. Clear his tongue from his airway by pressing on his forehead with one hand and lifting his chin with the other to tilt his head back. (If you think his neck might be injured, keep his head still and thrust his jaw forward.)

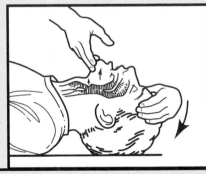

c. Look in his mouth for gum, food, or other obstructions. Remove them by sweeping them out with your index finger.

Someone who is choking on food might grasp his throat to signal that he is unable to breathe. Treat by performing the Heimlich maneuver (see pages 296–97).

d. Protect the airway of any accident victim. If he begins to vomit, turn him on his side so that the vomit comes out his mouth rather than getting into his lungs.

2. If the airway seems to be open and the victim is still not inhaling and exhaling, begin rescue breathing:

a. Place a mouth-barrier device over the victim's mouth. That will protect both of you from orally transmitted diseases.

b. While maintaining the head-tilt or jaw-thrust position, pinch the nostrils, seal your mouth over the victim's mouth, and blow into it to fill his lungs. (For a child, seal your mouth over both the mouth and nose, then breathe gently.) Watch to see if the chest rises.

c. Remove your mouth and take another breath. Look for the victim's chest to fall as he exhales.

d. Repeat every 5 seconds for any-one over 9 years of age, every 3 seconds for anyone 9 or under.

If the victim's chest does not rise and fall, no air is reaching the lungs. Follow these steps:

e. Reposition his head and jaw so that the tongue does not block the airway.

f. Check again for obstructions in his mouth.

g. Perform the Heimlich maneuver to remove anything lodged in the throat.

Resume rescue breathing. Continue until a medic tells you to stop or it becomes physically impossible for you to keep going.

Techniques for performing rescue breathing are constantly being improved. Check with your local Red Cross chapter for current methods and training opportunities.

Heimlich Maneuver

During a meal, a man lurches from his chair and clutches his throat. His face turns red and he seems unable to breathe.

Ask, "Are you choking?" If the victim nods yes and he cannot speak, cough, or breathe, perform the *Heimlich maneuver.*

Do not interfere with a person who is conscious and can speak, cough, or breathe. He is still getting air into his lungs. Encourage him to cough up the object, and be ready to administer first aid if it is needed. Have someone call for help.

HOW TO DO THE HEIMLICH MANEUVER

Food caught in the throat is like a cork stuck in the neck of a plastic bottle. Nothing can get in, but squeeze the bottle the right way and the cork will pop out. That's the principle behind the Heimlich maneuver. Here's how to do it:

1. Stand behind the victim. Put your arms around his waist and clasp your hands together. The knuckle of one thumb should be just above his navel but below his rib cage.

2. Thrust your clasped hands inward and upward with enough force to pop loose the obstruction.

3. Repeat this Heimlich maneuver until the obstruction clears or medical help arrives.

If a choking person is very large or has lost consciousness, use this version of the Heimlich maneuver:

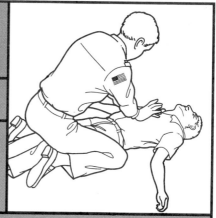

1. Lay him on the floor and sit straddling his thighs.

2. Place the heel of one hand on the victim's upper abdomen, slightly above his navel but below the rib cage.

3. Place your other hand on top of the first and press upward with quick thrusts.

4. With your index finger, probe the mouth of an unconscious victim to remove any obstructions. Be ready to start rescue breathing.

5. Repeat this Heimlich maneuver until the obstruction pops loose or medical help arrives.

If **you** ever choke on food and cannot breathe, clutch your throat with your hand. That's the universal sign for choking, and it might bring someone to your aid. If there is no one nearby, perform the Heimlich maneuver on yourself by pulling your fist into your upper abdomen, or you can bend over the back of a chair and force it against your belly.

Thrusts to the abdomen can cause rib fractures and other injuries. Use only mannequins or other training devices to practice or demonstrate Heimlich maneuvers.

NO HEARTBEAT

An accident or medical condition that causes a person to stop breathing can also stop his or her heart. You can try to provide both oxygen and blood circulation for such a victim by performing *cardiopulmonary resuscitation (CPR)*.

Learning CPR requires careful instruction from a certified teacher. Perhaps you can learn and practice CPR at Scout meetings. The Red Cross offers CPR classes, too. Your Scout leaders can help you find training to learn this lifesaving skill.

Cardio- **means "heart," and** *pulmonary* **comes from the Latin word for "lung." Thus, cardiopulmonary resuscitation includes breathing for a victim and keeping his or her blood circulating.**

Heart Attack

Heart attack is one of the major causes of death in the United States. Exercise, a good diet, and avoiding tobacco and drugs will help you keep your own heart healthy. First aid training will prepare you to help someone else who is having heart trouble.

Five Common Warning Signals of Heart Attack

1. Uncomfortable pressure, squeezing, fullness, or pain in the center of the chest behind the breastbone. The feeling might spread to the shoulders, arms, and neck. It can last several minutes or longer, and it might come and go. It isn't always severe. (Sharp, stabbing twinges of pain usually are **not** signs of heart attack.)

2. Unusual sweating—for instance, perspiring even though a room is cool.

3. Nausea—stomach distress with an urge to vomit.

4. Shortness of breath.

5. A feeling of weakness.

Should anyone display these symptoms, get medical attention for the victim right away. Be ready to begin CPR if his or her heartbeat and breathing stop.

SEVERE BLEEDING

A broken window. A car crash. A careless moment with a knife, ax, or power tool. Suddenly blood is spurting from a nasty wound. Without quick first aid, a person suffering a severe cut can bleed to death in a matter of minutes.

BOY SCOUTS OF AMERICA RECOMMENDATION

Treat all blood as if it were contaminated with blood-borne viruses. Do not use bare hands to stop bleeding; always use a protective barrier, preferably latex gloves; always wash exposed skin areas with hot water and soap immediately after treating the victim. The following equipment is to be included in all first aid kits and used when rendering first aid to those in need:

- **Latex gloves, to be used when stopping bleeding or dressing wounds**

- **A mouth-barrier device for rendering rescue breathing or CPR**

- **Plastic goggles or other eye protection to prevent a victim's blood from getting into the rescuer's eyes in the event of serious arterial bleeding**

- **Antiseptic for sterilizing or cleaning exposed skin areas, especially if there is no soap or water available**

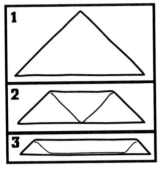

Cravat Bandage

Make a cravat bandage from a Scout neckerchief or triangular bandage *(1)* by folding the point down to the long edge *(2)*. Finish by folding two more times to the long edge *(3)*. Tie all bandages in place with square knots.

FIRST AID FOR SEVERE BLEEDING

1. Direct pressure on a wound will stop most bleeding. Put on latex gloves from your first aid kit. With a clean cloth or sterile dressing as a pad, use the palm of your hand to apply firm pressure directly over the wound. Don't waste time—when clean material is not close by, use a neckerchief, shirt, or whatever else you can reach.

2. While pressing on the wound, raise the injury above the level of the victim's heart.

3. Direct pressure is almost always the treatment of choice. Bleeding can sometimes be further slowed by pressing hard on an arterial pressure point in the victim's armpit or groin. Try using pressure points if direct pressure over broken bones will cause further injury or if the nature of a wound makes direct pressure ineffective.

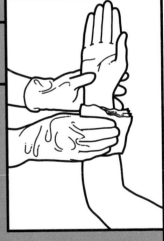

4. Don't remove a direct pressure pad that has become soaked with blood. Instead, place a fresh pad over the first one and continue applying pressure.

5. When the bleeding has stopped, hold the pad in place with a cravat bandage, an athletic wrap, strips torn from clothing, or something else close at hand. Bind the pad firmly but not so tightly that circulation is cut off. If the bandage is on an arm or a leg, periodically feel for a pulse further out on the limb— at the wrist or just behind the anklebone. No pulse is an indication the bandage is too tight. In all cases of serious bleeding, get the victim under medical supervision.

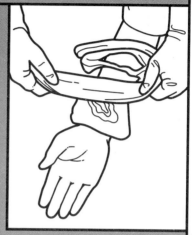

6. If you have touched any blood or other bodily fluids, wash your skin with soap and water or cleanse with an antiseptic as soon as possible, and change out of clothing that might have come in contact with blood.

INTERNAL POISONING

Among children, poisoning is the most frequent cause of accidental death. Young children will swallow almost anything: fuels, poisons, insecticides, battery acid, peeling wall paint, pills from a medicine cabinet, weed killer from garden supplies. If you see items in your home that could be dangerous to a child, move them to safe storage.

Some mushrooms, fungi, berries, and leaves are poisonous if swallowed. Eat no wild plants unless you are certain they will not harm you. Overdoses of drugs can also be poisoning emergencies.

A poisoning victim might suffer nausea and stomach pains. He might vomit and there might be burns around his mouth. His breathing might be different from normal. Often the most important sign of poisoning is the presence of the poison—open pill bottles, spilled household cleansers, or other evidence of what might have been swallowed.

FIRST AID FOR INTERNAL POISONING

1. Immediately take any poison containers to a telephone. Call the poison control center toll free at 1-800-764-7661, or your local emergency center at 911, or an operator, and follow the instructions you are given.

2. Treat the victim for shock and monitor breathing. Do not give anything by mouth unless you are told to do so by medical professionals.

3. Save any vomit (use a bowl, cook pot, or plastic bag). It will help a physician identify the poison and give the right treatment.

SHOCK

When a person is injured or under great stress, his circulatory system might not provide enough blood to all parts of his body. That's called *shock*. A shock victim could have some, all, or none of these symptoms:

- A feeling of weakness
- Confusion, fear, dizziness
- Skin that is moist, clammy, cool, and pale
- A quick, weak pulse
- Shallow, rapid, and irregular breathing
- Nausea and vomiting
- Extreme thirst

Injuries are almost always accompanied by some degree of shock, but the victim might not be affected right away. Treat every accident victim for shock, even if no symptoms appear. Prompt first aid could prevent shock from setting in.

FIRST AID FOR SHOCK
1. Eliminate the cause of shock by restoring breathing and heartbeat, controlling bleeding, relieving severe pain, and treating wounds.
2. Make sure the airway stays open for breathing.
3. Have the injured person lie down. Raise his feet ten to twelve inches to move blood from his legs to his vital organs.
4. Keep him warm by placing plenty of blankets, coats, or sleeping bags under and over him.
5. Call or send someone for emergency medical care.

Never leave an accident victim alone. Fear and uncertainty can increase shock. In a calm voice, assure him everything is being done to care for him. A person who appears to be unconscious might still be able to hear you—keep letting him know you are there.

OTHER FIRST AID CASES

FAINTING

Fainting occurs when the brain does not receive enough oxygen. It can be caused by getting up too quickly, standing too long, or by fright, bad news, or breathing foul air. A person about to faint might become pale and dizzy, then fall to the ground.

FIRST AID FOR FAINTING

Keep the victim lying down until he recovers. Loosen his collar and raise his feet. If he does not improve right away, treat for shock and get medical help.

Anytime you feel faint, sit down and put your head between your knees, or lie down and raise your legs.

CUTS AND SCRATCHES

Cuts and scratches are *wounds*—openings in the skin and tissues that can allow germs to enter the body and cause infection.

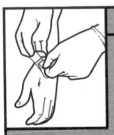

FIRST AID FOR SMALL WOUNDS

Wash scratches and minor cuts with soap and water. Applying antiseptic can help prevent infection. Keep the wound clean with an adhesive bandage. On camping trips, clean and rebandage small wounds daily.

FIRST AID FOR LARGER CUTS

Treat large cuts by using direct pressure to stop bleeding, then keep the wound as clean as you can to limit infection. Cover an open wound with a sterile gauze pad or clean cloth folded into a pad. Hold the pad in position with tape, a cravat bandage, or other binder.

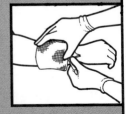

Anyone suffering a serious wound should be treated for shock and seen by a physician.

PUNCTURE WOUNDS

Puncture wounds can be caused by pins, splinters, nails, and fishhooks. All can be dangerous because they allow germs into a wound that is hard to clean.

FIRST AID FOR PUNCTURE WOUNDS

Encourage the wound to bleed to help remove anything that might have been forced inside. Use tweezers sterilized over a flame or in boiling water to pull out splinters, bits of glass, or other objects you can see. Wash the area with soap and water, apply a sterile bandage, and get the victim to a doctor.

REMOVING A FISHHOOK

Someone snagged by a fishhook should cut the line and, if possible, let a doctor remove the hook from the flesh. In the backcountry you might have to do the job yourself:

1. Push the hook farther in until the barb comes through the skin.

2. Snip off the barb with pliers, wire cutters, or nail clippers.

3. Ease the shank of the hook back out through the point of entry.

4. Wash and bandage the wound.

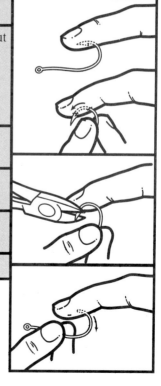

NOSEBLEED

A nosebleed can look bad, but it will usually stop in just a few minutes.

FIRST AID FOR NOSEBLEED

Have the victim sit up and lean forward to prevent blood from draining into his or her throat. Pinch the nostrils together to maintain pressure on the flow. Apply a cool, wet cloth to the victim's nose and face.

If bleeding is severe or if there are other injuries to the face and head, position the victim to keep blood out of his airway. Treat for shock and call for help.

BURNS AND SCALDS

A spark from a campfire, boiling water spilled from a pot, rays of the sun on bare skin, a bolt of lightning—the causes of burns are many. Treatment for a burn depends upon its degree.

FIRST AID FOR BURNS AND SCALDS

Get the victim away from the source of heat that caused the burn and treat any hurry cases—stopped breathing, no heartbeat, or severe bleeding. Then try to assess the degree of burn:

First-Degree Burn

A mild burn will cause the skin to be tender and it might also become red. Treat immediately by holding the burn under cold water or applying cool, wet compresses until there is little or no pain.

Second-Degree Burn

If blisters form, the burn is more serious. Place the injury in cool water until the pain goes away. Let the burn dry, then protect it with a sterile gauze pad. Do not break the blisters—that makes

them open wounds. **Do not apply butter, creams, ointments, or sprays**—they are difficult to remove and can slow the healing process.

Third-Degree Burn

This is the most severe burn. Skin might be burned away and some flesh will be charred. Since nerves are damaged, the victim might feel no pain. **Do not try to remove any clothing,** as it might be sticking to the flesh. **Do not apply creams, ointments, or sprays.** Wrap a clean sheet around the victim, treat him or her for shock, and get immediate medical attention.

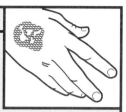

Do not apply salves, ointments, jellies, or anything else to burns. The one exception is the gel pad, a sterile dressing made especially to cover first-, second-, or third-degree burns. The gel pad provides pain relief and helps shield wounds from infection. Physicians can remove it easily when further treatment is required.

SUNBURN

Sunburn is a common injury among people who enjoy being outdoors. Repeated burns can cause long-term skin damage and the potential for skin cancer. People with lighter skin are most at risk, though others are not immune. Prevent sunburn by using plenty of sunscreen with a sun protection factor (SPF) rating of at least 15. Reapply sunscreen after swimming or if you are perspiring. A broad-brimmed hat, long-sleeved shirt, and long pants provide even more protection.

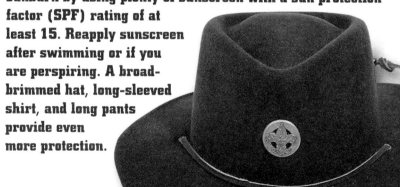

BLISTERS ON THE FOOT AND HAND

Blisters are pockets of fluid that form as the skin's way of protecting itself from friction. Blisters on the feet are common injuries among hikers. Avoid getting blisters by wearing shoes or boots that fit, by changing your socks if they become sweaty or wet, and by paying attention to how your feet feel.

FIRST AID FOR BLISTERS

A *hot spot* is a warning that a blister might be forming. As soon as you notice it, treat a hot spot or blister with a "doughnut bandage" to relieve the pressure on your skin.

Cut moleskin in the shape of a doughnut and fit it around the injury. Shape several more "doughnuts" and stack them on top of the first. The doughnut bandage will keep pressure off the injury.

A gel pad made of the same material used to treat burns can be applied directly over a blister to reduce friction and speed healing. Follow the instructions on the package. Used together, a gel pad and a moleskin doughnut provide maximum relief for blisters and hot spots.

If you must continue hiking even though you think the blister will break, it might be a good idea to drain the fluid. First, wash the skin with soap and water, then sterilize a pin in the flame of a match. Prick the blister near its lower edge and press out the liquid. Keep the wound clean with a sterile bandage or gel pad and surround it with a doughnut bandage.

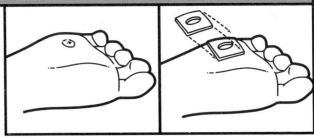

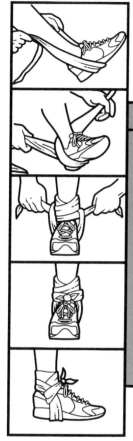

SPRAINED ANKLE

A sprained ankle occurs when you bend your foot far enough to strain tendons and ligaments. Minor sprains cause only mild discomfort, but more serious twists can temporarily disable you.

FIRST AID FOR A SPRAINED ANKLE

If you suffer an ankle sprain during a hike and must keep walking, don't remove your shoe or boot. It will support your ankle, and if you do take it off, the injury might swell so much you won't be able to get your footwear back on. Reinforce the ankle by wrapping it, boot and all, with a triangular bandage, neckerchief, or some other strip of cloth.

As soon as you no longer need to walk, take off your shoe and rest with your leg raised. Reduce swelling with cold, wet towels or an ice pack. The compression of an athletic bandage might also help. Seek medical care.

HEAD INJURIES

A head injury can be very serious and should be handled with extreme urgency and care. A cut to the head can cause severe bleeding; call for help immediately. If the victim is bleeding but conscious, have the victim hold a clean cloth over the wound and apply pressure. Keep the victim as comfortable as possible and wait for help to arrive. Use the triangular bandage, described below, when the entire scalp must be covered.

BITES OR STINGS OF INSECTS, TICKS, CHIGGERS, AND SPIDERS

The bites or stings of insects, spiders, chiggers, and ticks can be painful. Some can cause infection.

FIRST AID FOR BITES AND STINGS

Bee and Wasp Stings

Scrape away a bee or wasp stinger with the edge of a knife blade. Don't try to squeeze it out. That will force more venom into the skin from the sac attached to the stinger. An ice pack might reduce pain and swelling.

Tick Bites

Ticks are small, hard-shelled arachnids that bury their heads in the skin of warm-blooded vertebrates. Protect yourself whenever you are in tick-infested woodlands and fields by wearing long pants and a long-sleeved shirt. Button your collar and tuck the cuffs of your pants into your boots or socks. Inspect yourself daily, especially the hairy parts of your body, and immediately remove any ticks you find. If a tick has attached itself, grasp it with tweezers close to the skin and gently pull until it comes loose. Don't squeeze, twist, or jerk the tick, as that could leave its mouth parts in the skin. Wash the wound with soap and water and apply antiseptic. After dealing with a tick, thoroughly wash your hands.

Chigger Bites

Chiggers are almost invisible. They burrow into skin pores, causing itching and small welts. Try not to scratch chigger bites. You might find some relief by covering chigger bites with calamine lotion or by dabbing them with clear fingernail polish.

Spider Bites

The bite of a female black widow spider can cause redness and sharp pain at the wound site. The victim might suffer sweating, nausea and vomiting, stomach pain and cramps, severe muscle pain and spasms, and shock. Breathing might become difficult.

The bite of a brown recluse spider doesn't always hurt right away, but within two to eight hours there can be pain, redness, and swelling at the wound. An open sore is likely to develop. The victim might suffer fever, chills, nausea, vomiting, joint pain, and a faint rash.

Victims of spider bites should be treated for shock, then seen by a physician as soon as possible.

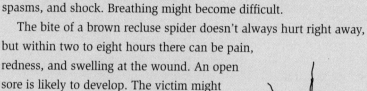

JELLYFISH STINGS

The jellyfish and Portuguese man-of-war have stinging cells on their tentacles. When touched, the toxins in those cells attach to the skin and cause a sharp burning pain.

FIRST AID FOR JELLYFISH STINGS

Call for medical help immediately. People who are allergic to jellyfish stings might go into deep shock. Do not wash the affected area with fresh water, as that will cause the release of more toxin. Instead, soak the injury for thirty minutes (unless medical help arrives sooner) in alcohol or vinegar, then use tweezers to remove the remaining tentacles.

CHAPTER 11

312

When helping victims of bites or stings, do whatever you must to avoid being stung or bitten yourself. A first-aider who becomes injured could greatly complicate any emergency situation.

ANIMAL BITES

If the bite of a dog, cat, or any other warm-blooded animal breaks the skin, it is not an ordinary wound. The animal might have *rabies,* a deadly disease that can be transmitted through the saliva of some mammals. The only way to learn if an animal is infected is to have it caught and tested by medical experts.

FIRST AID FOR ANIMAL BITES

1. Scrub the bite with soap and water to remove saliva.

2. Cover the wound with a sterile bandage and get the victim to a doctor.

3. Do not put yourself at risk by trying to catch the animal. Call police, rangers, or animal control officers who are trained to do the job safely.

SNAKEBITES

Snakes are common in many parts of the country, but bites from them are rare. Snakes try to avoid humans, and normally strike only when they sense danger. Snakebites seldom result in death.

The bite of a nonpoisonous snake causes only minor puncture wounds.

Red and black—friendly jack

Red and yellow—deadly fellow

The bite of a poisonous snake can cause sharp, burning pain. The area around the bite might swell and become discolored; however, a poisonous snake does not inject venom every time it bites.

Use a hiking stick to poke among stones and brush ahead of you when you walk through areas where snakes are common. Watch where you put your hands as you collect firewood or climb over rocks and logs.

FIRST AID FOR NONPOISONOUS SNAKEBITES

The bite of a nonpoisonous snake requires only ordinary first aid for small wounds—scrubbing with soap and water, then treating with an antiseptic. Snakes are not warm blooded, so they cannot carry rabies.

FIRST AID FOR POISONOUS SNAKEBITES

1. Get the victim under medical care as soon as possible so that physicians can neutralize the venom.

2. Remove rings and other jewelry that might cause problems if the area around a bite swells.

3. If the victim must wait for medical attention to arrive, have him lie down and position the bitten part lower than the rest of his body. Encourage him to stay calm. He might be very frightened, so keep assuring him that he is being cared for.

4. Treat for shock.

5. If available within 3 minutes of the bite, apply a venom extractor such as a Sawyer Extractor® directly over the fang marks and leave in place for no more than 10 minutes. Properly used, the extractor can remove up to 30 percent of the venom. **Do not make any cuts on the bite**—that's an old-fashioned remedy that can harm the victim much more than help him.

6. **Do not apply ice to a snakebite.** Ice will not help the injury, but it can damage the skin and tissue.

OBJECT IN THE EYE

A bit of dust or other foreign object in the eye is almost always painful, and it can endanger vision.

FIRST AID FOR OBJECT IN THE EYE

Have the person blink his eyes; tears might flush out the object. If that doesn't work, wash your hands with soap and water and then pull the upper lid down over the lower one. The lower lashes might brush out the speck.

For an object under the lower lid, place your thumb just below the lid and gently pull the lid down. Use the corner of a sterile gauze pad or clean handkerchief to lift out the speck. If that also fails, get the person to medical care.

HYPERVENTILATION

A person who is anxious or frightened might react by breathing too quickly and deeply. That's not unusual, but if rapid breathing continues too long, it can lead to *hyperventilation*, an abnormal loss of carbon dioxide from the bloodstream. The victim might feel as though he or she is suffocating, and might become dizzy, disoriented, and increasingly fearful.

FIRST AID FOR HYPERVENTILATION

1. Talk quietly to the victim and encourage him or her to calm down and breathe slowly.

2. Having the victim breathe into a paper bag might help restore carbon dioxide to the body.

3. While hyperventilation is usually not a serious concern, it is sometimes a symptom of asthma or diabetes. Dizziness and anxiety can be warning signs of a heart attack. For these reasons, someone who has experienced hyperventilation should be checked by a physician.

BROKEN BONES

A fall, a violent blow, an automobile accident, and someone might suffer a *fracture*—a broken bone.

When you suspect a fracture, do not move the person. Look for these symptoms:

- There is an abnormal shape or position of a bone or joint.

- There is swelling or a bluish color at the fracture site.

- The victim might have heard or felt a bone snap.

- The victim feels pain when you press on the skin over the fracture.

- The victim might not be able to move the injured limb.

FIRST AID FOR BROKEN BONES

1. Treat "hurry cases" (severe bleeding, stopped breathing, no heartbeat).

2. Treat for shock.

3. Allow the patient to lie still right where you found him. Make him comfortable by tucking blankets, sleeping bags, or clothing under and over him.

4. Call a doctor or rescue squad.

5. If the victim must be moved, first splint the broken bone. The saying, "splint it where it lies," is usually good advice.

CLOSED AND OPEN FRACTURES

A broken bone that does not cut through the skin is a *closed (simple) fracture.*

A broken bone piercing the skin is an *open (compound) fracture*—a fracture plus an open wound.

An open fracture is especially dangerous because it can allow bacteria to infect the wound and the bone. Keep an open fracture as clean as possible.

Splints

A *splint* is any stiff material that can be bound to a fractured limb in order to prevent the broken bone from moving and causing further injury and pain. A splint should be long enough to immobilize the joints above and below a fracture.

Make splints from whatever is handy—boards, branches, hiking sticks, ski poles, shovel handles, cardboard, folded newspapers and magazines, sections of tent poles.

Padding allows a splint to fit better and can make the victim more comfortable. Cushion a splint with clothing, blankets, pillows, crumpled

paper, a sleeping pad, or other soft material. Hold splints and padding in place with neckerchiefs, handkerchiefs, roller bandages, strips of cloth, or whatever else you have.

Lower-Arm Fracture

Splint to hold the hand and forearm motionless. Placing the splinted arm in a sling with the forearm slightly raised will also immobilize the elbow joint.

Upper-Arm Fracture

Tie a splint to the outside of the upper arm. Place the arm in a sling with the forearm raised about three inches above level, then use a cravat bandage to hold the upper arm against the side of the body. The body itself acts as a splint to immobilize the elbow and shoulder.

Collarbone or Shoulder Fracture

Place the forearm in a sling with the hand raised higher than the elbow, then tie the upper arm against the side of the body with a wide cravat bandage. No splint is necessary.

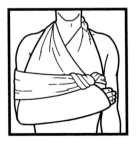

HOW TO MAKE A SLING

Support an injured hand, arm, collarbone, or shoulder with a sling made from a Scout neckerchief or large triangular bandage.

Tie an overhand knot in the largest angle of the triangle. Place the sling over the chest with the knot at the elbow of the injured limb and one end over the opposite shoulder. Bring the free end of the sling up to the other shoulder and tie the ends together behind the neck with a square knot.

Lower-Leg Fracture

Use two splints that are long enough to reach from the middle of the thigh to past the heel. Place one splint on each side of the injured limb and bind them together.

Thigh Fracture

Apply two padded splints, one outside the leg extending from heel to armpit, the other inside the leg from heel to crotch. Bind the splints together.

Note: The muscles of the upper leg are strong enough to pull the ends of a broken

thighbone into the flesh, which can cause serious internal bleeding. For this reason, the first aid described here for a thighbone *(femur)* fracture is early emergency care. The patient should not be moved until a traction splint has been applied by trained personnel. A thigh fracture can pose a serious threat to the victim's life. Get medical help immediately.

SKIN POISONING FROM PLANTS

For information on first aid for poison ivy, poison oak, and poison sumac, see chapter **3**, "Tenderfoot Scout," page 59 **T**.

POISON IVY

POISON OAK

POISON SUMAC

HEAT EMERGENCIES

IN HOT WEATHER, your body adjusts to keep you comfortable. Help it do that by drinking plenty of fluids and resting in the shade when you feel too warm. It might be wise to plan summertime work and play for early morning and evening hours instead of the middle of the day when the temperature is highest. Wear light-colored clothing and shade your head with a hat.

HEAT EXHAUSTION

Heat exhaustion occurs when the body's cooling system becomes overworked. Think of it as an air conditioner running wild. Heat exhaustion can affect a person outdoors or in a hot room. Symptoms can include the following:

- Pale skin that is clammy from heavy sweating

- Nausea and fatigue

- Dizziness and fainting

- Headache, muscle cramps, and weakness

FIRST AID FOR HEAT EXHAUSTION
1. Have the victim lie in a cool, shady place with his feet raised. Remove excess clothing.
2. Cool the victim by applying cool, wet cloths to his body and by fanning him.
3. If he is fully alert, let him sip from a glass of water into which you've stirred a pinch of salt.
4. Recovery should be rapid. If symptoms persist, call for medical help.

HEATSTROKE

Heatstroke happens when a victim's cooling system is so overworked it stops functioning. In simple terms, the body's air conditioner is broken. The victim's temperature soars to a life-threatening level. Symptoms of heatstroke can include the following:

- Very hot skin

- Red skin, can be either dry or damp with sweat

- Rapid and quick pulse, noisy breathing

- Confusion and irritability, unwillingness to accept treatment

- Unconsciousness

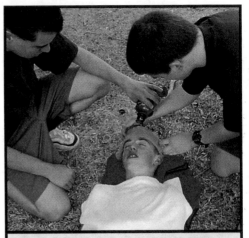

FIRST AID FOR HEATSTROKE

The victim must be cooled immediately. He is in danger of dying, so act quickly.

1. Move him to a cool, shady spot.

2. Cool him any way you can. Remove outer clothing and sponge him with cold water. Cover him with wet towels, wet clothing, or whatever else is handy and fan him. Place him in a stream, in a bathtub filled with cold water, or in front of an air conditioner running full blast in a house or car. Use combinations of all available treatments.

3. Keep the victim lying down and comfortable with his head and shoulders slightly raised.

4. Monitor the victim closely. His temperature could go up again, he might vomit, and he might require rescue breathing.

5. Get emergency medical help right away.

DEHYDRATION

Water is essential for nearly every bodily function, including digestion, respiration, brain activity, and regulation of body temperature.

Moisture is lost through breathing, sweating, digestion, and urination. If a person gives off more water than he takes in, he is suffering from *dehydration.* It can affect him in any of the following ways:

- Fatigue

- Headache and body aches

- Confusion

Heat exhaustion, heatstroke, and hypothermia can all be caused in part by dehydration.

FIRST AID FOR DEHYDRATION

Protect yourself from dehydration by drinking plenty of fluids. That's easy to do on hot summer days when you are thirsty. It is just as important in cold weather when you might not feel like drinking. Drink enough so that your urine stays clear.

Having plenty of drinking water in the backcountry can sometimes be a challenge, but you must make the effort. It might involve purifying stream water, melting snow, or carrying all you need from home. For information on safe drinking water for the backcountry, see pages 255–56.

COLD EMERGENCIES

WHEN YOU HEAR of someone freezing to death or dying of exposure, the killer was probably *hypothermia*—from *hypo*, meaning "low," and *thermia*, meaning "heat." It occurs when the body is losing more heat than it can generate.

Flesh exposed to low temperatures or cold wind can freeze. Far from the body's core heat, toes and fingers are especially vulnerable, as are the nose, ears, and cheeks.

Avoid cold emergencies by wearing enough clothing to stay warm and dry, and don't forget your hat. Eat plenty of food for energy and drink lots of fluids. If bad weather catches you in the backcountry, put up your tent and crawl into your sleeping bag.

HYPOTHERMIA

Hypothermia is a danger to anyone who is not dressed warmly enough. Wind, rain, hunger, dehydration, and exhaustion increase the risk. The temperature doesn't have to be below freezing. A lightly dressed hiker caught in a windy rainstorm is at great risk. So is a swimmer too far out in chilly water.

A victim of hypothermia might show any of these symptoms:

- Feeling cold and numb

- Fatigue and anxiety

- Uncontrollable shivering

- Confusion, irritability; makes bad decisions

- Stumbling and/or falling down

- Loss of consciousness

While one person is being treated for hypothermia, the rest of the group could also be at risk. Be sure to protect yourself and others from getting too cold. Everyone should take shelter, put on dry, warm clothing, and have something to eat and drink. Look out for one another.

FIRST AID FOR HYPOTHERMIA

Treat a victim of hypothermia by preventing him from getting colder and, if necessary, helping him rewarm to his normal temperature. Try any or all of the following methods. Be gentle and patient with anyone suffering hypothermia.

1. Take the victim into the shelter of a building or a tent and get him into warm, dry clothes.

2. Zip him into a dry sleeping bag.

3. Offer an alert victim warm or hot liquids (cocoa, soup, fruit juices).

4. Give him water bottles filled with warm fluid to hold in the armpit and groin areas.

5. If hypothermia is advanced, helping the victim breathe warm, moist air will aid in rewarming.

6. Be ready to provide other first aid if needed.

7. Seek medical care for the victim.

FROSTBITE

A victim of frostbite might complain that his ears, nose, fingers, or feet feel painful and then numb. Another frostbite victim won't notice anything. You might see grayish-white patches on his skin—a sure sign of frostbite.

FIRST AID FOR FROSTBITE

Get into a tent or building, then warm the injury and keep it warm. If an ear or cheek is frozen, remove a glove and warm the injury with the palm of your hand. Slip a frostbitten hand under your clothing and tuck it beneath an armpit. Treat frozen toes by putting the victim's bare feet against the warm skin of your belly. Avoid rubbing frostbitten flesh, as that can damage tissue and skin.

You can also warm a frozen part by holding it in warm—not hot—running water. Or wrap it in a dry blanket. Have the patient exercise injured fingers or toes, and don't let the injured area freeze again. Get the victim to a doctor.

Avoid cold emergencies by wearing enough clothing to stay warm and dry, and don't forget your hat.

LONG-TERM FIRST AID CARE

YOU'VE TREATED AN accident victim's hurry cases, protected him from further injury, and sent for help. It's time to decide what to do next.

The best plan in most cases is to make the victim comfortable and wait for medics to arrive. Continue to treat for shock, keep the airway open, monitor his condition for any changes, and be ready to provide any other treatment the victim might require.

In the backcountry, medical help could be hours in coming. It might be wise to set up camp and shelter the victim with a tent. (Rather than lifting a badly injured person into a tent, you can slit the floor of a standing tent and then place the tent over him where he lies.)

Be aware of your own needs, too, and those of others around you. Stay warm and dry, and have enough to eat and drink. Some group members might be frightened or disoriented by what they have seen. Don't let them wander off. Giving people specific jobs to do—fixing a meal, gathering firewood, making camp—can focus their attention and help calm their concerns.

MOVING AN INJURED PERSON

The decision to move an accident victim should be made carefully. A victim of serious injuries should be moved by first-aiders only in case of immediate danger—out of a river or the path of a fire, for example, or away from an unstable avalanche area. Even if you must hurry, use your hands to stabilize injuries as much as you can to minimize further injury.

Victims of less serious injuries can sometimes move on their own or with assistance.

RESCUE FROM A SMOKE-FILLED ROOM

A smoke-filled room is a hazardous environment. Moving an injured or unconscious person should be done quickly, but you must also avoid putting yourself at risk. Rushing into a dangerous place to help someone will do no good if you also become a victim. If your safety will be threatened, wait until trained rescuers arrive.

A few of the ways a person can be moved to safety from a smoke-filled room are these:

- With both hands, grasp his clothing and drag him toward you.

- Roll him onto a coat, blanket, tablecloth, or whatever else is handy, and drag him on that.

- Get behind the victim, reach under his arms, grab his wrists, and haul him out of the room.

Assists and Hand Carries

Walking Assist

Someone who has suffered a minor accident or who feels weak can be assisted as he walks. Bring one of his arms over your shoulder and hold onto his wrist. Place your free arm around his waist.

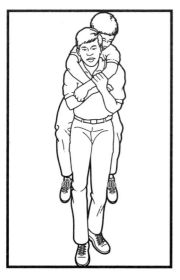

One-Person Carry

Kneel in front of the victim with your back to his belly. Grasp his hands over your chest, and carry him piggyback. Avoid straining your back by keeping it straight and lifting with your legs.

Four-Handed Seat Carry

Two first-aiders can transport a conscious person with this carry. Each bearer grasps his own right wrist with his left hand. The two bearers then lock hands with each other. The patient sits on their hands and places his arms around their shoulders.

Two-Person Carry

The bearers kneel on either side of the victim. Each bearer slides one arm under the victim's back and one under his thighs. The bearers grasp each other's wrists and shoulders, then rise from the ground with the patient supported between them.

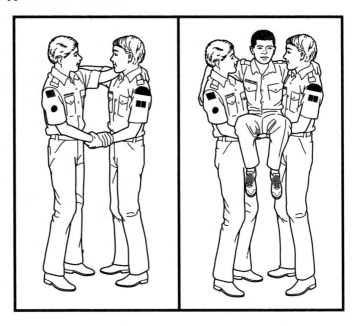

Stretchers

When a person must be moved for some distance or his injuries are serious, he should be carried on a stretcher.

Moving someone on a stretcher can be difficult and exhausting work requiring a large number of rescuers. Whenever possible, use a litter or rescue basket made specifically for transporting injured persons. If none is available, consider the following:

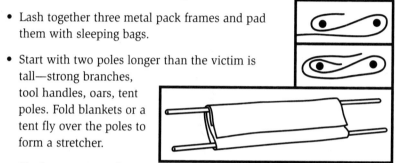

- Lash together three metal pack frames and pad them with sleeping bags.

- Start with two poles longer than the victim is tall—strong branches, tool handles, oars, tent poles. Fold blankets or a tent fly over the poles to form a stretcher.

During an evacuation, stretcher bearers should trade off with each other to conserve their strength. At least one rescuer should monitor the patient at all times in order to note any changes in his or her vital signs.

DOING THE BEST YOU CAN

GOOD SAMARITAN LAWS legally protect anyone making a good-faith effort to help the victim of an injury or illness. Whenever you are confronted with a first aid emergency, use the skills you have to the best of your ability. Remember to watch out for your own safety as well as that of others in the area. Treat hurry cases first, then put together a plan to get professional medical attention for the victim.

No one expects you to have the knowledge of a physician. However, Scouting's history is filled with stories of Scouts who used their training to help others, sometimes even saving lives. Learn all the first aid you can and review it often. Perhaps one day you will be able to do just the right thing at a time when your actions make all the difference.

CITIZENSHIP

TRAILHEAD

12

CITIZENSHIP

"This was a good country in the past. It is a good country today. It will be a good country tomorrow unless we fail it."

—*Daniel Carter Beard (first BSA National Commissioner),* Hardly a Man Is Left Alive

Being part of a community means taking an active role in making it a good place for everyone.

Ours is a nation bursting with possibilities. The United States of America embraces over 3.5 million square miles, from Arctic tundra to tropical wetlands, from sun-baked desert to old-growth forest, and from crowded cities to great prairies, farmlands, and mountain ranges stretching as far as the eye can see.

We Americans are as diverse as the land upon which we live. We can trace our heritage to every part of the globe, a rich and varied resource that has enabled us to create a society capable of tremendous achievement. When we work together, we possess the energy, optimism, and ability to accomplish almost anything we set out to do.

America is made up of all of us. It has become a strong nation because of the efforts of every person living upon its soil. Ours is a good country, and it will continue to be in the future, but only if we do not fail it. That is where you have a vital role to play.

HOW OUR NATION CAME TO BE

THE UNITED STATES OF AMERICA was born out of a desire for freedom. The colonists who settled much of the eastern coast of North America were ruled by a British government that increasingly limited rights the colonists believed they should have. For example, Americans had to let British soldiers stay in their homes. They were required to obey British laws and pay British taxes even though they had no legal way to make changes when they felt those laws and taxes were unfair.

The Declaration of Independence helped set the course for America as a nation of its own.

The colonists decided they would be better off if they governed themselves. They declared their independence from Great Britain on July 4, 1776, but the British did not want the colonies to slip out of their control. Armies arrived to put down the rebellion, and the Revolutionary War dragged on for five bitter years. Many lives were lost before a treaty signed in 1781 signaled the end of the war and the recognition of the United States as an independent nation.

Representatives of the thirteen states gathered to write the United States Constitution—the blueprint to build a government for the new nation. Even in the 1700s there were too many people to meet together every time a law had to be made. The Constitution solved that problem by making ours a *representative* democracy, in which citizens vote for officials who then represent them in the government. A country governed in this way is called a *republic*.

The authors of the Constitution could not have imagined the world we would live in more than two hundred years later. But in their wisdom they designed a government flexible enough to meet the needs of a nation that would continue to grow and change.

During the last two centuries, the strength of the Constitution has been tested many times. One of the most difficult issues for the young nation was the question of slavery. When the Constitution was written, many people believed slaves did not have the same rights as free Americans. Many others believed just as strongly that slavery was wrong and that the Constitution should treat everyone equally, regardless of their race.

The struggle became so profound that in 1861 the states that were supporting slavery and the rights of states to determine their own laws tried to break away and form a separate country. Citizens of the other states fought against them in order to hold the nation together, and when the Civil War ended, America was still united. Constitutional liberties had been extended to all people regardless of race, but those bloody years of war will always be a dark reminder that our freedoms have a high price.

Your Rights As an American

Do you like to get together with your friends? Read all sorts of books and newspapers? Live in a home no one can enter unless invited? Those are rights that cannot be taken from you. You have the right to believe in any religion you want. You enjoy freedom of speech, and can travel freely.

Your rights, guaranteed by the Constitution and amendments, including the Bill of Rights, are shared by all Americans. It doesn't matter where we live, how much money we have, the color of our skin, whether we are male or female, or what we think— we are all equal under the law. Rarely in human history have the rights of every person been so respected.

Throughout our history, hundreds of thousands of Americans have paid that price by sacrificing their lives to defend the Constitution and the principles it embraces.

WHAT YOUR NATION ASKS OF YOU

AMERICA IS YOUR LAND. Its laws protect your right to life, liberty, and the pursuit of happiness. By supporting the Constitution, you help preserve these rights. Defend the same rights for others, even when you do not agree with the ways in which they exercise them.

Written by our representatives, the laws of our communities, states, and nation govern much of what we do every day. You can help your government respond to the needs of the people by learning about laws, obeying them, and seeking to improve them through Constitutional processes if you disagree with them.

America relies on its citizens to keep it safe. The men and women of the armed forces stand ready to defend the nation against threats from beyond our borders. But ignorance, prejudice, and apathy are enemies of our country, too. Do your part to defeat those threats by taking advantage of educational opportunities. Stand up for the rights of others. Play an active role in making your neighborhood, county or parish, state, and nation good places in which to live.

Your Responsibilities As a Citizen

A strong America can exist only if its citizens are informed. You can begin by studying our nation's history and understanding how our government works. When you are old enough it will be your right and your duty to learn about issues and candidates for public office, and then to vote at election time.

Our country needs dedicated teachers, engineers, scientists, writers, bus drivers, farmers, and merchants. The nation counts on capable coaches, pilots, soldiers, and computer programmers. It depends upon people committed to protecting the environment, caring for the sick, sheltering the homeless, and helping others in need.

America especially needs young people like you who are doing something good with your lives. You are the future of the country, but you can contribute to the health of the nation right now. When you do your best in school, keep yourself fit, and are of service to your family and community, you are strengthening the fabric of America.

KNOW OUR NATION'S MOTTO— IN GOD WE TRUST

IN 1861, the secretary of the Treasury wrote a letter to the director of the United States Mint. "No nation can be strong except in the strength of God, or safe except in His defense," the letter said. "The trust of our people in God should be declared on our national coins."

A vote of Congress made the secretary's suggestion law, and the motto, In God We Trust, began to appear on various coins. Since 1955, the motto has been stamped on every coin produced by the U.S. Mint.

KNOW AMERICA'S PAST

AMERICA'S HISTORY is full of people acting with dedication, dignity, and heroism. Some of America's best-known people are remembered for their leadership, others for their educational skills, their writings, or their inventions. Some served their country by sacrificing their lives. While each of these people represents the achievements of one individual, he or she also shows how the lives of all Americans are important to our nation.

Most of America's greats, though—pioneers, parents, youth group leaders, teachers, community volunteers, and millions of others—have made their contributions quietly. They shared their knowledge with others, offered a helping hand to those in need, and strove to keep their communities on the right course. Through their deeds, they have changed our country and the world.

The history of the United States is also full of significant places and monuments, each with stories to tell. You might have visited some of the most famous—the White House, perhaps, or Gettysburg Battlefield, the USS *Arizona* monument at Pearl Harbor, or Yellowstone National Park. Your town is sure to have locations that are important to its past. Reading about American history and visiting museums, historical sites, and library exhibits can increase your understanding and appreciation of your nation and your place in it.

KNOW OUR NATION'S FLAG

THE FLAG OF THE UNITED STATES represents the men and women who built America. It reminds us of the Native Americans who inhabited

the continent for thousands of years, of Pilgrims finding a place to worship God in their own way, of pioneers building homes in a new land, of George Washington leading a young nation, of Abraham Lincoln holding that nation together, of Martin Luther King's dream of justice and equality for all, and of people of all races and beliefs who have fought and died for our country.

Respect the flag and the ideals it represents by always handling, displaying, folding, and saluting it in the right way.

For more on greeting and displaying the flag, see pages 42–44.

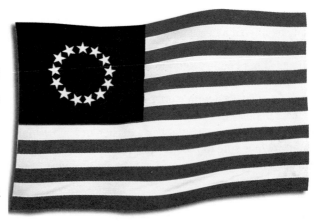

The first official flag of the United States of America was created by a resolution of the Continental Congress in 1777.

KNOW THE PLEDGE OF ALLEGIANCE

THE PLEDGE OF ALLEGIANCE TO THE FLAG OF THE UNITED STATES OF AMERICA

I pledge allegiance to the flag

of the United States of America

and to the republic for which it stands,

one nation under God,

indivisible, with liberty and justice for all.

Written in 1776, the Declaration of Independence set in motion the creation of the United States of America.

Boy Scouts have always stood ready to serve their nation. Helping out in their communities, doing their best in school, learning about current events, and standing up for what is right are all ways that today's Scouts strengthen America.

KNOW OUR NATIONAL ANTHEM

DURING THE WAR OF 1812, a British fleet attacked U.S. Fort McHenry near Baltimore. A young man named Francis Scott Key watched as the bombardment lasted through the night. He did not know if the American fortress could withstand the assault.

When the smoke cleared the next morning, Key saw a United States flag—the Star-Spangled Banner—still flying over the fort. He wrote down the feelings he'd had during the night and the hope he felt for his nation's future. Soon the words were being sung throughout the country. What Francis Scott Key had written became our national anthem.

Whenever you hear our national anthem played or sung, show your respect by standing up. Give the Scout salute if you are in uniform. Otherwise, place your right hand over your heart.

The Star-Spangled Banner

O say can you see, by the dawn's early light,

    What so proudly we hail'd at the twilight's last gleaming,

Whose broad stripes and bright stars through the perilous fight

    O'er the ramparts we watch'd, were so gallantly streaming?

And the rocket's red glare, the bomb bursting in air,

    Gave proof through the night that our flag was still there,

O say does that star-spangled banner still wave

    O'er the land of the free and the home of the brave?

KNOW YOUR STATE

EACH OF THE FIFTY STATES shares America's national history. Each is also proud of its unique origins, development, and character. Emblems and mottoes on the flags symbolize much about the states' pasts. A state flag, song, bird, motto, and flower further identify each state. A state's name often reflects its historic roots, and its capital city has special significance to its residents.

Do a little research to learn the emblems of your state and write them in the following blanks. What do they tell you about your home?

My state's name _____

My state's capital city _____

My state's motto _____

My state's flower _____

My state's bird _____

Title of my state's song _____

My state's flag

KNOW YOUR COMMUNITY

MANY AMERICAN TOWNS and cities are hundreds of years old. They might have been founded near rivers and harbors where ships could dock, or they might have been built along the trails and railroad lines that crossed the continent long ago. Other communities are much younger, growing up at the edges of cities or established close to sites of industry, agriculture, or tourism.

Most libraries have information about local history. There might be museums or monuments honoring historical events. People who have lived in your neighborhood for a long time are often eager to share their memories of what your community was like in years gone by. You might enjoy discovering why your hometown is located where it is, who started it, and how it has changed over the decades.

Neighborhood Maps

You can learn a great deal about your city or town by looking at a street map available from your local chamber of commerce, city hall, library, or a tourist information center.

Pinpoint your neighborhood on the map. Find nearby schools, stores, churches, synagogues, and parks. Spot the locations of your troop meetings and the homes of others in your Scout patrol. Trace the routes you travel.

Get to know your neighborhood well enough to give useful directions to visitors who need help finding their way. By developing a sense of place about your community, you can also increase your own sense of belonging.

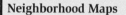

KNOW YOUR NEIGHBORS

NEIGHBORS ARE THE PEOPLE who live in houses near yours, on farms down the road, or in apartments in your building. You see them working and playing in their yards, going to the store, and coming home in the evening. Take time to introduce yourself. Explain that you are a neighbor and a Scout, and that you would be pleased to learn a little about them.

When you know your neighbors, you will find yourself surrounded by the most exciting of all community resources. Every one of them has stories to tell and skills to teach. As you get acquainted and share with your neighbors what you know, you will be reminded that a community is more than just a collection of buildings. It is the unified strength of people sharing with one another.

There are some special neighbors you won't want to overlook:

Senior Citizens

Older Americans are important members of any community. They can draw on many decades of experience to help solve local problems. If they are retired, they often have more time to devote to their neighborhood. Because their children and grandchildren might live far away, senior citizens appreciate the friendship of neighbors, especially of young people like you.

Persons with Disabilities

Each of us must overcome challenges in our lives. Perhaps you or another Scout in your troop gets around with crutches or in a wheelchair. A few of your neighbors might experience impaired hearing or a loss of sight. Some people must adjust to developmental disabilities, as well.

We all wish we could have perfect health and awareness. However, illnesses and accidents can leave people of any age with impairments and disabilities. Someone in your family might have faced physical or mental limitations since birth.

While they might have special ways of overcoming certain conditions, people with disabilities are full members of our communities. They often have much to offer. Be sensitive to their needs, but then look beyond their limitations and get to know them as the people they really are.

Ethnic Groups

Everyone has an ethnic background. For Native Americans, that means being part of the tribes that lived in North America before European explorers arrived. The ethnic origins of everyone else lie outside the borders of the United States. Your parents, grandparents, or other ancestors might have come from Africa, Asia, Europe, South America, or another area of the world. Perhaps your family arrived in America hundreds of years ago. Maybe you've lived in the United States just a few months.

Americans try hard to make our nation a place where people of all backgrounds and races can live and succeed together. At the same time, we take great pride in our ethnic roots. Ethnic songs, clothing, languages, foods, and religious beliefs help each of us identify with our past. Ethnic festivals and holidays encourage us to celebrate our own heritage and to enjoy those of our neighbors.

Watch for posters in store windows telling of local celebrations and festivals, and read the newspapers for announcements of ethnic events. You can have a good time learning about other cultures. By accepting the differences among us, you will realize the wonderful variety and strength that different ethnic groups bring to a community.

WHAT A COMMUNITY GIVES YOU

DO YOU CHEER for a sports team in your town? Are you pleased when your school band marches in a parade? Are you proud of the troop number on the sleeve of your Scout shirt? That's because you know you belong. You are a part of that team, that school, and that troop.

You probably feel the same way about your community. You're glad to say, "I am from that place." You can take pride in your neighborhood, and rightly so. It is your home. It gives you an identity. It provides the *support, safety,* and *services* you need.

Support

At a court of honor, you've known the warmth of having your friends and family watch you receive a new badge. If you play on a sports team, you understand how good it feels to have local fans cheer you on. When you do your best in school, your neighbors might give you a pat on the back.

People in a community support each other through the bad times as well as the good. Perhaps you have known a family whose home was damaged by fire. Right away, neighbors brought them food, blankets, clothing, and furniture. Some might have pitched in to repair the smoky rooms, and they might have raised money to help the family get started again. That's what a community can do.

Safety

People who care about their neighbors and the places where they live want to keep their communities safe. You can help in many ways—shoveling snow from sidewalks, sweeping glass out of the street, reporting a downed stop sign or a broken street light. With your knowledge of first aid, you are always ready to assist injured persons. You can also support the police, fire departments, and rescue squads that handle more serious safety matters. They are part of your community, too.

Services

If there were no communities and your family lived by itself, you would need to find your own food and water every day. At night you could burn a candle or a lantern, but there would probably be no other light. If you became sick, you would have to heal yourself.

Thanks to communities, though, clean drinking water is as close as the nearest faucet, lights come on at the flip of a switch, and if someone in your family becomes injured or ill, help is available at clinics and hospitals.

Fresh water, electrical power, medical attention, and dozens of other services exist because people in a community work together. By sharing the labor and the cost, you and your neighbors provide yourselves and your community with the necessities of life.

You might want to plan a patrol or troop outing to visit a fire department, police station, sewage treatment plant, utility company, or other community service. Call in advance to set up the visit. Officials are often eager to show you around and let you see your community services at work.

LEARN HOW YOUR COMMUNITY IS RUN

A BIG CITY usually has a large full-time government. Officials in a smaller town might be men and women who serve part-time, often without pay. In either case, a city council and a mayor, city manager, or tribal leader are elected by the people of the community to look after local affairs.

City council meetings are usually open to the public. The same is true of county, state, and federal sessions of elected bodies. By watching meetings, you can see how decisions affecting the public are made. That's one of the ways you and other citizens can determine whether or not officials are making the choices you want them to make. Talk with your Scoutmaster about taking the troop to see a government meeting.

You can also visit directly with many local leaders. Write or call their offices for an appointment. Public officials are busy, but they enjoy talking with the people they represent. Before you go, write down the questions you would like to have them answer. Perhaps you are interested in how a mayor does his or her job. Maybe you have seen a problem in your neighborhood that you feel a city council member should know about,

and you want to suggest a solution. By answering your questions now and by being supportive of your interests, leaders are helping to ensure a better community tomorrow.

VOLUNTEER ORGANIZATIONS

A mayor or city council member will tell you that government cannot provide every service a community needs. That's where volunteer organizations step in—groups whose members donate their time and energy to get things done.

A good example is the parent-teacher organization your parents or guardian might belong to at your school. They aren't paid to go to the meetings, and they aren't forced to pay their membership dues. However, they know that teachers and parents working together can make your school a better place in which to learn.

Your Scout troop couldn't exist without volunteers. Volunteers organize and run it. They find funding to pay for tents and cooking gear. On their own time, Scout leaders receive training, hold troop meetings, and go with you on campouts.

Many churches, temples, synagogues, and mosques also help with community needs. So do volunteer fund-raising organizations such as the United Way. Neighborhood block-watch and crime-stopper groups do much to increase the safety of homes and businesses. In some towns, even the fire department and rescue squads are made up of people who have other jobs but are ready at a moment's notice to go to someone's assistance.

You can be a volunteer, too. Perhaps you could help an organization at your school that informs students about the dangers of drug abuse and drunk driving, or you and your friends might spend one Saturday each month completing a service project such as collecting food and used clothing for homeless people.

OTHER COMMUNITY RESOURCES

Every time you run across a playground, visit a museum or a zoo, or read a book in a library, you are using community resources. The same is true of the hiking trails, beaches, sports fields, and picnic areas you enjoy in your city parks.

Of course, a library without readers has no purpose. A zoo without visitors won't stay open long. A concert hall lacking an audience is doomed to close. You can help keep community resources full of life by using them.

WORLD COMMUNITY

SEEN FROM THE MOON, Earth
looks like a glowing blue marble floating
in the blackness of space. From that distance,
the differences between people and between nations
would appear to be very small.

We think of people in other lands differently when we view them as
neighbors. Instead of being fearful of them, we learn that many people
beyond our borders are contributing to the good of the world community.
We also begin to understand their hopes and concerns.

We see examples of international cooperation whenever drought, flood,
earthquake, or famine threaten some part of the globe. Nations that are
able to do so send food, supplies, and medical aid to people in trouble.

Many problems we face today are so great they cannot be solved by
one nation. The list is long—air pollution, AIDS, the destruction of rain
forests, the endangerment of whales and other species, and the threat
posed by nuclear weapons are just a few.

But these challenges are not hopeless. They all have solutions. In fact,
you might someday hold some of the answers. You can begin by learning
about people around the world. Then be willing throughout your life to
make the Earth a
better place—not
just for yourself or
just for Americans,
but for everyone.
That is what you as
a good neighbor
can do. That is
what truly builds
a community,
a nation, and
a peaceful world.

Reaching out to meet people who are different from you can lead to understanding and friendship.

Held every four years, world jamborees bring together Scouts of many nations for fellowship and fun.

PREPARED FOR LIFE

MAKING THE MOST OF YOURSELF

Good judgment, self-reliance, initiative,

the ability to learn—the BSA can help you

achieve them all.

MAKING THE MOST OF YOURSELF

DO YOU ENJOY MUSIC? Maybe you can play an instrument and sing a song. You might like sports, too. Do you know the rules of soccer? When you throw a baseball, is it right on target?

You might be able to draw cartoons and faces. Math and science might seem easy for you. Maybe you can make people laugh by telling funny stories. Your friends might respect you as a leader and a good listener. Perhaps you are gentle with animals and like to spend time caring for them.

You are a collection of wonderful talents, ideas, and experiences. Your skills and interests are possibilities. They are hints of what you can become. To make the most of these gifts, be open to the joy of learning.

How to Gather Information
Something you don't understand is a mystery just waiting to be solved. Gather clues by:
• Looking and listening
• Asking
• Reading
• Writing
• Learning by doing
• Learning by teaching

LOOKING AND LISTENING

YOUR EYES AND EARS can be powerful tools of discovery. Pay attention as you help a neighbor plant a garden. Study the way a window washer ties a safety rope around his waist. Watch where birds near your home like to roost, and notice what they seem to be doing.

Learning by observing is especially important when you are hiking

and camping. You can make sense out of a map only if you are aware of landmarks around you. When you see changes in the clouds, you can pitch your tent before a storm breaks. Sit quietly in the woods and you might observe wildlife that would otherwise stay hidden.

Practice using your other senses, too. The smell of rain, the taste of a huckleberry, and the feel of the wind in your face can deepen your enjoyment of adventures and teach you much about the outdoors.

ASKING

"CAN YOU SHOW ME HOW THIS WORKS?" "Would you tell me why this happens?" "Is there a better way to get this done?"

When you are curious about something, ask. People are almost always willing to share what they know. Be polite, of course, and if someone is busy you might need to arrange another time when he or she can talk with you. But there are no silly questions and there are no questions that are too simple. Questions are stepping stones to knowledge. Unless you ask, you might never know.

READING

STRAP YOURSELF into the pilot's seat of a rocket and feel its engines blast you into space. Hoist the anchor of an old wooden ship and sail the open seas with pirates and explorers. Shrink yourself to the size of a blood cell and swim through the human body. Become a dinosaur and stride across prehistoric lands with long, thundering steps.

READING CAN
PROVIDE ANSWERS.

Through the magic of reading, you can do almost anything. A book is a flying carpet, a time machine, a spyglass. Open a book and you can travel to the far corners of the Earth, to the inside of an atom, and to the most distant stars. Do you know what people ate a thousand years ago? What makes a computer work? How to find a summer job? Reading can give you the answers.

School and public libraries are full of exciting books. Librarians will show you how to locate books about subjects you like—just ask. They will also explain how you can use library videos, recordings, and other forms of stored information. Find out about getting a borrower's card so you can take home books and other library resources.

Reading aloud to someone is a generous act of sharing. Read to your parents, your brothers and sisters, and your friends. Perhaps you know of elderly neighbors who would love to hear a story. If there are younger children in your family, encourage them to read to you. That's a fine way to spend time together as you help them improve their own reading skills.

Reading is a window into the past and the future. It is a doorway to discovery and adventure. Read, read, and read some more. It will entertain you, expand your mind, and fill you with worlds of fresh ideas.

WRITING

TRAVELERS GOING INTO NEW TERRITORY keep track of what they see by writing in a journal. Scientists make notes of their experiments. Sailors keep records in a ship's log. Many Scout patrols have a trip log in which they write about each of their hikes and campouts.

Try keeping a journal of your own. Get a notebook and write a little every day about what you have done and seen. Write about school, activities with your friends and family, and what you observe in your neighborhood. You can include drawings, photos, stories you have cut from newspapers, and anything else that interests you.

No one but you ever has to read your journal, though you might want to share it. Some people write in journals every day for many years and can use them to remember what they were doing long ago. But even if you write just once in a while, putting your words on paper will give you a new way of understanding yourself and your world.

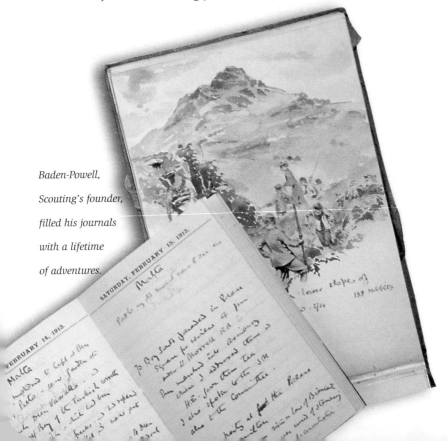

Baden-Powell,

Scouting's founder,

filled his journals

with a lifetime

of adventures.

LEARNING BY DOING

DO YOU REMEMBER how you learned to ride a bicycle? Perhaps you saw somebody else riding and thought you would like to do that, too. You climbed on a bike, started pedaling, and fell over. You got back on and probably fell again.

You kept at it, though, and finally figured out how to ride. Today, bicycling might seem so easy that you've forgotten it was ever difficult.

Much of learning is like that. You try something and grasp a small piece of it. You try again and understand a little more. The key is to keep at it and to learn from your successes **and** from your failures.

LEARNING BY TEACHING

SCOUTS HAVE MANY OPPORTUNITIES to share their knowledge with others. You might show your patrol how to use a compass. Once they have the idea, give them the compass and let them try it. They might make mistakes, but that's all right. Encourage them to keep at it, and provide more guidance when they're stuck. Before long they'll have the new skill mastered, thanks to you.

Teaching is good for the teacher, too. As you share your knowledge, you'll find yourself thinking carefully about how to explain it. Helping someone else learn will increase your own understanding of what you know.

WATCHING TELEVISION

TELEVISION offers many opportunities for learning and for entertainment. Coverage of sporting events lets you feel as though you are sitting in the stands. News and information programs keep you informed about current affairs, history, science, and the arts.

But television must be used wisely. Many families look through the program listings together at the beginning of each week and pick a few good shows they want to watch. Otherwise, they leave the television off and use their free time for reading, playing sports, learning music, helping neighbors, working on Scout projects, and enjoying each other.

In addition to filling so many hours, television programs and commercials often present fantasy views of life. Actors neatly solve all their problems by the end of each show. They sometimes use violence to settle differences with others. Smoking, drinking, unwise sexual activity, and illegal drug use are sometimes shown as being glamorous.

Of course, solving real problems takes lots of hard work. Hitting or shooting real people causes pain and death, not peace. Tobacco, alcohol, and drug abuse can make real people ill and dependent.

Talk with your family about what you see on television. Do you agree with the way the actors are treating one another? Could the story really have happened the way it was presented? By discussing programs, you can better separate the make-believe of television from the realities of life.

USING
THE INTERNET

COMPUTERS allow access to a vast amount of knowledge. By logging onto the Internet, you can contact sources of information around the world and download material about any subject. You might already be using the Internet for schoolwork, hobbies, or simply for enjoyment. You can also develop on-line friendships with Scouts anywhere on the globe.

For all of its benefits, though, the Internet can also present hazards you should know about and avoid. Most people using the Internet are friendly and honest. However, there are some who use the Internet to take advantage of others. There are also Web sites with content that is unsuitable for young people. Use the following guidelines to protect your privacy and gain the most good from your time on-line:

- Don't respond to messages or Web sites that make you feel uncomfortable or that you know are meant only for adults. If you come across information or images that you don't understand, talk about it with your parent or guardian.

- Don't give out personal information, including your address, telephone number, photograph, school name, or your parents' work address or telephone number.

- Never agree to meet anyone who has contacted you on-line unless your parent or guardian comes with you.

HAVING INITIATIVE

"Thinking is good, knowledge is

good, but no man ever gets very far with

either if he does not have initiative."

Boy Scout Handbook, 6th edition, 1959

It's fun to learn about adventures through reading, computers, and television, but it is even more exciting to have experiences of your own. Grab your pack and head for the hills with your patrol or troop whenever you can. Paddle a canoe, climb a mountain, and sleep under the stars. Catch a fish, repair a trail, cook a meal outdoors, and hike in the rain.

See new places, too. Explore neighborhood parks, city museums, and zoos. Visit factories and public utilities. Your travels as a Scout might take you to a high-adventure base far from home, or even across the ocean to a world jamboree.

Take time to meet people, too. Greet neighbors down the street and Scouts from other troops. Visit with new students at school and with

hikers you meet on the trail. Who are they? What do they do? Everyone has a story. Listen, learn, and discover.

Have the initiative to increase your knowledge. Family members, teachers, and neighbors have much to share. Develop good study habits and then use them.

To complete big projects, you might need to aim for small goals along the way. Hikers who walk the two thousand miles of the Appalachian Trail from Maine to Georgia don't do it all in one day. Each morning they set out to walk about a dozen miles. That might not seem like much when there are so many miles to go, but a few miles every day carries them over mountains, through valleys, and past sparkling lakes. Late one afternoon they come to a windy mountaintop that is the end of the trail. By setting reasonable goals and then sticking to their plan, they can walk the entire Appalachian mountain range.

You can meet many challenges that way. Map out a route to reach a goal of where you want to go, what you want to learn, or what you would like to achieve. Figure out the small steps that will take you there, then complete them one at a time.

The hardest part of making your own adventures might simply be getting started. But once you've laced up your hiking boots and are standing at the beginning of a trail, nothing can hold you back. Once you've said hello to someone and been greeted with a smile, the tough part of making a new friend is over. And as soon as you open a book and start reading, the words will seem to flow.

MAKING YOUR OWN GOOD LUCK

A SCOUT TROOP CAMPING in the mountains was hit by a storm. Even though they had snug tents and warm sleeping bags, some of the Scouts began to complain. They were sure the weather was ruining their trek, and they wished they hadn't come.

But one Scout thought it was great to be in the middle of a mountain storm. He loved to hear thunder crashing down the long valleys. He saw the beauty of a forest full of mist. He knew that bad weather would put his camping skills to the test, and he welcomed the chance to improve.

"I always hope for the best, prepare for the worst, and accept whatever comes my way," he told the others. "And then I have fun no matter what." With a smile on his face, he had a fine campout.

Rain falls on everyone. There is not much you can do about that. But you can decide to see the hard times as opportunities rather than obstacles. You can choose to make the most of a situation rather than giving up and wishing you were somewhere else.

The world around you is bursting with opportunities. Jump into life, celebrate it, live it well, and help others. Make the most of every moment, do nothing that is not of value, and live every day to the fullest.

SELF-RELIANCE

AS A SCOUT, you learn how to cook camp meals for yourself. You can pitch a tent and get your bed ready for the night. You know ways to care for your clothing and gear.

You can do those things at home, too. Helping with the cooking in your own kitchen is really not much different from the way it is in camp. The same goes for taking care of your clothes, making your bed, and keeping your part of the house neat.

The time you spend outdoors studying animals, finding your way, and working with other Scouts can increase your patience and concentration at home and in school. When you lead a patrol on a hike, you are learning leadership skills that will be valuable in your family and in your community.

Scouting teaches independence. By knowing what to do, you develop trust in your own abilities, and you have the quiet confidence that you can always do your best no matter what happens.

GOOD JUDGMENT

GOOD JUDGMENT is the ability to make wise decisions even in diffi-cult situations. You don't need great knowledge to use good judgment; you just have to do your best with what you already know.

Each of us has been around people who seem to do the right thing at the right time. Your patrol leader might be that kind of person. He comes up with ideas at meetings. He gives you a hand with Scout skills when you need a little help, and he leaves you alone when you want to do them yourself. He looks out for the safety and well-being of others, both in the patrol and beyond the troop. Some people would say he is using common sense while others might call it wisdom. What they are really talking about is good judgment.

"Good judgment," says an old Scoutmaster, "comes from hav-

ing lived through and learned from lots of bad judgment."

Your patrol leader didn't become wise without making lots of little errors, but he doesn't let that discourage him. Instead, he learns all he can from each failure and then moves on.

He knows that he can often learn more from his mistakes than from his successes.

If you examine the end of a log, you will see a series of rings expanding out from the center. Each ring represents a period of growth. Together, they made the tree strong and helped it withstand the worst storms.

Your experiences, both good and bad, are like those rings. Each adds a little bit to your wisdom and to the strength of your judgment. Good judgment can't be taught, but through the gathering of many experiences, it can be learned.

GETTING ALONG WITH OTHERS

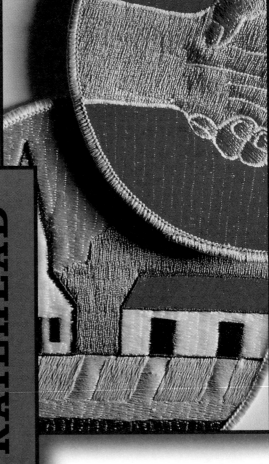

Extending friendship and understanding to others opens a world of fresh ideas, experiences, and cultures. Scouting offers guidance on getting along with others in ways that are healthy and fun.

GETTING ALONG WITH OTHERS

MOST OF US are surrounded by people. Every day we have opportunities to be with others at school, at work, and at home. Sharing experiences with them can be a wonderful part of being alive. Getting along is also the foundation for a community, a country, and a world where people can live together in peace.

Over 270 million Americans share our nation. There are nearly 6 billion people on the planet, all with their own needs, hopes, and dreams. Learning about the extraordinary mix of cultures, histories, and religions can be great fun, and can lead to a deeper understanding of other people.

MEETING PEOPLE

HAVE YOU EVER moved to a different neighborhood or started classes at a new school? Have you gone to the first day of practice with a sports team you didn't know, or showed up for a meeting of a Scout troop you've never attended before? Not knowing anyone can be scary.

But remember how good you felt when someone said hello and started to show you around? Suddenly you were no longer a stranger. You knew that people valued you and were happy you were there.

You can be the one who takes that first step toward welcoming another person. Is there a new student at your school, someone attending your church for the first time, or a family that has just moved into your neighborhood? Introducing yourself and asking people about themselves is an act of kindness that can help them feel at home.

Meeting people is a skill that grows with practice. You might be uneasy about stepping forward to greet someone you don't know. Talking to a person of a different race, religion, or generation might at first seem awkward, but others are probably just as shy as you are. Focus on making someone feel welcome, and you can open the door to understanding and friendship.

"The good scout is always at work—working to improve himself and to improve the daily lot of others."

Handbook for Boys, 1st edition, 1911

LISTENING TO OTHERS

SOMETIMES we don't listen very well. Your little sister might be learning how to play soccer, for instance, and is eager to tell you about it. At first you think it's boring—you already know how to play.

But then you pay attention and think about what your sister is saying. She wants to share her excitement with you and to gain your support. Maybe you can go outside with her and kick the ball back and forth. It's enjoyable for both of you, and you can give her pointers on playing the game. By taking time to really listen, you are building her confidence and strengthening the bonds in your family.

Listening is just as important when someone is angry. Perhaps a friend is mad at you because of something you did. Instead of getting mad yourself, wait until both of you are calm, and then listen carefully to what your friend is saying.

Maybe you were wrong and can make things better by apologizing. Even if you were right, your friend might have misunderstood something you said or did. Or it could be that your friend actually was upset over something else and took it out on you. By listening rather than returning his anger, you are helping to improve the situation.

CHOOSING FRIENDS

YOUR FRIENDS are among the most important people in your life. You enjoy being with them and going places together. They understand you. You depend on them to be there for you through good times and times that are not so good.

Choose friends whose values you admire, but don't turn down the chance to get to know someone because he or she is not just like the rest of your friends. Differences of race, culture, and language might keep some people at a distance. For others, physical disabilities can be a barrier to friendships.

Look beyond the differences that might separate you from others and accept them for who they are. You might be surprised how much you have in common and how much your differences can enrich friendships.

PEER PRESSURE

ONCE IN A WHILE, you might discover that a few people you know are using tobacco, alcohol, or drugs. Or they might be cheating on tests, taking things that don't belong to them, or being unkind to someone. They might pressure you to join them, even though you know what they are doing is wrong. When you refuse, they might say that you can't be part of their group or that they won't be friends with you anymore.

But real friends would not want you to do anything that could put you and others at risk. If the people you spend time with are smoking, drinking, getting high, or doing anything else that is unwise, you don't have to go along with them. You might need to look for new friends who are interested in healthier activities. Don't worry, they're out there. Be true to your beliefs, and you will find them.

YOUR FAMILY

FAMILY is a word that means belonging, support, and love. For many Scouts, a family is made up of parents, brothers, and sisters all under the same roof. Grandparents, aunts, uncles, and cousins might live nearby.

There are other kinds of families, too. Perhaps you live in a family with one parent, or you share time with your father and mother who live in different places. Your grandparents and other relatives might live far away, even in other countries. Maybe your family has no parents at all, but instead is made up of relatives or guardians who want the best for you. The most important thing is that they care for each other and want to share their lives with you.

Of course, there might be times when you feel that others in your family don't understand you. You might disagree with some of their ways of doing things. As you grow older, you will want to be more independent. All of the changes you are going through as you grow and mature can cause strain at home, but you can make the most of family life by being patient and putting energy into developing healthy relationships with family members.

For instance, you might have a curfew that gives you the freedom to explore, but within reasonable limits. Now and then you and your parents or guardian might discuss family rules to see if they are fair and if you are doing your part to follow them. By respecting those guidelines, you are proving that you are responsible, and your parents or guardian might respond by gradually pushing back the boundaries they have set.

Family members can also offer solutions to problems you are facing. You might be having difficulty with a subject in school, or you might not understand why your friends are acting a certain way. If you ask them, your parents and your older brothers and sisters might be able to help.

Consider earning the Family Life merit badge. It will help you better understand your family, your role in it, and how important you are to other family members.

"As a Scout you will learn skills that

will make you even better qualified

to help at home than you were before

joining. If someone in the family gets

sick, you know how to get a doctor.

If somebody has an accident, you can

give first aid. If a package needs to

be tied up, you know the knot for

doing it. If the family has a picnic,

you can make the fire and broil the

steak. There are dozens of things

you can do for the family that will

make life so much easier. . . ."

Boy Scout Handbook, 6th edition, 1959

FAMILY TIME

The demands of school, Scouts, sports, friends, and other activities might fill most of your days and evenings. Older family members often have jobs and projects of their own. Although you live in the same house, you and others in your family might be rushing past one another with hardly a word.

Make a real effort to spend time together, even if that means scheduling an hour now and then and writing it down on a calendar so everyone can plan around it. Sit down for a meal together, play a game, or go for a walk. The activity is not important—what matters is that you share time together.

FAMILY JOBS

On a patrol campout you pitch in to set up tents, cook meals, and leave a clean campsite. Doing your part goes a long way toward making an adventure a success.

The same is true at home. Keeping a household running smoothly takes a lot of work. The more you help out, the better. You might already keep your room neat, do your own laundry, care for pets, and wash dishes after meals. Of course, you don't have to wait to be asked to do family jobs. Look around for what needs to be done and help do it.

> A part-time job can help you learn work habits as you earn money to pay some of your own expenses. However, your most important job for the next few years is to get a good education. Manage your time and your spending habits so that schoolwork always comes first.

YOUR FAMILY AND SCOUTING

When you join the Boy Scouts of America, your whole family can become a part of Scouting. Your relatives can attend special Scout gatherings. Some of them might help run the troop or assist with special events. Many people want you to have all the valuable experiences that Scouting offers and to reach the goals you set for yourself. By supporting you, each of them can share in the spirit of Scouting.

CARING FOR YOUNGER CHILDREN

ONE OF YOUR family jobs might be looking after younger brothers and sisters. Perhaps you will be asked to take care of other children in the neighborhood, too.

Be aware of the ways you treat people younger or smaller than yourself. Everyone deserves respect. Sometimes it can seem easy to respond to the poor behavior of others by name-calling or physical force, but you should always find other ways to resolve conflicts.

Before taking responsibility for young children, find out the following:

- Know where their parents or guardian can be reached.

- Know a neighbor who will lend a hand if you need it.

- Have emergency phone numbers ready in case of illness or accident.

- Ask if the children are to eat, and if so, what they are supposed to eat.

- Ask what time the children are to go to bed.

- Ask about the use of televisions, computers, stereos, or radios.

While children are in your care, remember these rules:

- Keep children out of danger areas.

- Lock the doors. Don't open them for anyone unless you know the person.

- After the children are in bed, check every half hour to be sure they are all right.

- Stay awake until a parent or guardian returns.

TAKING CARE OF YOURSELF WHEN YOU ARE ALONE

DISCUSS WITH YOUR FAMILY
what you should do when you must be home alone. That might happen once in a while when your parents or guardian are gone for an evening. If they work, you might be alone every day after school.

Ask your parents or guardian what you should do if someone knocks on your door and wants to come in while you are alone. In most cases, it's best to leave the door locked and ask the visitor to wait outside while you call one of the numbers on your list.

HOUSE KEYS

Decide how you should answer if a stranger calls on the phone. A good response is this: "My parent can't come to the phone right now. Would you like to leave your name and a message?"

Your parents or guardian might set other guidelines for you to follow when you are in the house by yourself. They might ask that you not invite friends over during those hours, or that you call if you want to leave.

Make a list of emergency phone numbers and tape it near the telephone. Write down the numbers for general first aid emergencies (see page 292). Then add the following:

Parents or guardian
  at work _____

Family friend _____

Nearest relative _____

Neighbor _____

The list will give you plenty of trusted people you can call if you need help.

SEXUAL RESPONSIBILITY

AS YOU GROW into manhood, you are maturing in many remarkable ways. You are becoming stronger, wiser, and better able to make good decisions. Young women you know are also maturing both physically and emotionally. Your relationships with them will become closer and more meaningful, both to you and to them.

You are maturing sexually, too. The ability to father a child is a responsibility with powerful consequences in your life and in the lives of others. The choices you make require your very best judgment.

It's important to remember that sex is never the most grown-up part of a relationship. It is never a test of manliness. True maturity comes from acting responsibly in the following ways:

Your Responsibility to Young Women

Whenever you like to be with someone, you want the best for that person. A healthy relationship is supportive and equal. You can have a terrific time together enjoying life and growing socially and emotionally. However, the difficulties created by an unplanned pregnancy can be enormous. Don't burden someone you care for with a child neither of you is ready to bear.

Your Responsibility As a Future Parent

When you are fully grown and have become secure in yourself and in your relationship with another person, the two of you might decide to marry and become parents. That is a wonderful choice full of challenges and rewards. By waiting until you are prepared, you can give a child a close, loving family in which to grow.

Your Responsibility to Your Beliefs

For the followers of most religions, sex should take place only between people who are married to each other. To do otherwise might cause feelings of guilt and loss, while waiting until after marriage provides a foundation for a lasting relationship and a strong family. Abstinence until marriage is a very wise course of action.

Your Responsibility to Yourself

An understanding of wholesome sexual behavior can bring lifelong happiness. Irresponsibility or ignorance, however, can cause a lifetime of regret. AIDS and other diseases spread by sexual contact can ruin your health and that of others. An unplanned pregnancy before you are ready could severely limit your chances for education, occupations, and travel.

You owe it to yourself to enter adulthood without extra hurdles to overcome. Learn what is right. Your religious leaders can give you moral guidance. Your parents or guardian or other responsible adults can provide the facts about sex that you must know.

If you have questions about growing up, about relationships, or about sex, **ask.** Talk with your parents, religious leaders, teachers, or Scoutmaster. They want what is best for you. Let them know your concerns.

ABUSE

MOST RELATIONSHIPS WITH OTHERS can be warm and open.
That is because they are built on trust. A pat on the back, a hug of
encouragement, or a firm handshake are ways we can show people we
care about them.

However, it is a sad fact that some adults and teenagers use their size
and their power over others to abuse them. You need to know about
abuse so that you will understand what to do if you are ever threatened.

Those who abuse young people know they are doing something
wrong. They usually try to keep their actions a secret from other adults.
They might frighten their victims to prevent
them from telling anyone what is happening.
They might try to make the abused person
feel that he or she is to blame.

No one should live in fear of abuse. You
do not have to let people touch you in
ways you find uncomfortable. If you are
ever asked to do something you know is
wrong, you have the right to refuse.

How to
Protect Your Children
from Child Abuse:
A Parent's Guide

Boy Scouts of America

PROTECTING YOURSELF FROM SEXUAL ABUSE

**MOST SEXUAL ABUSE CAN BE
PREVENTED** if young people
know and follow these three R's:

- *Recognize.*

- *Resist.*

- *Report.*

Recognize

Recognizing a situation that could become sexual abuse can help you get
away before you are in serious danger.

People who sexually abuse young people are called *molesters.* Most often, the molester is known by his or her victim. The molester might be anyone—a family member, schoolteacher, religious leader, or youth group leader.

An adult attempting sexual abuse might begin by touching you in ways that are confusing. He or she might try to touch your groin area and pretend it was an accident. You might be asked to pose for photographs in your underwear or swimming suit, and then in no clothing at all.

Some adults or older youths might try to use your natural curiosity about sex as an opportunity to attempt sexual abuse. Sex is a normal bodily function you need to understand. Be on guard around anyone who makes it seem dirty or secretive.

A Time to Tell

- Shows some ways to prevent child molestation
- Intended for viewing by boys 11 through 14 years old
- Valuable for families, youth groups, schools, and churches
- A unique approach to a sensitive subject

At the head of this tape is a 4-minute, 40-second Presenter's Orientation for leaders of youth groups to preview before showing *A Time to Tell* to the 11- to 14-year-old male audience.

Copyright 1989 • Boy Scouts of America

Resist

If anyone ever attempts to do something to your body that makes you feel bad or that you know is wrong, you have the right to stop them. Run, shout, or make a scene in public to protect yourself. Faced with resistance, most molesters will back off.

Report

Anytime you believe that someone has tried to abuse you or someone else, report it. Talk to a trusted adult or call an abuse hot line—you can get the number from the phone book or by dialing an operator. Abuse is an adult-sized problem. By talking about it with adults, you can let them solve it.

For more information on dealing with abuse, you and your parents or guardian can read together the pamphlet *How to Protect Your Children from Child Abuse: A Parent's Guide,* found inside the cover of this handbook.

TO HAVE A FRIEND, BE ONE

THE BSA has always encouraged its members to be independent, to stand on their own two feet, and to use good judgment rather than being swayed by peer pressure. Trusting in yourself is an important quality to have.

But just as important is the willingness to get along with others. The Scout Law reminds you to be friendly and helpful. When you help others, always remember the rules of safety. The Scout Oath and Law do not require you to put yourself in danger. You should discuss with your parents how to be a good Scout and be safe. A Scout is courteous, too, as well as cheerful and kind. These points of the Scout Law provide

clear guidance for meeting new people, developing friendships, appreciating differences, and playing an active role in your family and community.

The first *Scout Field Book* put it this way:

"If you see a Scout Badge on a boy's coat lapel, give the Scout Salute and watch him smile. Maybe you can be of assistance to him. He may be a stranger in your town. By greeting him, you have made him feel that he is not alone."

We all depend on others for connection, fellowship, support, and love. When you do everything you can to help others feel appreciated, you will find that you are also not alone.

PHYSICALLY STRONG

TRAILHEAD

15

PHYSICALLY STRONG

CLIMB A MOUNTAIN. Swim a mile. Run a race. Paddle a canoe. Be alert throughout the school day. To get the most out of life, you need to be rested, fit, and ready, and that means doing all you can to keep yourself physically strong.

Everyone is different. Your body might be long and lean or thick and muscular. The color of your skin might be a rich brown, black, yellow, red, or white. Your hair might be straight, curled, or wavy. You might walk with a strong, steady stride, or get around in a wheelchair. However your body looks, you can be proud of it. It is like no one else's in the world. It is a sign that you are special.

While we can celebrate our differences, there is also much about our bodies that is the same. Each of us has over two hundred bones, more than six hundred muscles, and miles of blood vessels. They work with the organs, nerves, and thousands of other body parts like a finely tuned machine.

When you say the Scout Oath, you promise to do your best to keep yourself physically strong. Follow wise health practices and you will be ready for action. Best of all, healthy habits you develop now will stay with you for a lifetime.

A STRONG BODY

THE HUMAN BODY thrives on exercise. It is meant to be used. Opportunities for daily exercise are everywhere. Walking, jogging, bicycling, and working around the house are all good. So are the canoeing, backpacking, swimming, and climbing you might do on Scout outings. You might already take part in team sports at school or on neighborhood leagues.

The key to exercise is that it must be regular. Get in a routine of playing hard or working out at least three times a week. Once you have started, you will come to enjoy it so much that you won't ever want to miss a chance to be active.

STRETCHING

Before beginning a sports event, an exercise routine, a hike, or any other physically challenging activity, it's a good idea to take a few minutes to stretch. Stretching relaxes the tendons and ligaments of your joints. It warms the muscles and gets them ready to work. It makes your body more flexible and lessens the chance of injury. Stretching after an activity can help prevent stiffness and soreness in your muscles and joints.

Try the following stretches, doing each with just enough effort to put a little strain on your muscles. Stretch without bouncing. At first you might feel tight, but over time your range of motion will increase.

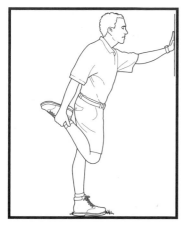

Thigh Stretch

Place your left hand on a wall for support. Grab your right ankle with your right hand and gently pull your heel up toward your buttocks. Hold for 30 seconds, then repeat with your left ankle.

Achilles Tendon and Calf Stretch

To stretch your calf muscles and Achilles tendons, stand about three feet from a wall and place your palms flat against it. Keep your heels on the floor and your back straight, as you lean closer to the wall. Hold that position for 30 seconds.

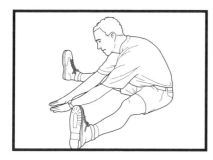

Straddle Stretch

Sit on the floor and spread your legs out flat. Lean forward as far as you can, sliding your hands on the floor. Hold the position for 30 seconds. The straddle stretch is good for the muscles in your back and the backs of your legs.

A STRONG HEART

The most important muscle in your body is your heart. Every day it pumps the equivalent of more than two thousand gallons of blood through your arteries and veins, carrying oxygen and nourishment to cells throughout your body.

Regular aerobic exercise will strengthen your heart muscles. A diet low in fat will keep your arteries clear. Don't smoke or use illegal drugs— they can weaken your heart.

EATING RIGHT

Good nutrition will build up your body, keep it in good repair, and serve as a source of energy for everything you do. Eat a balanced diet that includes foods from the basic food groups. (For more information on good nutrition and the basic food groups, see chapter 10, "Cooking," page 259 ✳.)

How Much Should You Weigh?

The number of pounds that show up on a scale give only a general picture of what your weight should be. How much you weigh depends on many factors, including how quickly your body processes the food you eat and whether your basic build is stocky, slender, or somewhere in between.

Eat a balanced diet in moderation, get plenty of exercise, and your body will probably find its own ideal weight. If you do have concerns or questions, a family physician can provide the answers you need.

Take pride in caring for your body and staying active. The habits you develop now will serve you well in the years to come. And whether you are a boy or an adult, it's never too late to begin paying attention to your fitness.

DRINKING WATER

Did you know that 70 percent of your body is made up of water? Water helps your system digest food. It washes wastes through your intestines and kidneys. When you perspire, the evaporation of moisture from the surface of your skin cools you. Drink plenty of fresh water every day, at least six to eight glasses. For more on drinking water during outdoor activities, see chapter 9, "Camping," page 233 .

WHAT ABOUT CAFFEINE AND SUGAR?

Coffee, tea, and many cola drinks contain *caffeine,* a mild stimulant that temporarily stirs up the nervous system and speeds the heart. Caffeine can make you irritable and cause you to have difficulty sleeping. None of these beverages has much food value. Water, fruit juices, and milk are far better for you.

Sugar is an ingredient in many candies, cereals, and other foods. Sugary foods and sodas will give you a quick surge of energy, but it wears off quickly. The resulting letdown can leave you feeling tired and irritable. Try to limit the amount of sugary foods and beverages you eat and drink. Fresh fruits and juices are nutritious substitutes.

GETTING RID OF WASTES

Eat the right foods, exercise regularly, drink plenty of water, and your body will take care of eliminating wastes. Grains and fresh vegetables provide *roughage* that keeps food moving smoothly through your system. Your digestive tract will develop its own rhythm for bowel movements.

CLEANLINESS

YOUR SKIN is your body's largest organ. Sweat glands in the skin help control body temperature. Nerve endings are sensitive to heat, cold, and touch. Skin is also the outer armor protecting you from injury and disease.

Skin is very tough, but it requires regular care. Keep it clean. When you are in the sun, protect your skin from harmful rays by applying plenty of sunscreen with a sun protection factor (SPF) of 15 or more. If your skin becomes dry or irritated, soothe it with lotion.

BATHING

Bathe regularly—once a day if you can. A shower or bath is best, or you can wash your whole body with a wet cloth. In camp and on the trail, carry water at least two hundred feet (seventy-five steps) from lakes, streams, and springs before you wash so that there is little chance of getting soap in open water where it could harm plants and animals.

YOUR HANDS

When you work and play hard, your hands will get dirty. Don't be ashamed of that, but when you are done, scrub your hands with soap and water, just as you do before handling food and after using the bathroom. Clean under your nails, too, and keep them trimmed with clippers or nail scissors.

YOUR FEET

Your feet contain one-fourth of all the bones in your body. They give you balance. They absorb the impact of millions of footsteps. Your feet twist, turn, and spring back for more.

Wash your feet thoroughly whenever you bathe. Cut your nails straight across to prevent them from becoming ingrown. For hiking and hard play, wear properly fitted shoes or boots that support your feet and offer good traction. Blisters, bunions, and aching feet are often caused by shoes that are too narrow or too short. On the trail and on the playing field, treat "hot spots" and blisters as soon as you notice them. (For more on treating hot spots and blisters, see chapter 11, "First Aid," page 308 ⊞).

YOUR HAIR

Shampoo your hair often enough to keep it clean. Exercise your scalp by massaging it with your fingertips.

YOUR TEETH

Your teeth can last a lifetime, but only if you care for them. Gentle brushing removes sticky, colorless *plaque* that causes tooth decay and gum disease. Flossing loosens food particles and scrapes plaque from between your teeth. Brush and floss your teeth at least twice a day. Eat a well-balanced diet and have a dentist check and clean your teeth every six months.

YOUR EYES

Look in a mirror. Are your eyes clear and bright? If they're bloodshot or if they hurt, you might have eyestrain. The cause can be wind or smoke, lack of sleep, staring too long at a television or computer screen, or a need for glasses. Have your eyes examined by a specialist if you have any concerns.

Rest your eyes when you are studying by looking out a window now and then and focusing on distant objects. Wear sunglasses in bright light, especially on open water and snow. Goggles or a snorkel mask will keep swimming pool chemicals from irritating your eyes. Wear safety goggles whenever you use power tools.

YOUR EARS

Clean the outside of each ear with a damp washcloth wrapped over the end of a finger. Let the inside of your ears take care of themselves. Never dig in your ears—that could infect them or even damage the eardrums.

Very loud noises, especially those that persist, can damage your hearing. Wear ear protection around noisy machinery and on firing ranges. When you listen to music, keep the volume at a reasonable level, especially if you're listening with headphones.

An earache, constant ringing, or fluid running out of an ear are all signs of trouble. See a doctor if you suffer from any of these symptoms.

Being in top physical condition helps you enjoy outdoor adventures to the fullest.

FRESH AIR

THE AIR YOU BREATHE provides the oxygen your body must have. Breathe the cleanest air you can by staying away from exhaust fumes, smoke, and chemical vapors. Use paints, glues, and sprays only outside or in well-ventilated areas. Refuel and light camp stoves and lanterns outdoors, and never bring them into a tent.

REST AND SLEEP

SLEEP IS ONE OF YOUR BODY'S ways of renewing its energy. Rest also gives your body a chance to replace old tissues and build new—in other words, to grow. How much sleep is enough? Most boys of Scouting age need nine to ten hours each night.

On campouts, you will probably be very tired by nightfall. When you crawl into your sleeping bag, you'll probably fall asleep right away and not awaken until dawn.

It can be a little different at home. With school activities, Scout meetings, homework, and reading for pleasure, there is much to do in the evening. Sometimes sleep might not seem very important. Do some planning, though, so that you can get enough sleep and also finish everything else you want to do. Go to bed at the same time each night and get up at the same time in the morning. As you get used to the schedule, you'll fall asleep quickly and awaken refreshed.

PROTECTING YOURSELF AGAINST DISEASE

A HEALTHY DIET, regular exercise, and plenty of sleep will help you stay strong and well. So will immunizations that guard against diseases such as tetanus, polio, mumps, and measles. A doctor can tell you if you have received all the shots you need. In addition, do the following:

- Wash cups and utensils used by others before you drink or eat from them.
- Use your own bath towel, washcloth, and handkerchief.
- Stay clear of persons who are coughing or sneezing.
- Keep flies away from yourself and your food.
- Wash your hands often, and always after using the bathroom.

LEARN SKILLS TO KEEP YOU SAFE

THERE ARE SAFE WAYS to do almost everything: swimming, bicycling, paddling a canoe, using an ax, and playing team sports. Learn and follow the rules of the activities you enjoy. Hike and camp with care. Anytime you aren't sure how to do something safely, ask. Understand the dangers of an activity and know how to avoid them.

Lifting Safely

Protect your back from injury by practicing the proper lifting technique. Instead of leaning over at your waist and grabbing a heavy object, bend your knees, keep your back straight, and lift with the strong muscles of your legs.

COMMONSENSE SAFETY

It doesn't take much skill to cross a railroad track, but if a train is coming, common sense tells you to wait. It is common sense to use a sturdy stepladder instead of a wobbly chair when you have to reach high. It is good judgment to stay away from strange dogs and to sweep up broken glass before someone steps on it and gets hurt.

Be on the lookout for hazardous situations and do something to correct them. Is a campfire getting too large? Douse it. Is a sidewalk crowded? Keep your skateboard under your arm.

PROTECTING YOURSELF FROM TOBACCO, ALCOHOL, AND DRUGS

ON A HIKE, you trust your map and compass to show you the way. When it comes to drugs, alcohol, and tobacco, you can trust that part of the Scout Oath in which you promise to keep yourself physically strong and mentally awake. Just as you trust your compass, trust what you know is right.

Tobacco

Advertisements in magazines and newspapers often pretend that smoking is very exciting. You might have friends who think smoking makes them look grown up.

Don't be fooled. Smoking shortens your breath and makes it harder for you to be good at sports. Smoke coats your lungs with sticky tars that have been shown to cause cancer and emphysema, diseases that kill hundreds of thousands of people every year. Chewing tobacco and snuff are known causes of gum disease and cancer of the mouth.

Tobacco contains an addictive drug called *nicotine* that raises blood pressure and increases the heart rate. A smoker gets in the habit of expecting those changes, and becomes uncomfortable without nicotine. Many people find that it's very hard to quit once they've begun using tobacco.

It's best never to start smoking in the first place. If you do smoke, stop now. Your lungs will slowly heal, and you can look forward to a much healthier and longer life.

Alcohol

Like tobacco advertisements, attractive commercials for beer, wine, and liquor are all around us. But flashy images don't change the fact that drinking will cloud your mind and affect your good judgment. Alcohol can injure your body, especially your liver and brain.

Alcoholism—a dependence on liquor—destroys many people. The craving for alcohol saps their resources and their health, ruins families, and can lead to early death. If you want to make the most of your life, don't drink.

Although you might be too young to drive a car, be aware of the dangers of drinking and driving. Even a modest amount of alcohol can make a person an unsafe driver, and the results are too often tragic. Thousands of teenagers die every year in crashes involving drivers who have been drinking.

Never ride in a car driven by someone who has been drinking. You can always find another way home, but you won't always live through a crash caused by a drunk driver.

Drugs

Drugs are chemicals that alter the body's chemistry. When you are sick, drugs given by a doctor can help you get well. Unfortunately, many young people use illegal drugs that don't come from a physician. Marijuana, cocaine and crack, codeine, depressants, LSD, heroin, inhalants, and steroids have powerful effects on the mind as well as the body. They can produce temporary feelings of pleasure, energy, and peace. However, they can also cause nightmares, fear, and loss of reason. Users might lose interest in the rich life going on all around them. Because the amount of an illegal drug that is swallowed, smoked, inhaled, or injected is not controlled by a doctor, a user never knows how much of a drug he or she is taking. An overdose can lead to serious illness, disability, or death.

Many drugs are addictive. If you begin using a drug, you might soon find that you want more and more of the substance, and that trying to stop using is physically and emotionally painful. You might lie, cheat, and steal to get it. Using drugs can become more important to you than your friends, your family, and even your own life.

Since alcohol, tobacco, and illegal drugs can have such dangerous effects, why would anyone ever start using them? Here are some reasons users might give you, followed by ways you can respond:

- *"All of my friends are doing it."* Sometimes it seems as though everyone is doing something. To be like them, you might be tempted to try it, too. But if their actions are wrong, you don't have to follow the crowd. Show your friends there's a better way to live. Get more involved in Scouts, school activities, sports, and clubs. If you have to, find new friends who aren't developing dangerous habits.

- *"I want to get away from problems."* Scouts learn on campouts that life in the outdoors is not always easy. Perhaps you've been caught in a thunderstorm. Maybe a Scout fell and twisted his ankle. You didn't run away from those problems. Instead, you used your skills to make a safe camp or to give first aid. You faced the tough times squarely and made the best of them.

  At home and in school, demands can seem very heavy. You might feel as though there's a lot of weight on your shoulders, or that parents and teachers expect too much of you. Instead of turning to drinking and drugs to escape problems, look for ways to solve them. Use your skills to find solutions. You don't have to do it all alone. Friends, parents, teachers, school counselors, and Scout leaders might all be able to help.

- *"I want to feel grown up."* Because of the way smoking, drinking, and using drugs are often shown in movies and on television, they might seem like adult things to do. But hurting your body and your future is really very childish.

  You can prove you are becoming an adult by accepting worthwhile responsibilities. Helping with household chores shows you are doing your part to make family life better for everyone. Earning Scout badges and holding troop leadership positions are signs you are maturing. So is doing your best in class and in school activities. Those are the real ways to let the world know you are becoming a respected adult.

- *"There's nothing else to do."* Some young people say they use drugs, alcohol, and tobacco because they are bored. What they're really saying is that they're too lazy to go out and take part in the real excitement of being alive.

  If you look around, boredom should be the furthest thing from your mind. Athletics, books, Scouting, school projects, music, exercise, travel, helping others—the world is full of opportunities.

What to Do About Tobacco, Alcohol, and Drugs

Baden-Powell, the founder of Scouting, had faith that Scouts were smart enough to figure out what is healthy and right. Have faith in yourself and in your judgment. Don't let others pressure you into harming your body and your mind with drugs, alcohol, or tobacco. And if you have been foolish, there is no law that says you have to stay that way.

Finally, you can simply turn your back on anything that would harm you. That's a real sign of courage. Nobody can make you do something wrong if you don't want to do it. With a strong body and clear mind, you will be far ahead of those who choose instead to risk their friends, their families, and their lives on the dangers of using drugs, tobacco, and alcohol.

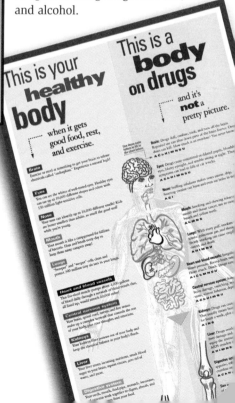

ADVENTURE

& OPPORTUNITY

OUTDOOR ADVENTURES

16

TRAILHEAD

OUTDOOR ADVENTURES

"*Scouting* is three-quarters *-outing.*"

The first Boy Scout summer camp was held in 1907. Lord Baden-Powell, the founder of Scouting, brought together a group of twenty-two Scouts on Brownsea Island off the coast of England. They were divided into four patrols—the Wolves, Bulls,
Curlews, and Ravens. After setting up their tents and cooking areas, they devoted seven days to woodcraft, nature observation, lifesaving, and Scout skills. Around the evening campfires they told stories, sang songs, and performed skits. The Scouts agreed that their summer camp had been a terrific success.

Today's camporees and summer camps can be just as exciting as that first one on Brownsea Island. You can spend your days hiking, swimming, mastering the lore of Scouting, and learning about nature. You'll have plenty of chances to pass requirements for badges and to practice no-trace camping methods. You might even get to know Scouts from other areas.

CAMPOREES

A CAMPOREE is usually a weekend of fun, fellowship, and Scouting activities shared by two or more troops camping together. Your patrol can show its skill as you make camp and take part in camporee activities. You can also share good times and fresh ideas with Scouts from other troops. What are they cooking for meals? How do they set up their dining fly? Can they show you how to lash together a signal tower or how to paddle a canoe?

Perhaps your patrol will lay out an orienteering course that other Scouts can use to test map-and-compass skills. A knot rack could help everyone learn to handle rope, and an obstacle course can give you a real workout. Camporee games might require that the members of your patrol cooperate with each other in order to reach a goal. Some games can't be won unless all the patrols pool their efforts and work as one big group.

Camporees can be great experiences. They are also a perfect way for a patrol to get ready for summer camp.

SUMMER CAMP

SOME SCOUT CAMPS lie in deep forests or at the bases of high, windy peaks. Others are tucked back in the woods along rivers and lakes. A few are located in deserts or along seashores. Every camp is different, but here's a small sampling of what you are likely to find:

- Nature hikes with instructors who really know their stuff
- Map-and-compass courses
- A wood yard for practicing proper use of knives, saws, and axes
- Archery and rifle ranges
- Conservation projects, meadow repair, trail maintenance, and erosion control
- Instruction in the best no-trace methods of backcountry travel
- Project COPE (Challenging Outdoor Personal Experience) courses that improve your balance, fitness, and ability to solve problems
- Aquatics programs in swimming pools, lakes, or streams
- Crafts areas

Summer camp allows you to devote a full week to living the Scouting life. Your own troop leaders will be there to help you work on many outdoor skills and to enjoy some tremendous adventures. A camp staff of experienced older Scouts and adults can give you a helping hand whenever you need it. You can form new friendships with Scouts from other troops and learn how they do things in their patrols.

Scout camps come in many shapes and sizes, but they all share one thing in common—they offer as much adventure and excitement as a Scout can have anywhere. For many troops, a week at summer camp is a high point of the year.

When winter comes, don't put away your outdoor gear. Many BSA high-adventure bases offer exciting challenges throughout the year.

COUNCIL HIGH-ADVENTURE BASES

HIGH-ADVENTURE bases operated by BSA councils can drop you right into the middle of terrific action. Whitewater kayaking, extended backpacking, rock climbing, and sailing are just a few of the activities older Scouts will find. The BSA publication *Passport to High Adventure*, No. 4310, describes these and other high-adventure opportunities.

NATIONAL HIGH-ADVENTURE BASES

FOR REAL EXCITEMENT beyond your council, it's hard to beat the national high-adventure bases of the Boy Scouts of America. Designed for older Boy Scouts, Varsity Scouts, and Venturers, each base offers the training, equipment, and support you will need to set out on wilderness treks that challenge your skills, strength, and willpower.

Philmont Scout Ranch

Explore the rugged high country of northern New Mexico on a backpacking trek, as a member of a conservation work crew, or by taking part in an advanced wilderness adventure. Covering more than 137,000 acres of mountains, forests, prairies, and streams, Philmont is an inspiring backpacker's paradise. Staffed camps in the backcountry offer program opportunities including rock climbing, black-powder rifle shooting, living history, horseback riding, archaeology, environmental awareness, and many others.

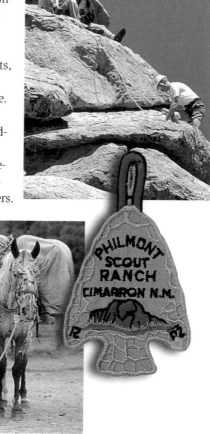

Florida National High Adventure Sea Base

Explore the clear waters of the Florida Keys and Bahamas by various kinds of watercraft, including sailboats. Snorkel and scuba dive among schools of brilliantly colored tropical fish. Investigate a primitive island, search for the wreckage of galleons, cast your bait for sailfish in the Gulf Stream waters, practice windsurfing, and study the marine life of North America's only living coral reef.

Northern Tier National High Adventure Programs

The Sioux and Chippewa once traveled this northern lake country. French-Canadian trappers followed, their canoes loaded down with furs. Headquartered in the beautiful Superior-Quetico boundary waters of Minnesota, Ontario, and Manitoba, the Northern Tier offers wilderness canoeing expeditions and programs featuring fishing and winter camping.

JAMBOREES

AS SCOUTING SPREAD around the world in the early years of the twentieth century, Lord Baden-Powell invited Scouts from all nations to a jamboree in London. He wanted young people of many countries to camp with each other, share their knowledge, and develop friendships. The 1920 jamboree was such a success that world jamborees continue to be held every four years. BSA national jamborees, also four years apart, bring together thousands of American Scouts for a week of fun, learning, and fellowship.

Baden-Powell hoped that get-togethers of boys from around the world would, as he put it, "establish friendships among Scouts of all nations and help to develop peace and happiness in the world and goodwill among men."

AWARDS AND RECOGNITION

TRAILHEAD

17

AWARDS AND RECOGNITION

IN ADDITION TO BADGES of rank and merit badges, Scouts are eligible to earn a number of other awards that reflect their achievements. The requirements for these awards are listed in the *Boy Scout Requirements* book, No. 33215, and on application forms.

Snorkeling, BSA

Earn this award by completing the requirements on the application form.

BSA Lifeguard

Earning this special Scout certification will give you practice in lifeguarding, boat rescues, and advanced rescue skills. Check with your Scout leaders or local council service center for names of approved BSA Lifeguard counselors.

Mile Swim, BSA

Want to train for and complete a swim covering a full mile? Check out the *Swimming* merit badge pamphlet for more information.

Hornaday Awards

William T. Hornaday was the first director of the New York Zoological Society, and one of the most earnest pioneers of conservation in our nation's history. The recognition that bears his name is granted to Scouts who have done exceptional and distinguished service in conservation. It is granted in five forms:

- *Unit certificate* to a den, pack, patrol, troop, team, crew, or a group of five or more Scouts or Venturers for unique projects involving conservation or in improving environmental quality.

- *Badge* to a Scout or Venturer for outstanding service in conservation or in improving environmental quality within a council.

- *Bronze medal* to a Scout or Venturer for exceptional service in conservation or in improving environmental quality within a council.

- *Silver medal* to a Scout or Venturer for unusual or distinguished service in conservation or in improving environmental quality on a state or regional basis. No more than six silver medals are awarded each year. The silver medal is the highest conservation award available to a Scout or Venturer.

- *Gold medal* to an adult Scouting or Venturing leader for unusual and distinguished service in conservation or in improving environmental quality on a state, BSA region, or national basis. No more than one gold medal is awarded each year.

World Conservation Award

Receive this award by completing the requirements for the following merit badges: Environmental Science, Citizenship in the World, and either Soil and Water Conservation or Fish and Wildlife Management.

Leave No Trace Awareness Award

Receive this award by completing the following requirements: Recite and explain the principles of Leave No Trace. On three separate camping/backpacking trips demonstrate and practice the principles of Leave No Trace. Earn the Camping and Environmental Science merit badges. Participate in a Leave No Trace–related service project. Give a ten-minute presentation on a Leave No Trace topic approved by your Scoutmaster. Draw a poster or build a model to demonstrate the differences in how we camp or travel in high-use and pristine areas.

Interpreter

A Scout wearing the interpreter strip must be able to carry on a conversation in a foreign language or in sign language, write a letter in the foreign language (not required for signing), and translate orally and in writing from one language to another.

50-Miler Award

The 50-Miler Award is presented to Scouts who have taken part in a troop event involving a wilderness trip covering at least fifty consecutive miles over at least five consecutive days. Requirements also include doing service projects to improve the environment.

Historic Trails Award

Along with other members of your troop, research a historic trail or site and learn about its significance. Hike and camp for two days and one night along the trail or near the site, then work with adults to mark and restore the trail or site.

Totin' Chip

When a Scout demonstrates that he knows how to handle woods tools, he may be granted totin' rights. For requirements, see page 85.

Paul Bunyan Woodsman

Earn the Totin' Chip, then help another Scout earn his. Show your skill with a three-quarter ax or a saw to do a forestry job, and teach other Scouts how to use woods tools safely.

Firem'n Chit

The owner of a Firem'n Chit has demon-strated knowledge of safety rules in building, maintaining, and putting out camp and cooking fires.

Den Chief Service Award

Den chiefs who complete certain service and training requirements can receive this special recognition.

World Crest

All members of the Boy Scouts of America may wear the World Crest as an expression of world brotherhood.

RELIGIOUS EMBLEMS

"A SCOUT IS REVERENT." Scouts show their faith by doing their duty to God. Some also undertake special service and learning that could qualify them for religious emblems. These are not Scouting awards. Faith groups develop their religious emblems program including the requirements. The BSA Religious Relationships Committee oversees the religious emblems programs.

Armenian—Ararat

D.R.E., Diocese of the Armenian Church of America (Eastern Diocese), 630 Second Avenue, New York, NY 10016.

Armenian—Saint Mesrob

Armenian Apostolic Church of America, Western Prelacy, 4401 Russell Avenue, Los Angeles, CA 90026.

Association of Unity Churches— Light of God

The Association of Unity Churches, P.O. Box 610, Lee's Summit, MO 64063.

Baha'i—Unity of Mankind

Baha'i Committee on Scouting, Baha'i National Center, Wilmette, IL 60091.

Baptist—God and Church

Local council service center or PRAY, 8520 Mackenzie Road, St. Louis, MO 63123.

Buddhist—Sangha

National Buddhist Committee on Scouting, 701 E. Thrift Avenue, Kingsland, GA 31548-8213.

Christian Church (Disciples of Christ)— God and Church

Local council service center or PRAY, 8520 Mackenzie Road, St. Louis, MO 63123.

Church of Jesus Christ of Latter-day Saints— On My Honor

Church of Jesus Christ of Latter-day Saints, Church Distribution Center, 1999 West 1700 South, Salt Lake City, UT 84104.

Churches of Christ— Good Servant

Members of Churches of Christ for Scouting, ACU Station, Box 27938, Abilene, TX 79699-7938.

Eastern Catholic— Light Is Life

Local council service center, diocesan Scout office, or National Catholic Committee on Scouting, P.O. Box 152079, Irving, TX 75015-2079.

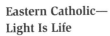

Eastern Orthodox— Alpha Omega

PRAY, 8520 Mackenzie Road, St. Louis, MO 63123.

Episcopal— God and Church

Local council service center or PRAY, 8520 Mackenzie Road, St. Louis, MO 63123.

First Church of Christ, Scientist— God and Country

PRAY, 8520 Mackenzie Road, St. Louis, MO 63123.

General Church of the New Jerusalem— Open Word Award

Chairman, Boy Scout Relations Committee, General Church of the New Jerusalem, P.O. Box 277, Byrn Athyn, PA 19009.

Hindu—Dharma

North American Hindu Association, 411 Park Avenue, Suite 202, San Jose, CA 95110.

Islamic—In the Name of God

National Islamic Committee for Scouting, P.O. Box 51931, Indianapolis, IN 46251-0931.

Jewish—Ner Tamid

Local council service center or PRAY, 8520 Mackenzie Road, St. Louis, MO 63123.

Lutheran— God and Church

Local council service center or PRAY, 8520 Mackenzie Road, St. Louis, MO 63123.

Protestant— God and Church

Local council service center or PRAY, 8520 Mackenzie Road, St. Louis, MO 63123.

Meher Baba— Compassionate Father

Committee for Meher Baba and Scouting, 912 Ninth Avenue South, North Myrtle Beach, SC 29582.

Religious Society of Friends (Quakers)— Spirit of Truth

PRAY, 8520 Mackenzie Road, St. Louis, MO 63123.

Moravian— God and Country

The Moravian Church, Drawer Y, Winston-Salem, NC 27108.

Reorganized Church of Jesus Christ of Latter Day Saints—Liahona

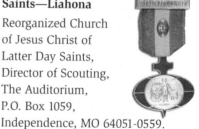

Reorganized Church of Jesus Christ of Latter Day Saints, Director of Scouting, The Auditorium, P.O. Box 1059, Independence, MO 64051-0559.

Polish National Catholic—God and Country (Bog I Ojczyzna)

Mr. Arthur Wyglon, 115 Heather Hill Drive, Buffalo, NY 14224.

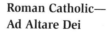

Roman Catholic— Ad Altare Dei

Local council service center, diocesan Scout office, or National Catholic Committee on Scouting, P.O. Box 152079, Irving, TX 75015-2079

Presbyterian Church (U.S.A.)—God and Church

Local council service center or PRAY, 8520 Mackenzie Road, St. Louis, MO 63123.

The Salvation Army— God and The Salvation Army

The Salvation Army, P.O. Box 269, Alexandria, VA 22313.

United Methodist— God and Church

Local council service center or PRAY, 8520 Mackenzie Road, St. Louis, MO 63123.

United Church of Christ—God and Church

Local council service center or PRAY, 8520 Mackenzie Road, St. Louis, MO 63123.

Zoroastrian— Good Life

Zoroastrian Association, c/o Villy Gandhi, Corresponding Secretary, The Good Life Program, 704 Harristown Road, Glen Rock, NJ 07452-2334.

ORGAN DONOR AWARENESS

THANKS TO MODERN medical techniques, many people can benefit from the transplant of organs and tissues. A transplanted cornea, for example, can give sight to a blind person. Liver, heart, and lung transplants can save many lives, and new transplant opportunities are being developed all the time.

As a Presidential Good Turn, the Boy Scouts of America set out in 1986 to educate Americans about the importance of organ donation. To learn more about how to become a donor and how to educate others on the importance of donor contributions, contact local donor organizations.

LIFESAVING AWARDS

THE NATIONAL COURT OF HONOR presents awards for rare Scoutlike action and for saving life.

Honor Medal

The highest special award in Scouting is the gold Honor Medal for saving life. It is given to Scouts and Scouters who show heroism, resourcefulness, and skill by saving or trying to save life at great risk of their own. In cases of *exceptional skill or resourcefulness and extreme risk of life,* the medal is awarded with crossed palms.

Heroism Award

This is awarded for heroic action involving minimum risk to self.

Medal of Merit

The Medal of Merit is awarded to Scouts who put into practice the skills and ideals of Scouting through some great act of service. This act need not involve a rescue or risk to self.

OPPORTUNITIES FOR OLDER SCOUTS

TRAILHEAD

18

OPPORTUNITIES FOR OLDER SCOUTS

SCOUTING IS PACKED WITH ADVENTURES for older members. Many continue to be active in the troops they first joined. They take on leadership roles of increasing responsibility and play key roles in making a troop's program effective and exciting. The wisdom and experience of older Scouts give a troop strength. Experienced Scouts can be role models for younger boys, and can help them learn skills and take part in campouts and other troop activities.

Of course, Scouts of any age can continue to work on requirements and merit badges leading to the rank of Eagle Scout. Older Scouts can also set off on expeditions to council and national high-adventure bases, attend national and world jamborees, and be eligible for other BSA opportunities including Order of the Arrow membership.

Many troops are associated with Venturing crews or Varsity Scout teams designed for older Scouts. And many troops have a Venture patrol that provides enhanced program possibilities beyond those available to younger boys.

VENTURE PATROLS

A VENTURE PATROL is an *optional* older-boy patrol (ages 13 through 17) within a troop. It is led by a youth member elected as *Venture patrol leader.* Like a Varsity Scout team, the Venture patrol features exciting and demanding *ultimate adventures* and sports activities. For example, a Venture patrol might spend two or three months learning how to paddle and portage canoes, brushing up on orienteering, and researching the food and gear needed for long journeys. With the skills mastered, they plan and set out on a canoe-camping ultimate adventure—miles of canoe travel along lakes and rivers, finding their way with a map and compass, and pitching their tents each evening on the shore. Venture patrols might also select a sport such as basketball or soccer, and spend a season (usually three months) sharpening their skills, competing among themselves, and challenging other Venture patrols.

Venture patrol members may continue to advance through Scouting's ranks and to hold positions of troop leadership. Venture patrol members wear the Boy Scout uniform with the Venture identification strip above the right pocket.

Venture and Varsity Program Features

Venture patrols and Varsity Scout teams offer older Scouts plenty of terrific program opportunities. Members can choose from among the following high-adventure and sports features, each lasting about three months. Activity pamphlets, available at local Scout shops or service centers, provide how-to information and program outlines.

High Adventure Program Features
Backpacking
Canoe Camping
Caving
Cycling
Discovering Adventure
Fishing
Freestyle Biking
Frontiersman
Mechanics
Orienteering
Rock Climbing and Rappelling
Snow Camping
Survival
Whitewater Canoeing

Sports Program Features
Basketball
Bowling
Cross-Country Skiing
Roller Hockey
Shooting Sports
Soccer
Softball
Swimming
Tennis
Triathlon
Volleyball
Waterskiing

VARSITY SCOUTING

VARSITY SCOUT TEAMS

The Varsity Scout team is made up of young men ages 14 through 17 in a stand-alone program of the Boy Scouts of America, separate from the troop. Each of its five fields of emphasis is managed by a Varsity Scout team member who serves as *program manager,* and by an adult from the Varsity Scout committee who serves as *program adviser.* They work together in a manner similar to that of a player and a coach.

A Varsity Scout team is divided into *squads* of four to eight members—just the right size to take maximum advantage of a great range of exciting activities and to have plenty of opportunities for everyone to serve as leaders. Every squad elects a *squad leader.* The *team captain*—a Varsity Scout elected by all the team members—conducts meetings and works closely with adult leaders (the Varsity Scout team Coach, assistant Coaches, and Varsity Scout committee members) to develop and carry out an effective program.

A Varsity Scout may wear Scout shorts and a tan knit Varsity Scout shirt as an activities uniform. For more formal occasions, Varsity Scout team members wear traditional Boy Scout uniforms with orange shoulder loops and a Varsity Scout identification strip above the right pocket.

VARSITY SCOUTING'S FIVE FIELDS OF EMPHASIS

Advancement

Team program activities are arranged to help members complete the qualifications for the Eagle Scout rank and, for current Eagles, the Eagle Palms. Varsity Scouts may also pursue and achieve other Scout awards and recognitions.

High Adventure and Sports

Varsity Scouts plan and take part in tough physical and mental activities—endeavors as wide-ranging as snow camping, whitewater rafting, backpacking, swimming, and roller hockey. In addition to learning and practicing the skills they need in order to enjoy the activities they choose, many Varsity Scout teams also set their sights on extended once-a-year experiences at a council-operated or national high-adventure base, or at another location selected by the team.

Personal Development

Varsity Scouting stresses personal development through spiritual growth, leadership, citizenship, and social and physical fitness. The program manager responsible for personal development assists each member of the team in selecting and participating in activities that will enhance the personal development of all team members.

Service

Varsity Scouts upholding the Scouting habit of doing a Good Turn daily participate in group service projects for the benefit of their church, school, community, and needy individuals. In addition, each team member may conduct service projects on his own initiative.

Special Programs and Events

Providing the time, means, and encouragement for Scouts to participate in special programs and events is an important feature of Varsity Scouting. Special events might be national Scouting activities (jamborees, Order of the Arrow functions), district or coun-

cil events (Scout shows and camporees), or activities conducted at the team level (cookouts, ski trips, etc.).

VENTURING

VENTURING IS A STAND-ALONE PROGRAM of the Boy Scouts of America for young men and women ages 14 through 20, who have completed the eighth grade and who subscribe to the Venturing Oath and Code. Venturing crews are operated by chartered organizations just like Cub Scout packs and Boy Scout troops. The chartered organizations match their program resources to the needs and interests of their youth members who are called *Venturers*. The adult leaders are called *Advisors,* and the top youth member is called the *crew president.*

A Venturing crew may pursue a special avocation or hobby of its youth members and adult leaders. These special interests include the outdoors, sports, arts/hobbies, youth ministry, and Sea Scouting.

Venturing offers an advancement program based on achieving proficiency in a variety of skill levels. The awards include the Venturing Bronze, Venturing Gold, Venturing Silver, Venturing Ranger, and Sea Scouting Quartermaster awards.

Male Venturers who have achieved the First Class rank as a Boy Scout in a troop or Varsity Scout team may continue working toward the Star, Life, and Eagle ranks up to age 18.

THE VENTURING OATH

As a Venturer, I promise to help strengthen America, to be faithful in my religious duties, to help others, and to seek truth, fairness, and adventure in our world.

ALPHA PHI OMEGA NATIONAL SERVICE FRATERNITY

BASED ON THE PRINCIPLES of the Scout Oath and Law, Alpha Phi Omega National Service Fraternity (APO) is a national college service fraternity active on many campuses. APO's service program encourages its members to continue their Scouting involvement through college connections. Many chapters are coeducational. For more information, contact APO's national office:

Alpha Phi Omega National Office
14901 East 42nd Street
Independence, MO 64055
816-373-8667
E-mail: aponed@aol.com

NATIONAL EAGLE SCOUT ASSOCIATION

NATIONAL EAGLE SCOUT
ASSOCIATION

THE NATIONAL Eagle Scout Association (NESA) is a fellowship of men who have achieved the Eagle Scout Award. The NESA journal, *Eagletter,* highlights the accomplishments of members and brings news of Eagle Scout activities to readers. Applications for joining NESA are available at local council service centers.

ORDER OF THE ARROW

THE ORDER of the Arrow (OA) is Scouting's national honor society. It sets out to recognize those youth and adult campers who best exemplify the Scout Oath and Law in their daily lives, to develop and maintain camping traditions and spirit, to promote Scout camping, and to crystallize the Scout habit of helpfulness into a life purpose of leadership in cheerful service to others. The Order of the Arrow was founded in 1915 by Dr. E. Urner Goodman and Carroll A. Edson at Treasure Island, the summer camp of the BSA's Philadelphia Area Council. The Order of the Arrow became an official part of the Boy Scouts of America in 1948.

To gain membership in the Order of the Arrow, a registered Boy Scout or Varsity Scout must hold the First Class rank or higher. He must have taken part in a minimum of 15 days and nights of Scout camping in a 2-year period, including a 6-day and 5-night camping experience at a local or national council facility operated and accredited by the BSA. Eligible Scouts must then be elected to the Order by other members of their unit, following approval by their Scoutmaster or Varsity Scout team Coach.

The two membership levels of the Order of the Arrow are Ordeal and Brotherhood. During the Ordeal period, the first step toward full OA membership, a Scout is expected to strengthen his involvement in his Scout unit and encourage Scout camping. After 10 months of service and after fulfilling certain requirements, an Ordeal member may take part in the Brotherhood ceremony which places further emphasis on the ideals

of Scouting and of the Order. Completing this ceremony signifies full membership in the Order of the Arrow.

Following 2 years of service as a Brotherhood member, and with the approval of the National Order of the Arrow Committee, a Scout or adult leader may be recognized with the Vigil Honor for outstanding service to Scouting, his OA lodge, and his community. The Vigil Honor is granted by special selection, and is limited to not more than one person for every fifty members registered each year with a lodge.

Among the OA's national activities are service projects, college scholarships, American Indian camperships, matching grants for council camp improvements, and national leadership seminars. OA trail crews completing conservation projects at Philmont Scout Ranch provide invaluable service as they care for the environment. The national Order of the Arrow conference (NOAC), held every two years at a major university, trains leaders of local lodges and allows Scouts from across the country to share in the fellowship of OA membership.

While it recognizes both boys and adults, the Order of the Arrow is a youth-led program. Youth members are elected to serve as the *national chief, vice chief,* and *chiefs of four national regions.* Boys are also members of the National Order of the Arrow Committee to provide youth input on national OA policy, and they serve as the presiding officers for national and regional OA events.

The Order of the Arrow Handbook *explains the opportunities for, and the responsibilities of, OA members.*

HISTORY

1910

OUT OF THE PAST
INTO THE FUTURE

2000

OF

**THE BOY SCOUTS
OF AMERICA**

HISTORY OF THE BSA

TRAILHEAD

19

Renowned artist Norman Rockwell painted many pictures of Scouts in action. His images appeared on the covers of the third, fourth, sixth, and ninth editions of the Boy Scout Handbook.

HISTORY OF THE BOY SCOUTS OF AMERICA

SCOUTING CAME TO AMERICA because a boy did a *Good Turn*—an act of kindness for which he expected no reward. It happened many years ago on the foggy streets of London, England, when an American named William D. Boyce lost his way. A boy walked up and asked if he could be of assistance.

An early Boy Scout uniform and handbook

Mr. Boyce explained where he wanted to go. The boy led him to his destination, but when Mr. Boyce offered to give him some money, the boy said, "No, thank you, sir. I am a Scout. I won't take anything for helping."

William Boyce was so impressed by the boy's kindness that he met with Lord Robert Baden-Powell, the founder of the Boy Scouts in Great Britain. He liked what Baden-Powell told him, and he knew that boys in the United States would want to be Scouts, too.

On February 8, 1910, Mr. Boyce and a group of businessmen, educators, and political leaders founded the Boy Scouts of America. Scouts celebrate February 8 as the birthday of the BSA.

No one knows what happened to the boy who guided Mr. Boyce through the London fog, but he will never be forgotten. Like many acts of kindness, what was done proved to be far more significant than who did it. The boy's Good Turn helped bring Scouting to America.

BADEN-POWELL— SCOUTING'S FOUNDER

ROBERT BADEN-POWELL was a general in the British army who became famous for his leadership during the Boer War in South Africa between Britain and the descendants of Dutch settlers, the Boers. After the war, Baden-Powell wanted to use his fame to help boys become better men and to have fun while they were doing it.

In 1907, Baden-Powell invited a group of boys to Brownsea Island off the coast of England to attend the world's first Boy Scout camp. Its success led him to write a book called *Scouting for Boys.* Thousands of boys read it and wanted to join the new organization. Scouting spread like wildfire throughout England and, before long, around the world.

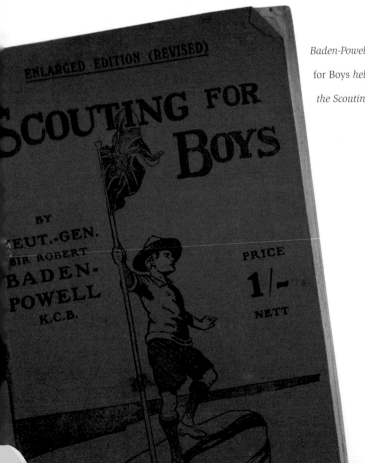

Baden-Powell's Scouting for Boys *helped launch the Scouting movement.*

SCOUTING'S EARLY LEADERS

Lord Robert Baden-Powell

In 1907, Lord Robert Baden-Powell founded the Boy Scout movement in Great Britain.

Ernest Thompson Seton

As the first Chief Scout of the Boy Scouts of America, Mr. Seton made nature study an important part of the Scouting program.

Daniel Carter Beard

A woodsman in a buckskin shirt, "Uncle Dan" helped establish the outdoor skills that are still at the heart of Boy Scouting.

James E. West

Mr. West was a dedicated leader who guided the Boy Scouts of America for over thirty years as it grew into a vigorous national organization.

THE BOY SCOUT HANDBOOK

BADEN-POWELL'S BRITISH SCOUTS had *Scouting for Boys* as their manual, but American Boy Scouts needed a guidebook of their own. Ernest Thompson Seton, a well-known author, artist, and wildlife expert, wrote the first edition of *The Boy Scouts of America Handbook for Boys* in 1911. It was packed with information about camping, hiking, swimming, wildlife, and other subjects Mr. Seton knew boys would like. The book also explained how to form troops and patrols, and listed all the requirements for Boy Scout ranks and merit badges.

The BSA has revised the handbook every eight or nine years to include the latest information about Scouting and outdoor adventures. The handbook you are reading is the eleventh edition, written to carry Scouting well into the twenty-first century. Nearly 40 million copies of *The Boy Scout Handbook* have been printed since 1911, making it one of the most popular books of all time.

Boys' Life Magazine

In 1912, the Boy Scouts of America began publishing a magazine called *Boys' Life*. Today, *Boys' Life* is received by 1.3 million Scouts every month. Each issue is filled with terrific stories, camping hints, and information for patrols and troops.

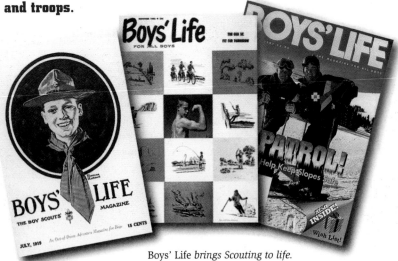

Boys' Life *brings Scouting to life.*

BOY SCOUT SERVICE

SERVICE TO OTHERS has always been a central part of Scouting. During World War I, Boy Scouts throughout the country collected paper and metal for recycling, and sold bonds to raise money for the war effort. In 1916, the United States Congress showed its thanks by granting the Boy Scouts of America a special congressional charter.

Scouts today carry on this tradition of service in their homes, communities, and nation by gathering food and clothing for needy neighbors, building playgrounds, and repairing parks and public buildings. They assist fire and police departments, aid disaster victims, and clean up after storms.

Recycling efforts allow Scouts to practice community service as they learn about wisely using natural resources.

Many Scouts also complete conservation work that protects and restores the land. The service projects required for different BSA ranks remind Scouts of the importance of contributing their time and energy to worthwhile efforts.

And in support of the President's Summit for America's Future held in 1997, the Boy Scouts of America committed each youth member to provide a minimum of twelve hours of community service annually through the year 2000. This will result in a total of two hundred million hours of community service rendered by the BSA and its youth.

The BSA Crime Prevention Program was created to use the collective resources of our youth, adult membership, law enforcement agencies, and the community to address the problem of crime in our communities.

The artwork of Joesph Csatari reflected the excitement and meaning of Scouting in the 1970s and 1980s.

THE SCOUTING FAMILY OF OPPORTUNITIES

IN ADDITION TO BOY SCOUTING, the BSA has developed programs for young people of different ages and interests:

- *Cub Scouting,* started in 1930, offers exciting activities for younger boys. *Tiger Cubs BSA* is for first-grade boys and their parents or guardians. Boys in the second and third grade (or ages 8 and 9) are *Cub Scouts.* Fourth and fifth graders (or boys who are 10) can join a *Webelos* den that prepares them to be members of a Boy Scout troop.

- *Varsity Scouting,* which began in 1978, allows older boys to add to their Scout experience by forming teams that take part in sports events and challenging outdoor adventures.

- *Venturing* is a program for young men and women ages 14 through 20. Venturing traces its origins to Sea Scouting, begun in 1912 as a branch of the BSA for older boys. Eventually it became Senior Scouting, then Exploring, and in 1998, Venturing was created. Venturing crews often choose an area of special interest such as sailing, mountaineering, youth ministry, sports, the outdoors, or arts/hobbies.

- *Lone Scouting.* The Lone Scouts of America was founded by William Boyce to provide Scouting experiences for boys living in sparsely populated areas of the country. Mr. Boyce's organization merged with the Boy Scouts of America in 1924. Today, the Lone Scout plan serves boys who cannot take part in the activities of a Boy Scout troop on a regular basis because of distance, disability, or other unavoidable factors.

- The *Direct Service Council* was established to make Scouting available to U.S. citizens and their dependents who live in countries outside the jurisdiction of the Transatlantic Council and the Far East Council (the BSA's two overseas councils). It is administered by the BSA's International Division at the national office in Irving, Texas.

   More than 4,500 youth members and 1,700 adult leaders belong to over 140 Direct Service Council units or are registered as Lone Scouts in isolated areas of the world.

   The program of Direct Service Council units is basically the same as that in the U.S., with some modifications when necessary due to circumstances and customs within a given country.

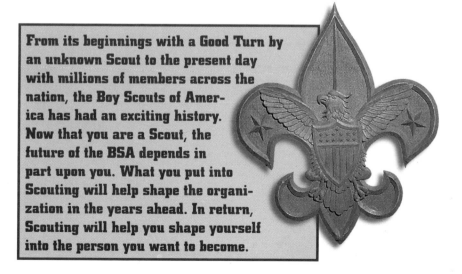

From its beginnings with a Good Turn by an unknown Scout to the present day with millions of members across the nation, the Boy Scouts of America has had an exciting history. Now that you are a Scout, the future of the BSA depends in part upon you. What you put into Scouting will help shape the organization in the years ahead. In return, Scouting will help you shape yourself into the person you want to become.

TENDERFOOT RANK REQUIREMENTS

✓		Leader initial and date
	1. Present yourself to your leader, properly dressed, before going on an overnight camping trip. Show the camping gear you will use. Show the right way to pack and carry it.	
	2. Spend at least one night on a patrol or troop campout. Sleep in a tent you have helped pitch.	
	3. On the campout, assist in preparing and cooking one of your patrol's meals. Tell why it is important for each patrol member to share in meal preparation and cleanup, and explain the importance of eating together.	
	4a. Demonstrate how to whip and fuse the ends of a rope.	1-31-01
	4b. Demonstrate that you know how to tie the following knots and tell what their uses are: two half hitches and the taut-line hitch.	1-31
	5. Explain the rules of safe hiking, both on the highway and cross-country, during the day and at night. Explain what to do if you are lost.	
	6. Demonstrate how to display, raise, lower, and fold the American flag.	
	7. Repeat from memory and explain in your own words the Scout Oath, Law, motto, and slogan.	
	8. Know your patrol name, give the patrol yell, and describe your patrol flag.	
	9. Explain why we use the buddy system in Scouting.	
	10a. Record your best in the following tests: **Current results** Push-ups _____ Pull-ups _____ Sit-ups _____ Standing long jump (_____ feet _____ inches) ¼-mile walk/run _____	

TENDERFOOT RANK REQUIREMENTS

		Leader initial and date
☐	**30 days later** Push-ups _____ Pull-ups _____ Sit-ups _____ Standing long jump (_____ feet _____ inches) ¼-mile walk/run _____	
☐	**10b.** Show improvement in the activities listed in requirement 10a after practicing for 30 days.	
☐	**11.** Identify local poisonous plants; tell how to treat for exposure to them.	
☐	**12a.** Demonstrate the Heimlich maneuver and tell when it is used.	
☐	**12b.** Show first aid for the following: • Simple cuts and scratches • Blisters on the hand and foot • Minor burns or scalds (first-degree) • Bites or stings of insects and ticks • Poisonous snakebite • Nosebleed • Frostbite and sunburn	
☐	**13.** Participate in a Scoutmaster conference.	
☐	**14.** Complete your board of review.	

NOTE: Alternate requirements for the Tenderfoot rank are available for Scouts with physical or mental disabilities if they meet the criteria listed in the *Boy Scout Requirements* book, No. 33215.

SECOND CLASS
RANK REQUIREMENTS

✓		Leader initial and date
	1a. Demonstrate how a compass works and how to orient a map. Explain what map symbols mean.	
	1b. Using a compass and a map together, take a 5-mile hike (or 10 miles by bike) approved by your adult leader and your parent or guardian.*	
	2a. Since joining, have participated in five separate troop/patrol activities (other than troop/patrol meetings), two of which included camping overnight.	
	2b. On one of these campouts, select your patrol site and sleep in a tent that you pitched.	
	2c. On one campout, demonstrate proper care, sharpening, and use of the knife, saw, and ax, and describe when they should be used.	
	2d. Use the tools listed in requirement 2c to prepare tinder, kindling, and fuel for a cooking fire.	
	2e. Discuss when it is appropriate to use a cooking fire and a lightweight stove. Discuss the safety procedures for using both.	
	2f. Demonstrate how to light a fire and a lightweight stove.	
	2g. On one campout, plan and cook over an open fire one hot breakfast or lunch for yourself, selecting foods from the four basic food groups. Explain the importance of good nutrition. Tell how to transport, store, and prepare the foods you selected.	
	3. Participate in a flag ceremony for your school, religious institution, chartered organization, community, or troop activity.	
	4. Participate in an approved (minimum of one hour) service project.	
	5. Identify or show evidence of at least ten kinds of wild animals (birds, mammals, reptiles, fish, mollusks) found in your community.	
	6a. Show what to do for "hurry" cases of stopped breathing, serious bleeding, and internal poisoning.	

*If you use a wheelchair or crutches, or if it is difficult for you to get around, you may substitute "trip" for "hike."

SECOND CLASS
RANK REQUIREMENTS

		Leader initial and date
☐	**6b.** Prepare a personal first aid kit to take with you on a hike.	
☐	**6c.** Demonstrate first aid for the following: • Object in the eye • Bite of a suspected rabid animal • Puncture wounds from a splinter, nail, and fishhook • Serious burns (second-degree) • Heat exhaustion • Shock • Heatstroke, dehydration, hypothermia, and hyperventilation	
☐	**7a.** Tell what precautions must be taken for a safe swim.	
☐	**7b.** Demonstrate your ability to jump feetfirst into water over your head in depth, level off and swim 25 feet on the surface, stop, turn sharply, resume swimming, then return to your starting place.†	
☐	**7c.** Demonstrate water rescue methods by reaching with your arm or leg, by reaching with a suitable object, and by throwing lines and objects.† Explain why swimming rescues should not be attempted when a reaching or throwing rescue is possible, and explain why and how a rescue swimmer should avoid contact with the victim.	
☐	**8.** Participate in a school, community, or troop program on the dangers of using drugs, alcohol, and tobacco and other practices that could be harmful to your health. Discuss your participation in the program with your family.	
☐	**9.** Demonstrate Scout spirit by living the Scout Oath (Promise) and Scout Law in your everyday life.	
☐	**10.** Participate in a Scoutmaster conference.	
☐	**11.** Complete your board of review.	

†This requirement may be waived by the troop committee for medical or safety reasons.

NOTE: Alternate requirements for the Second Class rank are available for Scouts with physical or mental disabilities if they meet the criteria listed in the *Boy Scout Requirements* book, No. 33215.

FIRST CLASS
RANK REQUIREMENTS

✓		Leader initial and date
✓	**1.** Demonstrate how to find directions during the day and at night without using a compass.	✓ 4/30/62
	2. Using a compass, complete an orienteering course that covers at least one mile and requires measuring the height and/or width of designated items (tree, tower, canyon, ditch, etc.).	
✓	**3.** Since joining, have participated in ten separate troop/patrol activities (other than troop/patrol meetings), three of which included camping overnight.	
✓	**4a.** Help plan a patrol menu for one campout—including one breakfast, lunch, and dinner—that requires cooking. Tell how the menu includes the four basic food groups and meets nutritional needs.	
✓	**4b.** Using the menu planned in requirement 4a, make a list showing the cost and food amounts needed to feed three or more boys and secure the ingredients.	
✓	**4c.** Tell which pans, utensils, and other gear will be needed to cook and serve these meals.	
✓	**4d.** Explain the procedures to follow in the safe handling and storage of fresh meats, dairy products, eggs, vegetables, and other perishable food products. Tell how to properly dispose of camp garbage, cans, plastic containers, and other rubbish.	
✓	**4e.** On one campout, serve as your patrol's cook. Supervise your assistant(s) in using a stove or building a cooking fire. Prepare the breakfast, lunch, and dinner planned in requirement 4a. Lead your patrol in saying grace at the meals and supervise cleanup.	
	5. Visit and discuss with a selected individual approved by your leader (elected official, judge, attorney, civil servant, principal, teacher) your Constitutional rights and obligations as a U.S. citizen.	
✓	**6.** Identify or show evidence of at least ten kinds of native plants found in your community.	✓ 5/1/02
	7a. Discuss when you should and should not use lashings.	
	7b. Demonstrate tying the timber hitch and clove hitch and their use in square, shear, and diagonal lashings by joining two or more poles or staves together.	

FIRST CLASS
RANK REQUIREMENTS

443

	Requirement	Leader initial and date
	7c. Use lashing to make a useful camp gadget.	
	8a. Demonstrate tying the bowline knot and describe several ways it can be used.	*(initials)* Joey
	8b. Demonstrate bandages for a sprained ankle and for injuries on the head, the upper arm, and the collarbone.	*(initials)*
	8c. Show how to transport by yourself, and with one other person, a person • From a smoke-filled room • With a sprained ankle, for at least 25 yards	
	8d. Tell the five most common signs of a heart attack. Explain the steps (procedures) in cardiopulmonary resuscitation (CPR).	
	9a. Tell what precautions must be taken for a safe trip afloat.	
	9b. Successfully complete the BSA swimmer test.*	
	9c. Demonstrate survival skills by leaping into deep water wearing clothes (shoes, socks, swim trunks, long pants, belt, and long-sleeved shirt). Remove shoes and socks, inflate the shirt, and show that you can float using the shirt for support. Remove and inflate the pants for support. Swim 50 feet using the inflated pants for support, then show how to reinflate the pants while using them for support.*	Austin
	9d. With a helper and a practice victim, show a line rescue both as tender and as rescuer. (The practice victim should be approximately 30 feet from shore in deep water.)	
	10. Demonstrate Scout spirit by living the Scout Oath (Promise) and Scout Law in your everyday life.	
	11. Participate in a Scoutmaster conference.	
	12. Complete your board of review.	

*This requirement may be waived by the troop committee for medical or safety reasons.

NOTE: Alternate requirements for the First Class rank are available for Scouts with physical or mental disabilities if they meet the criteria listed in the *Boy Scout Requirements* book, No. 33215.

STAR SCOUT
RANK REQUIREMENTS

✓		Leader initial and date
	1. Be active in your troop and patrol for at least 4 months as a First Class Scout.	
	2. Demonstrate Scout spirit by living the Scout Oath (Promise) and Scout Law in your everyday life.	
	3. Earn 6 merit badges, including any 4 from the required list for Eagle. **Name of Merit Badge** _Citizenship_____ (required for Eagle)* _Citizenship_____ (required for Eagle)* _Citizenship_____ (required for Eagle)* _1st Aid_____ (required for Eagle)* _Pioneering_____ _Camping_____	
	4. While a First Class Scout, take part in service projects totaling at least 6 hours of work. These projects must be approved by your Scoutmaster.	
	5. While a First Class Scout, serve actively for 4 months in one or more of the following positions of responsibility (or carry out a Scoutmaster-assigned leadership project to help the troop): **Boy Scout troop.** Patrol leader, assistant senior patrol leader, senior patrol leader, troop guide, den chief, scribe, librarian, historian, quartermaster, bugler, junior assistant Scoutmaster, chaplain aide, or instructor. **Varsity Scout team.** Captain, cocaptain, program manager, squad leader, team secretary, librarian, historian, quartermaster, chaplain aide, instructor, or den chief.	
	6. Take part in a Scoutmaster conference.	
	7. Complete your board of review.	

*A Scout may choose any of the 15 required merit badges in the 12 categories to fulfill requirement 3. See page 180 of this book for a complete list of required badges for Eagle.

LIFE SCOUT
RANK REQUIREMENTS

✓		Leader initial and date
☐	**1.** Be active in your troop and patrol for at least 6 months as a Star Scout.	
☐	**2.** Demonstrate Scout spirit by living the Scout Oath (Promise) and Scout Law in your everyday life.	
☐	**3.** Earn 5 more merit badges (so that you have 11 in all), including any 3 more from the required list for Eagle. **Name of Merit Badge** __Communication__ (required for Eagle)* _____ (required for Eagle)* _____ (required for Eagle)* __Geneology__ __Wilderness Survival__	
☐	**4.** While a Star Scout, take part in service projects totaling at least 6 hours of work. These projects must be approved by your Scoutmaster.	
☐	**5.** While a Star Scout, serve actively for 6 months in one or more of the positions of responsibility listed in requirement 5 for Star Scout (or carry out a Scoutmaster-assigned leadership project to help the troop).	
☐	**6.** Take part in a Scoutmaster conference.	
☐	**7.** Complete your board of review.	

*A Scout may choose any of the 15 required merit badges in the 12 categories to fulfill requirement 3. See page 180 of this book for a complete list of required badges for Eagle.

EAGLE SCOUT RANK REQUIREMENTS

✓		Leader initial and date
☐	**1.** Be active in your troop and patrol for at least 6 months as a Life Scout.	
☐	**2.** Demonstrate Scout spirit by living the Scout Oath (Promise) and Scout Law in your everyday life.	
☐	**3.** Earn a total of 21 merit badges (10 more than you already have), including the following: (a) First Aid, (b) Citizenship in the Community, (c) Citizenship in the Nation, (d) Citizenship in the World, (e) Communications, (f) Personal Fitness, (g) Emergency Preparedness OR Lifesaving, (h) Environmental Science, (i) Personal Management, (j) Swimming OR Hiking OR Cycling, (k) Camping, and (l) Family Life.*	

Name of Merit Badge

_____

_____

_____

_____

_____

_____

_____

_____

_____

| ☐ | **4.** While a Life Scout, serve actively for a period of 6 months in one or more of the following positions of responsibility:

Boy Scout troop. Patrol leader, assistant senior patrol leader, senior patrol leader, troop guide, den chief, scribe, librarian, historian, quartermaster, junior assistant Scoutmaster, chaplain aide, or instructor. | |

EAGLE SCOUT RANK REQUIREMENTS

	Leader initial and date
Varsity Scout team. Captain, cocaptain, program manager, squad leader, team secretary, librarian, quartermaster, chaplain aide, instructor, or den chief.	
5. While a Life Scout, plan, develop, and give leadership to others in a service project helpful to any religious institution, any school, or your community. (The project should benefit an organization other than Boy Scouting.) The project idea must be approved by the organization benefiting from the effort, your Scoutmaster and troop committee, and the council or district before you start. You must use the Life to Eagle Packet, BSA publication No. 18-927, in meeting this requirement.	
6. Take part in a Scoutmaster conference.	
7. Successfully complete an Eagle Scout board of review.	

77*You must choose only one merit badge listed in items *g* and *j*. If you have earned more than one of the badges listed in items *g* and *j*, choose one and list the remaining badges to make your total of 21.

NOTE: All requirements for Eagle Scout must be completed before a candidate's 18th birthday. The Eagle Scout board of review can be held after the candidate's 18th birthday. For more information, see *National BSA Advancement Policies and Procedures*, publication No. 33088.

If you have a permanent physical or mental disability you may become an Eagle Scout by qualifying for as many required merit badges as you can and qualifying for alternative merit badges for the rest. If you seek to become an Eagle Scout under this procedure, you must submit a special application to your local council service center. Your application must be approved by your council advancement committee *before you can work on alternative merit badges.*

EAGLE PALM REQUIREMENTS

		Leader initial and date
✓		
	Bronze Palm	
☐	**1.** Be active in your troop and patrol for at least 3 months after becoming an Eagle Scout or after the award of your last Palm.	
☐	**2.** Demonstrate Scout spirit by living the Scout Oath (Promise) and Scout Law in your everyday life.	
☐	**3.** Make a satisfactory effort to develop and demonstrate leadership ability.	
☐	**4.** Earn 5 additional merit badges beyond those required for the Eagle rank.* _____ merit badge _____ merit badge _____ merit badge _____ merit badge _____ merit badge	
☐	**5.** Take part in a Scoutmaster conference.	
☐	**6.** Complete your board of review.	
	Gold Palm	
☐	**1.** Be active in your troop and patrol for at least 3 months after becoming an Eagle Scout or after the award of your last Palm.	
☐	**2.** Demonstrate Scout spirit by living the Scout Oath (Promise) and Scout Law in your everyday life.	
☐	**3.** Make a satisfactory effort to develop and demonstrate leadership ability.	
☐	**4.** Earn 5 additional merit badges beyond those required for the Bronze Palm.* _____ merit badge _____ merit badge _____ merit badge _____ merit badge _____ merit badge	

EAGLE PALM REQUIREMENTS

		Leader initial and date
	5. Take part in a Scoutmaster conference.	
	6. Complete your board of review.	
	Silver Palm	
	1. Be active in your troop and patrol for at least 3 months after becoming an Eagle Scout or after the award of your last Palm.	
	2. Demonstrate Scout spirit by living the Scout Oath (Promise) and Scout Law in your everyday life.	
	3. Make a satisfactory effort to develop and demonstrate leadership ability.	
	4. Earn 5 additional merit badges beyond those required for the Gold Palm.* _____ merit badge _____ merit badge _____ merit badge _____ merit badge _____ merit badge	
	5. Take part in a Scoutmaster conference.	
	6. Complete your board of review.	
	You may wear only the proper combination of Palms for the number of merit badges you earned beyond the rank of Eagle. The Bronze Palm represents 5 merit badges, the Gold Palm 10, and the Silver Palm 15.	

*Merit badges earned anytime since becoming a Boy Scout may be used to meet this requirement.

NOTE: Scouts who earn three Palms may continue to earn additional Palms in the same order—bronze, gold, and silver. All requirements for Eagle Palms must be completed before a candidate's 18th birthday.

CREDITS

ACKNOWLEDGMENTS

The Boy Scouts of America gratefully acknowledges the contributions of the following people for their help in preparing the *Boy Scout Handbook*, 11th edition.

- Scouts and Scouters throughout the nation who participated in focus groups, photography efforts, and manuscript reviews
- Members of the National Council's Literature Review Committee: Gerard O. Rocque, chairman; Jeremia J. Arnold; Raymond Bellemore; Don S. Brereton; Walter M. Brown III; William D. Buchanan; Tony Fiori; Lawry Hunsaker; Raymona Johnson; Robert J. Longoria; E. C. Lupton Jr.; John C. Patterson; David E. Setzer, Ph.D.; Doyle E. Silliman; Ronald J. Temple, Ph.D.
- Subject experts who provided exceptional assistance: William W. Forgey, M.D.; William Hurst; Jan T. Perkins; K. Gregory Tucker; Bruce D. Walcott

National Office Publishing Team

Advisory council

Joseph P. Connolly; Rees A. Falkner; C. Michael Hoover Jr.; J. Carey Keane; Donald R. McChesney; Roger A. Ohmstede; Douglas S. Smith Jr.; James B. Wilson Jr.; J. Warren Young

Project director

Joe C. Glasscock, Boy Scout Division, BSA

Account executive

Maria C. Dahl, Electronic Publishing Division, BSA

Author

Robert Birkby, Eagle Scout, mountaineer, and former director of Conservation at Philmont Scout Ranch

Editor

Karen W. Webb, Winston Webb Editorial Services

Proofreader

Carolee P. Howard, Electronic Publishing Division, BSA

Concept designer

Brent H. McMahan, Sibley Peteet Design

Design manager

Laura E. Humphries, Henderson Humphries Design

Computer graphic artist
Melinda K. VanLone, Electronic Publishing Division, BSA

Computer graphic specialist
Melissa A. Brown, Electronic Publishing Division, BSA

Print coordinator
Kimberly Kailey, Electronic Publishing Division, BSA

Illustrator
John McDearmon, John McDearmon Illustration & Design

Photography manager
Michael Roytek, Electronic Publishing Division, BSA

Paintings
Joseph Csatari—pages 429, 436
J. C. Leyendecker—page 338
Dom Lupo—page 332
Norman Rockwell—produced from copyrighted art from the archives of
Brown & Bigelow Inc. and by permission of the Boy Scouts of America,
pages 428, 430

Photographs
Dan Bryant—pages vii (right), 87, 108, 179, 263, 342, 367, 406 (bottom)
Darrell Byers—pages 39, 52, 95, 202, 206, 211, 351 (top), 405 (bottom)
Phil Davis—pages 348 (bottom), 349 (bottom), 368, 398 (top)
Daniel Giles—pages 92, 350 (bottom), 384
Mark Humphries—page 176
Roy Jansen—pages 28 (bottom), 267 (bottom), 336 (top), 357, 364, 365, 463
Doug Knutson—page 241
Frank McMahon—pages 22, 75, 285 (top), 331, 344
Christian Michaels—page vi (top)
National Aeronautics and Space Administration—pages 348–49 (top)
Brian Payne—pages viii, 25, 51, 57, 72, 91, 94 (top), 98, 100, 126, 154, 167,
171, 212, 217, 221, 255, 320, 351 (bottom), 381, 386, 391, 398 (bottom), 406
(top), 420
Randy Piland—pages 19, 28 (top), 76, 89, 119, 247, 272 (top), 284 (top), 318
(top, bottom), 343, 346, 360 (bottom left, bottom right), 361, 380, 402, 419,
421 (top), 466
Scott Stenjem—front cover (mountain); pages 15 (mountain), 27, 169, 186,
195 (top), 222, 248, 265, 270, 281, 363, 399, 426
Gary M. Stolz—page vii (top)

Thanks to the Irving Public Library, Irving, Texas, for the use of its copy of
the Declaration of Independence, to the Bird of Prey Conservatory, San
Antonio, Texas, for the use of a live bald eagle, and to the National Scouting
Museum at Murray State, Kentucky for the use of the Scouting memorabilia.

INDEX

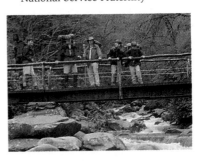

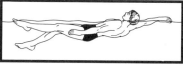

X

Y